THE
INSIDER'S GUIDE
TO THE
TOP TEN BUSINESS SCHOOLS

THE
INSIDER'S GUIDE
TO THE
TOP TEN BUSINESS SCHOOLS

Tom Fischgrund, *Ed.*

Third Edition, Revised

Little, Brown and Company
BOSTON   TORONTO

THIRD EDITION, REVISED

Library of Congress Cataloging-in-Publication Data

Main entry under title:

The Insider's guide to the top ten business schools.

1. Business education—United States.   2. Master
of business education degree—United States.
I. Fischgrund, Tom.   II. Title: Guide to the top ten
business schools.
HF1131.157   1983   650'.07'1173   83-13567

ISBN 0-316-28382-7

BP
DESIGNED BY DEDE CUMMINGS

Published simultaneously in Canada by
Little, Brown & Company (Canada) Limited
PRINTED IN THE UNITED STATES OF AMERICA

Dedicated to my parents, Cis and Herb,
to my wife, Lynne, to my
daughter, Beth, and to
my sons, Ted and Sam

TABLE OF CONTENTS

PREFACE TO THE THIRD EDITION

An MBA from a top ten business school still is a "golden passbook." The demand for top ten MBAs from major corporations, investment banks, consulting firms, and even new ventures continues to grow unabated. Graduates of the top ten now earn more than ever ($45,000 to $50,000 to start), while their skills and training have been improved and expanded with the latest management technology, theory, and practice.

While the value of a top ten MBA has not changed in recent years, the schools themselves have continued to refine and improve their programs. First, the trend toward general management continues. Schools that traditionally have been recognized as superior in a particular discipline, e.g., Wharton, MIT, and Chicago in finance and Northwestern in marketing, have strengthened their entire programs by developing other areas of study, adding courses, and revising their curriculum/requirements. Chicago, for example, has developed new areas of concentrations in general management, new products, marketing, and small business, has added new courses in competitive strategy, environmental analysis, and business ethics, and has encouraged liberal arts majors to enter its program through the Chicago Business Fellows Program. Kellogg (Northwestern) also has enhanced its program through internationalization of its curriculum and programming. In this vein, Kellogg has developed an international business concentration, incorporated international material into the regular program, and initiated several foreign exchange and internship programs. Significantly, while these schools have broadened their focus, it has not diminished their traditional strengths.

Second, the top ten schools continue to be in the forefront of management research. MIT is in the midst of a joint research project with ten major corporations, each of whom has contributed $5 million to study the impact of technology in the workplace. The project is entitled "Management in the 1990s." Chicago also is engaged in an unusual joint venture with the Argonne National Laboratory in which students work with scientists and researchers to advance the process of technology transfer by securing venture capital and developing business and marketing plans for commercially viable products.

A third trend is the continued investment by the top schools to improve recruiting facilities, classrooms, student housing, and their physical plants. UCLA recently received a $15 million gift from John E. Anderson, which it will use to develop a new management center for the renamed John E. Anderson Graduate School of Management. Other recent new facilities for recruiting, executive education, and administration were reported by Chicago (the Edelstone Center) and Northwestern (the Allen Center).

Fourth, the top ten schools are accepting even fewer students directly out of college. While just three years ago, up to 40 percent of one entering class came directly from college, no top ten business school now takes more than 13 percent. Most accept only a very limited number (2 to 4 percent) directly out of an undergraduate institution.

Fifth, tuitions continue to rise. The average yearly cost of a top ten MBA program is now $13,000 + for tuition. Only the public institutions, UCLA ($4,000 for out-of-state) and to a lesser extent Michigan ($11,000 for out-of-state), offer much lower tuitions. Offsetting this increase, however, is the continued escalation in salaries. Top ten MBAs now earn upwards of $50,000 to start, plus in many cases, bonuses and other benefits.

The final shift concerns the increasing number of top ten MBAs going into investment banking and consulting. Almost all the top ten reported an increasing number of their graduates entering these fields (up to 50 percent in some recent classes). It also is clear that investment banking and consulting offer the highest starting salaries ($60,000 + in most instances). Even with the upheavals and instability in the stock market, top ten MBAs will continue to enter these fields as long as their beginning salaries far exceed those in other areas.

There has been some recent criticism as to whether this shift in placement changes the basic mission of top business schools from developing general managers and business leaders to training financial whiz kids. This is troublesome, it is argued, because these financial types are not productive in a traditional manufacturing sense and, therefore, do not contribute to American business. Despite this criticism, it does not appear that the overall thrust of the top ten business programs has changed greatly to cater to the special interests of investment banking or consulting. The top ten schools do not appear to have altered their basic philosophy of management or business training. The shifts to consulting and investment banking seem to be driven more by the demands of the marketplace and high salaries, rather than by fundamental changes in the mission or programs of the top business schools.

The overall structure of each top ten program, its courses, requirements, and orientation, has not changed greatly. Even the academic and social environments are not that dissimilar from what they were a couple of years ago. Those changes that have taken place have been evolutionary and directional, rather than fundamental shifts in philosophy or training. Because each of the top MBA schools has developed a program that is already very successful, the absence of dramatic change is understandable.

A good measure of this success is demonstrated by the fact that a very large number of companies, in addition to investment banks and consulting firms, still compete for MBAs from the top ten schools and are willing to pay more for them each year. At the same time MBAs from the top programs continue to achieve prominence and leadership in all areas of business and society. Now more than ever an MBA from a top ten school is a very valuable and useful degree.

ACKNOWLEDGMENTS FOR THE THIRD EDITION

In preparing this revised edition, I sought and received the cooperation of all the top ten schools. Everything was updated, including course requirements, statistics, and other information within each chapter. Nevertheless, the opinions and viewpoints expressed in the write-ups on the schools remain those of recent graduates of each program. The opinions and viewpoints expressed in the book as a whole are those of this author.

I would like very much to thank the following individuals and schools for their cooperation:

Cathleen Watkins, Associate Director, Marketing and Communications, Anderson Graduate School of Management (UCLA)

Carol Scott, Associate Dean for Academic Affairs, Anderson Graduate School of Management (UCLA)

Leda Hanin, Director of Public Relations, Chicago Business School

Frederick Jacobi, Director of Public Affairs, Columbia Business School

William Hokanson, Director of Communications, Harvard Business School

Jean Thompson, Associate Director of Admissions and Financial Aid, Kellogg Graduate School of Management (Northwestern)

Ray Boyer, Assistant Dean and Director of Public Affairs, Kellogg Graduate School of Management (Northwestern)

Anneke de Bruyn Overseth, Associate Dean, School of Business Administration, University of Michigan

Margaret Daniels Tyler, Director of Master's Admissions, Sloan School of Management (MIT)

Cathy Castillo, News and Publication Office, Stanford Graduate School of Business

Paul Argenti, Adjunct Professor and Director of Communications, Tuck School of Business Administration (Dartmouth)

Stephen Morgan, Director, Media Relations, The Wharton School (University of Pennsylvania)

I would also like to thank Ken Werner, Tom Woll, and Howie Baskin for their advice and help; Debbie Jurkowitz, Barry Lippman, Michael Blaber, and Beth Rashbaum of Little, Brown for their editing and support; and Roslyn Fedro, Donna McIntyre, and Barbara Ball for their typing.

Tom Fischgrund

INTRODUCTION

Today, an MBA from a top business school is a golden pass-book. Graduates from these schools earn starting salaries of $50,000 and more, move rapidly up the corporate ladder, and have an unmatched blend of skills and confidence. An incredibly large number of today's corporate and business leaders are graduates of the top business schools.

It is not difficult, then, to understand why MBAs are so popular and competition for business school admission so intense. Harvard alone receives over 55,000 admission inquiries and almost 7,000 completed applications for an entering class of 785. Similarly, Wharton (University of Pennsylvania) receives almost 45,000 inquiries and 6,000 applications for its 660 enrollment slots. To satisfy this tremendous demand, many schools are developing part-time and evening business programs. As a result, more than 50,000 MBAs are awarded each year from business schools in the U.S.

While the number of MBA graduates continues to rise, the demand for MBAs in general is slackening. It is, therefore, becoming increasingly important to get an MBA from one of the top ten business schools. These top schools have purposely limited the size of their class enrollments to maintain the quality and integrity of their programs. At the same time, this insures that the limited number of students that graduate each year will be in great demand. A degree from one of the top schools can be worth as much as ten to fifteen thousand dollars more the first year than a degree from a lower-rated school. However, all the top business schools are not the same. They have different teaching methods, different areas of specialty, different strengths and weaknesses, and different personalities. For example, Harvard uses the case method, trains general managers, and has a "West Point" mentality. Wharton, on the other hand, uses a combination of case method and lecture, focuses on finance, and has a quantitative orientation.

Given this diversity among the top business schools, students should choose a school according to their academic needs, career goals, and personal interests. For instance, if a student is interested in finance and doesn't particularly want a high-pressure environment, the student should know which school would best meet those qualifications.

Deciding which of the top business schools to apply to has always been difficult because the information available is quite limited. The schools themselves send out brochures with very sparse and basic information. There are a few guidebooks that publish one-page summaries that are brief and restricted to general statistics. While these sources are valuable in providing such specifics as number of students, average GMAT scores, and course requirements, they fail to provide the in-depth information needed to make a well-informed decision. It is important to consider the academic, professional, and social environment of each school. For example: What is the school's strongest academic area? How competitive are fellow students? How much studying is required?

This book has been written specifically to provide this information for anyone who is considering applying to business school, anyone who is currently enrolled or about to begin an MBA program, or anyone who simply wants to know more about the top ten schools. It presents all the necessary inside information on each of these schools.

Each school is described and reviewed in depth by a recent graduate of that program who knows all the intimate details: the strengths and weaknesses, academic rquirements, social climate, and anything else you might wonder about. More specifically, this insider's guide will focus on seven areas for each school:

1. *The Program*

    a) What's it really like?
    b) What courses are required?
    c) How large are classes?
    d) How are classes taught — case method, lecture, or combination?
    e) What is the overall academic orientation (academic specialty)?
    f) What is the reputation of the school? Is it deserved?

2. *Getting In*

    a) Who gets admitted to the program?
    b) Are there quotas?
    c) What is the school looking for in prospective students?
    d) Are interviews necessary?

3. *Academic Environment*

    a) How is grading done?
    b) Do many students flunk out?
    c) Is it hard or easy to flunk out?
    d) What are fellow students like: friendly, competitive, cutthroat, etc.?
    e) What kind of interaction takes place in the classroom?
    f) Is there a lot of pressure?

4. *Social Life*

    a) Is there life at business school?
    b) Is there time to socialize?
    c) What do most people do?
    d) What kind of demands does the business school make on the student?
    e) What is it like to be married while going to business school?
    f) What is it like to be single while going to business school?
    g) How good is housing? On campus? Off campus?

5. *Recruiting and Job Search*

    a) What does business school train you for?
    b) What kind of placement record does the school have?
    c) What kinds of jobs do most students take?
    d) How is recruiting conducted?
    e) Is recruiting held on or off campus?
    f) When does recruiting begin?
    g) Do most students have summer jobs between the first and second year? What do they do?

6. *On the Job—First Years Out*

    a) How adequate or inadequate a preparation was the MBA program for a job?
    b) How useful was the degree?
    c) Is there much job switching after a year?
    d) Do salaries meet expectations?

7. *Summary Overview*

    a) What are the major strengths and weaknesses of the program?

b) Is there a general feeling that getting an MBA was the right decision?

The decision to go to business school represents a large investment. If you are enrolled in a full-time program in one of the nation's top schools, the direct out-of-pocket costs can reach $25,000 a year. When you consider that it is difficult to work at the same time that you are going to school, then the cost per year from lost salary and direct costs could reach $60,000. Since almost all of the programs are two years, the total cost of a business school education can reach $120,000. In addition, business school means an investment of two years of your life. Much could be accomplished in the working world during that same period.

Therefore, if the decision has been made to spend the enormous amount of time and money going to a top business school, then make a wise choice. Gather as much information as possible on the top schools and then decide which school is right for you.

SELECTING THE TOP TEN BUSINESS SCHOOLS

PICKING the top ten business schools is like choosing an economic policy — everyone has a strong opinion and is convinced he or she is right, but no consensus is ever reached. A number of ratings by business school deans and high-level corporate executives provide some insight into rankings, but as with any nonquantitative rating, the final decision must be somewhat subjective.

Still, there is a remarkably high degree of consensus among the ratings as to which schools are in the top ten. It is clear that the top programs are recognized as superior not only within the academic community by business school deans, but also by employers who have had direct experience with top ten MBA graduates. Moreover, it is evident that the top business school programs have maintained high ratings since the first edition of this book was published.

The top schools have well-defined philosophies, clear mission statements, and well-developed programs. Still, all the top schools continually strive to refine and improve their programs, which solidifies even further their position in the top ten. Based on the best information available and the most recent ratings, the following schools are included in this guide:

ANDERSON (UCLA)
CHICAGO
COLUMBIA
HARVARD
KELLOGG (NORTHWESTERN)
MICHIGAN
SLOAN (MIT)
STANFORD
TUCK (DARTMOUTH)
WHARTON (PENNSYLVANIA)

We hope the following chapters will be helpful to you in making your decision about business school and will aid you in your future success in one of the top programs. Then good luck in getting today's "Golden Passbook" — an MBA from a top business school.

OTHER TOP MBA PROGRAMS

IN the first edition, only the top ten business schools were listed and reviewed in depth. In doing this revision, some said that there are fifteen schools in the top ten. It is true that many other graduate business schools have excellent programs. Therefore, while the top ten still are profiled in this third edition, here is a list of other top MBA programs based on available rankings, subjective evaluations, and reputation:

University of California, Berkeley
Carnegie-Mellon
Colgate Darden (Virginia)
Cornell
University of Illinois, Urbana
Indiana University, Bloomington
New York University
University of North Carolina, Chapel Hill
University of Texas, Austin
Yale

While the majority of MBA programs are located in the United States, and American schools have certainly been in the forefront of management training and education, there are some good MBA programs outside this country. Students who are interested in international or foreign management should consider programs such as IMEDE (Institut pour l'Etude des Méthodes de Direction de l'Enterprise), which is located in Lausanne, Switzerland, and has an MBA course patterned after Harvard's program.

I

THE TOP TEN BUSINESS SCHOOLS

Chapter 1

*HARVARD BUSINESS SCHOOL**

THE PROGRAM

« *"There is no first day at the Harvard Business School,"* I *am told as I pick up cases the day before classes are to begin. "Classes at the B School are run like a business, that is, no excuses for undone work and no tardiness for class, short of death or a totally debilitating illness."*

With that advice in mind, I get to my first class early, at 8:15. Already half the class is there. The seats are arranged in a horseshoe formation facing three large blackboards in the front of the room. There are no windows in the large chamber. By 8:28, it appears as if all eighty-five students are there. By 8:29, the teacher comes in. At 8:30 sharp, class begins.

Like everyone else, I know the case method will be used, but I am not really sure how it actually works. Eight hundred cases and two years later, we will all be veritable experts in the case method. However, the first day it is still a mystery. I know very few of my fellow students. I had met three or four at a party the previous day, only to be overwhelmed by their impressive cre-

---

* BY TOM FISCHGRUND, MBA, HARVARD

dentials. *If they weren't bankers or CPAs, they had been economists with the Federal Reserve Board for seven years. I asked myself the eternal admissions question: "How did I get in?" There is clearly tension in the class the first day. Each student has read the case; some have prepared more than others. It is obvious no one feels really comfortable. The teacher looks around the room. The professor seems to eye each student individually. Finally, the professor stops, looks at one student, and says, "Mr. Canda, what is the problem faced by the XYZ Company?" Eighty-four students breathe a collective sigh of relief. We all know the time will come to open a case, but thank God it is not the first class on the first day.*

Mr. Canda hesitates a bit, but then speaks clearly and loudly — after all, he was good enough to get into the business school, so certainly he can do quite well in analyzing a simple marketing problem. The problem is quite simple according to Mr. Canda; the price for the product is too high. The answer is to lower the price and sell more product. The teacher asks, "Is that all?" Mr. Canda responds affirmatively. Ten hands shoot up. Then the analysis really begins. »

The Harvard Business School lives and dies by the case method. Luckily, it works. The case method relies on extremely bright students, extensive class participation, and a sharp teacher. All three elements are present at HBS.

The entering class at the Business School numbers 785. Each class is then divided into nine sections of eighty-five students. Each section is designated by a letter. These sections form the heart of the Business School program the first year. Students take all their courses the first year with their section-mates. In fact, all classes are taken in the same room. The teachers move from room to room instead of the students.

The demographics of the classes are remarkably similar from year to year. Most students (approximately two thirds) are twenty-three to twenty-six years old with one to four years' work experience under their belts. Only 2 percent come directly from college, and about one third are older than twenty-six. Women make up about one quarter of the class, international students one sixth, and minorities about one tenth. Over one half have majored in humanities and social sciences, 22 percent in engineering and 17 percent in business administration. The rest are scattered among a variety of fields such as pure science and preprofessional.

The students also have varied work experience. For example, in one section last year there were eight CPAs, three bankers, five computer jocks, five consultants, three government workers, one lawyer, two college professors, and one television reporter. The common thread that ties the students together is their intelligence and/or analytical ability. All are bright and capable of doing the work. Most work very hard. They are, as a sociologist might say, "achievement oriented." The quality of the student body is a major reason why the case method is so successful.

All students must take the same required courses the first year. Required courses include: Finance; Marketing; Control; Production and Operations Management; Organizational Behavior; Business; Government and International Economy; Managerial Economics; Human Resource Management; Introduction to Financial Statements; Managing Information Systems; Competition and Strategy; and Management Communications. Because all students must take the same courses the first year, it is not uncommon for CPAs to be taking accounting, or for economists to be studying introductory economics. In fact, this is done by design.

« I remember our third finance class. The case for the day was whether a bank should grant the John Doe Company a loan. The case was complicated because there was so much

contradictory information on the health of the company and its position in the market. In addition, there were enough numbers in the case to make a computer choke. The professor quickly surveyed the room and called on Mr. Rivers. Mr. Rivers then proceeded to do an in-depth financial analysis of the company. In addition to the normal analysis of the balance sheet and income statement, he did a pro forma for five years, presented all the financial ratios, and computed a statement of changes in financial position. Based on this financial analysis, he then looked at the management and the marketplace and concluded that the bank should not grant the loan. While his analysis was not perfect, I sat there in amazement that anyone could do such a complete analysis after only three days. Most of the ratios and many of the terms he used I had not even heard of. I wondered what kind of financial wizard this guy was and whether I was in the right school. It was only when I learned that Mr. Rivers worked for a bank for eight years, three of which were in its lending department, that I felt better. Several weeks later I began to understand and to use ratio analysis, not as well as Mr. Rivers, but competently enough. It was clear I was learning a lot, not only from the cases, but also from the experiences of my fellow students. Incidentally, Mr. Rivers was in my study group and provided much help in finance. »

The third essential ingredient to the case method is the right kind of teacher — bright, quick, and analytical. On the whole, HBS professors are very capable. They range from the highly experienced and renowned to those newly awarded Ph.Ds. All are extremely knowledgeable in their field, and most serve as consultants outside the school.

When you consider the experience and the ability of the eighty-five students, you realize that being a professor at the B School is not an easy task. Standing in the "pit," as the front of the classroom in the jaws of the horseshoe is called, the professor must be able to train students to analyze a case. It is a difficult process. The first-year program is standardized; all students read essentially the same cases. Eight or nine professors meet together to analyze the case. This helps the professor highlight the key elements, and his teaching reflects the combined thinking of all the professors involved.

Still, the case method is extremely hard to teach because the professor does not lecture from prepared notes. Although the central analytical process will remain constant, the data and conclusions will differ from class to class. The professor must help the class analyze the data, and other alternative courses of action. Students learn general principles from seeing and hearing similar themes and ideas repeated in case after case. It is a deductive process.

To paraphrase *The Paper Chase*, students teach themselves business while professors teach them how to think. There are no right or wrong answers in the case method; it is the process that is important. Students must learn these analytical skills quickly in order to succeed at the Business School. Almost everyone does.

Cases are always presented in problem form. For example, the class might be told that Polaroid is losing market share to Kodak. Then they might be asked what Polaroid should do. Or perhaps a factory cannot process all the raw materials it receives within a reasonable amount of time. What should it do? Data, such as market share, technological factors, and management style, are provided to aid in the analysis. As in real life, the data are often incomplete.

First, the student is called upon to identify the problem and those factors that affect it. Then the student is asked to outline alternate courses of action and to make a recommendation. Often it is difficult even to identify and pinpoint the problem. For example, if a company is losing market share, the problem could be pricing, production, marketing, advertising, management, the product itself, or any one of a dozen other factors. And the solutions can create as many problems as they solve. Cases are analyzed during the exchange between the students and the professor. Generally, a student is called upon to open or analyze a case by identifying the problem and stating the pertinent facts. At this point, other students are encouraged to join in and provide additional input. Defining the various alternatives and picking the "best" is a long discussion in and of itself. Most of the time, the course of action the company actually pursued is never revealed, since the analytic process itself is more important than the outcome. Implicit in this logic is the idea that in most cases rational analytical decision-making will produce the best result.

Quantitative methods such as decision analysis and linear programming are often used to aid in this process. Many cases require hours and hours of mathematical calculations. However, in almost all cases, quantitative methods are employed to support the qualitative analysis. They are means rather than an end in and of itself.

« *One of the most difficult cases we had to analyze our first year was the National Cranberry Case. It was about this cranberry processing plant that couldn't handle the millions of cranberries it was supposed to refine. The case itself was long and complicated. It took me three hours that night just to figure out how cranberries were processed. (There were seven machines, each with different functions and different capacities. They processed three different grades of berries and produced two different types of products.)*

The key analytical tool for that class was the flowchart or diagram of how the system worked. Solutions usually involved identifying that place or machinery which could not handle the workload. So the night before the class, I flowcharted the process and identified the bottleneck.

The next morning, despite my trying to look as inconspicuous as possible, my number came up. The professor said, "Mr. Fischgrund, what would you do first in this case?" A friend jokingly whispered to me to follow one cranberry through the system, since this was what was done in other cases. However, those cases involved small quantities, but here we were dealing with millions and millions of cranberries. I looked at the professor and in my most sincere tone of voice said, "Flowchart." The professor turned aside and said, "Smart boy," sending the class into hysterics. I spent the next half-hour outlining the process, calculating rates, capabilities, time requirements, machine costs, and so on. The solution was anything but clear.

I identified three options and then recommended that the growers build another machine to ease a bottleneck. It was not a great solution because it would take the growers years to recoup their investment in the machine. Other students immediately offered other solutions, a few of which were better than mine, but all had long payback periods or could not be profitably executed.

Finally, at the end of the class, the professor reported that the case had been used for years with many of the same suggested solutions. He then said that three years ago one student had come up with a remarkably simple solution. If the three mahine operators reported to work three hours earlier each day, the excess capacity could be stored within the system and the whole batch of cranberries could easily be processed each day. Compared to my $700,000 build-another-machine solution, this time shift alternative would cost maybe $36 per day. The professor then proceeded to explain that it was necessary to go beyond the data and think about what was or was not needed to get the job done. Thus, the professor was telling us that good business people continue to think beyond the flowcharts and bottlenecks. It was a most instructive class. »

Harvard trains its students to be general managers because it feels that good general managers are hard to find. Technical expertise, it is argued, can always be recruited from other top business schools. Thus, Harvard requires its students to take a well-balanced curriculum. During the first year, all courses are required, with no electives. One course is mandatory the second year. It is not necessary for students to declare a major, and none do. This is not to say that Harvard MBAs don't specialize and are not expert in their field. Many Harvard students bring with them some technical expertise; others develop their skills during the two years at the Business School. However, most students at the Business School receive a good general education and then refine their skills on the job.

Harvard Business School's reputation is legendary. As a credential for finding a job, a Harvard MBA is unparalleled. The successes of its graduates are constantly written up in the *New York Times*, the *Wall Street Journal*, and other top business publications.

The trials and tribulations of getting an MBA at Harvard are also legendary. *The Gospel According to the Harvard Business School*, which was published in 1974, portrayed the school as a highly pressurized, highly competitive, highly successful institution. It is viewed as a place with a lot of work, some fun, and some tragedy (i.e., suicides). It is also described as a training ground for top corporate leaders. While the book may exaggerate a bit, it does capture at least some of the basic elements of the program.

For most students the school is a lot of work, but that doesn't mean that there also isn't some fun. Students tend to work extremely hard, five to eight hours a night, in addition to the four class hours each day. Education is a serious business at the Harvard Business School, but there is a camaraderie and a shared "I've been through it" feeling among students. You become very close to your section-mates and many times long-lasting friendships develop.

Harvard has a reputation as a pressure-cooker environment. Although the movie and TV versions of *The Paper Chase* were about law school, they were also a remarkably accurate portrayal of life and classes at the Harvard Business School. Students are called on at random, and many times a lively, interesting, and sometimes embarrassing interchange takes place. Students must be prepared, willing, and able to take criticism. It is not an easy place to go to school.

« My best friend at business school, Bob Cole, was called on in a human behavior class to open a case about a company that had severe management problems. Nobody in the company could get along with anyone else. Sales were down and profit was declining precipitously. It was one of those cases in which it looked as if any positive action might help, but a clean sweep or reorganization was probably necessary. In cases like this, however, care must be taken not to recommend too many changes without considering all the implications and consequences. The case could have a red herring in it or some tricky twists that are not immediately obvious.

Bob Cole had done extensive preparation the night before and had developed an elaborate plan to restructure the entire company. He described his plan loudly and clearly to the class. The professor carefully wrote everything down on the blackboard. The moment Bob finished, twenty students raised their hands. Bob glanced at me with a slightly worried look. For the next thirty minutes, students took potshots at Bob's plan, listing numerous reasons why Bob's carefully laid out reorganization was faulty and how none of his recommended changes would enhance the company's profitability.

After listening to all the arguments, the professor walked up to the blackboard and proceeded to draw a big X through Bob's entire plan. The class was very quiet as the professor turned to Bob and said, "Now what do you think of your grand design?" Bob, looking only slightly concerned, rubbed his chin, thought for a minute, and said, "I should have gone to Wharton."

The class went wild. Later I found out that Bob aced the course. »

Harvard is not for the weak of heart. It is a difficult, highly structured educational experience. Students receive excellent training and learn the basics of business. The program has not changed significantly over the years but is constantly evolving through the updating of case material. Harvard's program works. It produces knowledgeable and highly desirable MBA graduates. Almost every Harvard B School graduate agrees that it was worth the effort.

GETTING IN

COMPETITION for getting into the Business School is intense. There are almost 7,000 highly qualified applicants for 785 places. The obvious question then is how does the Business School choose its class?

The Harvard Business School brochure says very little about admission standards except that "excellent top management potential [is] the only absolute admissions criterion." Admissions officers at the B School cite three primary factors: intellectual ability, leadership and management potential, and personal characteristics. The admissions staff says that they look at the entire person and his or her achievements and potential.

It is a given that all applicants who are accepted will be bright and capable. Many of my HBS friends tell me that people they meet at their current jobs can't compare as a group with the B School student body.

While Harvard maintains that there are no quotas, the classes are remarkably similar in terms of composition from year to year. The school tries to maintain a diversity by enrolling approximately 25 percent women, 10 percent minority, and 15 percent international students in each class. Similarly percentages and ranges that apply to age, college major, and work experience tend to remain relatively constant.

It is often said that the Business School program begins with the application. The application is ten pages long with seven essay questions. It takes forever to fill out. It provides an "opportunity" for the applicant to discuss accomplishments ("the three most substantial" ones), extracurricular and academic experiences, avocations and hobbies, strengths and weaknesses, and the decision to go to business school. The application is key to the admissions process. Interviews are not required and they are not factored into the selection process. Since the applicant's grades are already set, essays in the application are the one place where the candidate has the chance to affect the admissions decision.

Getting into the Harvard Business School takes some marketing skills. The prospective applicant must focus on what he or she can offer the Business School that is unique or outstanding, and convince the board to select him or her over the other 6,000 applicants. Also, the student should try to find a skill, quality, or achievement that is related to business and position this properly in the application.

« *One day one of my best friends at B School happened to mention to me that prior to entering the program, he had been a plant manager. While I was duly impressed, I also was surprised since I knew he had just graduated from college. I said, "Weren't you a bit young to be a plant manager?" He replied, "No, I really enjoyed being a gardener." Positioning.* »

13

ACADEMIC ENVIRONMENT

THE Harvard MBA program is to business what boot camp is to the Marines. The work is hard. The hours are long. There are constant tests of strength and endurance. The major difference is that the Business School program is three times as long.

Classes run from 8:30 in the morning to 2:30 in the afternoon, with 45 minutes for lunch. There are three classes on Monday, Wednesday, and Friday, two on Tuesday and Thursday. The schedule varies rarely except for an afternoon seminar or training session that might occur once a week. Each case takes approximately one and a half to two hours per night to prepare. Most students also spend one hour a night in study groups, especially during the first year. The average student spends a total of twelve to fifteen hours each day either in class or preparing for it. It is a very tough schedule.

Harvard recently announced that they have taken steps to reduce the heavy workload by 15 percent. This is designed to give students more time to prepare cases. While these changes should help somewhat, the program will remain intensive and the workload will stay very heavy.

On top of the heavy workload, there is the added pressure of grading. Students are graded on a bell curve: the top 15–20 percent receive excellents or high passes; the middle 70 percent receive satisfactories (called "sats"); and the bottom 10–15 percent receive low passes or an occasional unsatisfactory. What makes the system so tough for the student is that these percentages are fixed. Regardless of how good a class of students may be, 10 to 15 percent must get low passes. If a student gets too many low passes (9 or more credits), then his or her academic standing is reviewed and he or she may be asked to leave. This delightful process is called "hitting the screen" because students with marginal grades must go before a screen-

14

ing committee to explain their situation and tell why they should not be expelled. The number of students who actually hit the screen and are asked to leave is exceedingly small (less that 3 percent). However, the possibility of flunking out always exists. There is a constant strain to get satisfactory grades.

Good grades don't come easy. Grading is determined by two factors: class participation and exams. Students are expected to be prepared for every class every day. Generally, a student is called upon once a semester to open or analyze a case. The problem is that there is no telling which day it will be. In addition, students are expected to make insightful comments about whatever case is being discussed. Most courses at the Business School have a grueling four-hour written final. Some classes have midterm exams; most do not. The four-hour final is like playing Russian roulette — 50 percent of the grade depends on this one-shot exam.

« *Grades are a major concern at every school. At the B School, they are an obsession. Almost every student at the Business School was at the top of his or her undergraduate class. Most have received nothing less than A's and an occasional B since elementary school. So when 80 to 85 percent of the students don't receive excellents or high passes, you have to wonder how professors assign grades.*

In response to student questions, most professors said they divided students' papers or comments into quintiles and then gave the top quintile excellents, the middle three quintiles satisfactories, and the bottom quintile low passes. However, one professor told me she gave each student a numerical grade and then rank-ordered the grades numerically. Since she found the grades were so close (within one one-hundredth of each other), she put them into a computer to determine final grading. Another professor replied that he drew a smile face for each remark a student made. When queried as to how he told how good the remark was, the professor said, "The better the remark, the wider the smile." »

The pressure from grades could make the Business School highly competitive and cutthroat. In reality, Harvard is highly competitive, but it is not cutthroat. Students at the Business School probably wouldn't be there if they weren't aggressive. Moreover, the school also fosters that type of behavior. Students compete for air time in the class, since 50 percent of a student's grade depends on classroom participation. This encourages students to make comments critical of another student's ideas or analysis. However, it is important to note that it is the ideas that are criticized, and not the individual.

Because the school is so pressure-packed, students tend to work together in small study groups each night to discuss the next day's cases. The school encourages these study groups, recognizing that business is a cooperative effort. Most of the study groups form during the first week and generally last through the end of the first year.

« *The first week at Harvard is frightening. The classes are new and difficult and the people are overwhelming. But most of all, the workload is oppressive. During the first week, most of the cases seem incomprehensible, and those few I did understand took hours and hours to solve. Out of necessity and desperation, I decided to form a study group. I approached the twenty-two-year-old college grad sitting next to me, and we jointly tried to pick the brightest and most prepared students. We asked a banker and a CPA to join our group to help with the financial end; we asked a computer jock and an economic consultant to provide coverage for the economic and more quantitative courses. Finally, we asked the guy in front of us to join the group since he seemed to have more notes than the professor and always looked prepared. Everyone was flattered and ac-*

16

cepted. We were relieved. The study group turned out great. We all became close friends and together managed to survive the two-year program. »

Friendship and support from fellow students make the pressure and workload tolerable. Since all classes the first year are taken with the same group of people, there is a shared experience. Students get to know each other, and to understand each other's strengths and weaknesses. The dynamics of the classroom reflect this and benefit from it. Out of necessity, the Business School program involves cooperation among students. The program is stronger for it.

SOCIAL LIFE

STUDENTS eat, breathe, and live the Harvard Business School. From 8:30 in the morning to 12 or 1 o'clock at night, going to Business School is not only an occupation, it is a preoccupation. When B School students socialize, they socialize with their section-mates. When they talk, they talk about cases, cases, cases. Is there life at the Business School?

Yes and no. Life at the Business School is exciting. The people are bright and interesting. Most sections party together, drink together, and play sports together. A few sections hold obligatory get-togethers at the pub (the local on-campus bar) every day after class. The Business School fosters this camaraderie with a "work hard, play hard" ethic.

On the other hand, it is difficult to get away from the Business School and its cases. In many senses, it's like being part of a close-knit family in which you do everything with them and everything revolves around them. Most of the time it's good, but occasionally it is necessary to get away. A few students don't participate at all; some seek activities outside the

B School. Most students, however, see socializing with their section-mates as part of the B School experience.

Students at the Business School are lucky in having Boston to explore and enjoy when they want to get off campus. Boston is the premier college town. It has excellent restaurants, pre-Broadway shows, the Boston Symphony, the Celtics, the Bruins, and the Patriots, and enough attractions and landmarks to keep any student busy for two years. The problem is always time.

The program at the Harvard Business School consumes an inordinate amount of time. Students have to work hard to find time to enjoy themselves.

« *I was at the Business School two weeks when I became very concerned that I was spending so much time on my cases — five hours a night. I spoke with a few friends I had made during the first couple of weeks about my concerns. They were amazed. Their response was "How do you do it? How do you get your cases done so quickly?" The one fellow in our study group who was always prepared worked constantly except Friday evening and one afternoon during the weekend. While he was the exception, long hours for everyone are the rule.* »

The long and demanding hours take their toll on social relationships. Spouses of students get the worst of both worlds. They must share the daily academic pressure that their husband or wife constantly faces. Yet at the same time, they are excluded from much of the social life. Almost all parties and activities are with classmates who continually talk about the school in general or specific cases. Spouses may feel pretty neglected. Marriages that are strong can survive this pressure, while weak unions probably will not last.

Single students also feel pressure since there is little time to cultivate outside relationships. Most students, however, do find the time for some socializing, albeit even if most of it is with the section.

In the end, it is the individual section, a collection of eighty-five people, that makes or breaks the Business School social experience for most students. Since the majority of students get along very well with their section-mates, the social life is generally considered to be good and enjoyable.

« The Business School is not all work. There were three marriages, numerous engagements, two single births, and one set of twins in my section during the two years. My personal award for endurance and achievement goes to the family of the twins since not only did they manage to survive the two years, but the father also graduated with distinction. »

RECRUITING AND JOB SEARCH

IT is often said that the two-year program at the Business School is divided into two equal parts. The first year is spent in classes and the second year is spent recruiting. While this is probably an exaggeration, recruiting is a major activity during the second year. After all, that is what the MBA is all about.

The recruiting process, however, really begins in January of the first year. That is when students begin to search for the summer job between the first and second years. Students view the summer job as a opportunity to try out a new area or new company with very little risk and to test their newly acquired business and analytical skills. The types of jobs and positions that are available and accepted are similar to the jobs that students will have after they graduate, although they are hired at a much lower salary.

Finding a summer job, even for B School students, is not easy. Compared to the second year, fewer companies recruit on campus and when they do come, they have fewer openings. On the other hand, the B School's job resources are great and students often use professors, fellow students, and alumni to secure positions.

« I got a summer job in a most unusual way. I interviewed with a number of companies, but could not find anything I was really excited about. So I went to one of my professors and asked him if he knew of any interesting positions. He said he just heard of a great job that very morning that he thought was perfect for me. He then reached into his wastepaper basket, pulled out a crumpled piece of paper, and said "Here it is." I thought he was kidding, but he said he wasn't. I interviewed for the position and took it. It turned out to be a great summer job. »

The job search during the second year becomes almost a full-time occupation. Upon returning to campus in the fall, students immediately start to plan their search strategy. Most begin by reviewing the company and industry files in the library. They also visit the library once a week to look over job descriptions that are sent in by companies who will recruit on campus in the spring. Students then do exhaustive company analyses, applying all the sophisticated skills they picked up the first year. Actual interviewing on campus is not permitted the first semester. A few students, however, attend off-campus "get-togethers" held by aggressive consulting companies. The fall may also be spent investigating companies that do not recruit on campus, although the majority of students focus their efforts on the more than four hundred companies that visit the Harvard campus each year looking for MBAs.

During the fall term, students spend anywhere from 10 to 30 percent of their time on the job search. The effort really intensifies in the spring, when students devote 30 to 100 percent of their waking hours grasping for the golden ring. The weekly trips to the library become daily visits as students eagerly review each new job description.

The average student interviews with eight companies, although this may range anywhere from one to forty-five. The average student also receives four job offers, although again, this may vary from one to fifteen.

Interviewing is generally a two- or three-step process. Students initially interview with a company on campus for forty-five minutes. The company interviews anywhere from five to eighty-five students. The company then invites the most likely prospects to company headquarters at company expense for a second round of what usually turns out to be a full day of interviews. The student may be asked back for a third or fourth round of interviews, depending upon the company.

The popularity of different fields and industries apparently comes and goes in waves. In the 1950s marketing was the favorite. In the 1980s, consulting and investment banking are at the crest of the wave. Consulting and investment banking are highly sought after because they either pay enormously high starting salaries ($55,000 a year for both fields) or offer large financial rewards later on ($100,000 or more after five years in investment banking).

Obviously, not everyone in the class enters the most lucrative or the most popular fields. Approximately 20 percent go into consulting, and 30 percent enter investment banking. The rest take jobs in widely diversified areas such as real estate, commercial banking, or electrical and electronic machinery manufacturing. The HBS degree offers students a lot of choice of which most take full advantage.

« *The job search the second year is almost a ritual. To appreciate it fully, students generally go through rites of passage. The first stage involves going through the company books at the library. This is an absolute necessity. Students spend hours doing research. They sometimes are more prepared and know more about the company than the interviewer. It's almost like preparing cases, only the stakes are higher. Then, students must sign with at least two consulting companies, usually BCG and Booz Allen, HBO, Morgan Stanley, and a group of more traditional companies like ATT, GE, and GM. Preparing for the interviews would be hilarious if students didn't take it so seriously. New suits are bought and haircuts are obligatory. The day of their interview students come to class in suits (both men and women). It is an unwritten law at the B School that they will not be called on to open a case that day because they have more "important" matters on their mind. Second interviews and traveling are also part and parcel of the rites. Students proudly announce that they must go to New York on Tuesday to talk with Merrill Lynch and be in San Francisco on Thursday to speak to TransAmerica. It is a rough life, they say, but it is the price they must pay for their intelligence and popularity. Job offers and salary signal that the process is almost complete. Most students will remark offhandedly that they have six offers, but can't decide which company to honor. Salaries are never outwardly discussed other than to say, "I really am going to need a good accountant to figure out what to do with all my money." Finally, the decision itself — selecting the best job offer — is almost anticlimactic, but it does bring with it a certain security and serenity. The Harvard MBA has paid its first reward. The late nights, the pressure-filled days, and the two long years suddenly seem worth the enormous investment.* »

ON THE JOB — FIRST YEARS OUT

THE acid test for an MBA is how much it helps in getting, keeping, and advancing in a job. It is clear that Harvard MBAs get jobs at higher salary levels than most of their counterparts at other business schools. The degree is also helpful in providing basic on-the-job analytical skills and instilling confidence in the recent graduate.

The exact value of these newly acquired skills and confidence depends entirely on the job. Some industries and positions utilize MBAs better than others. It is my impression though, based on numerous discussions with my classmates, that Harvard MBAs generally feel they are better prepared for business than non-MBAs and have a slight edge over other MBAs at the same level.

« One friend told me "An MBA is not essential, but it helps." Compared with non-MBAs at the same level, most of my friends feel they have a broader perspective on business problems, and certainly a greater understanding of the numbers that tend to intimidate non–business school graduates. I remember doing one analysis that involved a lot of numbers and a somewhat difficult concept. I found I had an easier time explaining the concept to MBAs and they in turn generally understood it better. »

While MBA skills are important, the Harvard MBA credential carries a lot of weight. Harvard proudly boasts that 19 percent of the top three officers in Fortune 500 companies are Harvard Business School graduates. Chances are that if you work in a large company, your boss or your boss's boss, or someone higher, will have an MBA from Harvard.

Graduates of the B School form a kind of informal fraternity born out of a shared educational experience that has changed little over the years. Graduates remember cases and their section-mates, and they value their HBS contacts. These contacts can provide advice, help, and even a little push when necessary. This informal but useful network makes the HBS degree even more valuable.

B School graduates have a reputation for switching jobs frequently. Harvard MBAs are often accused of wanting only to be president or chief executive officer of the company. Most Harvard Business School graduates sarcastically respond that they are perfectly willing to wait two to three years before this happens. In reality, Harvard MBAs do have high expectations. After two grueling years at the Business School, most graduates feel they are ready to handle far more responsibility than they are initially given. As a result, some graduates quickly become frustrated. Because of this frustration or a desire to earn more money, many B Schoolers switch jobs after two years (estimates range from 20 to 50 percent of the class). Job switching is a fairly common practice during the first one to five years of employment.

The desire to earn more money is one of the chief reasons why most students go to business school in the first place (whether or not they publicly admit it). Generally, Harvard MBAs earn excellent salaries after graduating. The median starting salary for new Harvard MBAs is over $50,000 per year, with a range anywhere from $18,000 to $90,000.

Nevertheless, money (or lack of it) is also one of the most common complaints after graduating. Many B Schoolers enter companies that may have salary structures not generally accustomed to accommodating Harvard MBAs. Despite the fact that Harvard MBAs are being paid five to fifteen thousand dollars more than their non-Harvard counterparts, many MBAs, at least initially, desire to earn even more money. However, in the long run, after paying their dues, most Harvard graduates do very well financially.

SUMMARY OVERVIEW

THE MBA program at the Harvard Business School is generally considered to be the strongest in the country. As one professor stated, "What we do, we do very well." Harvard does an excellent job training general managers. The classes, the curriculum, and the entire program are designed to achieve this objective. The program requires that students take courses in all phases of management, e.g., finance, marketing, personnel, and so forth. Cases are usually structured to focus on the role of the general manager, and special afternoon training sessions and business games also emphasize general management.

One of the reasons Harvard is so successful at training general managers is that it utilizes a case method. Rather than just imparting facts, the case method helps students learn how to think. This enables students to deal with the multitude of problems general managers encounter.

The Harvard program also prepares students for this role by teaching basic analytic skills, and then by requiring students to use these skills in the public forum of the classroom. Once students learn such techniques as decision analysis, economic analysis, and marketing analysis, they must present, explain, and defend their thinking. The program rewards students who are able to think on their feet. As one student put it, "If you can talk in front of eighty-five people and succeed, a job should be easy. No one will ever be as critical as your eighty-five section-mates."

Despite this natural competitiveness, the Business School is actually a very supportive environment, both formally and informally. The faculty devotes a great deal of time to teaching and counseling students. There is also a tremendous amount of positive interaction between students both in and out of class. Harvard Business School classmates and alumni can be a most valuable asset throughout your career.

Finally, one of the School's greatest strengths is the employment value of the degree. The Harvard Business School is highly regarded by employers and provides a fast track in many companies. More than four hundred companies currently recruit on campus at the Business School.

Of course, the Business School program is not without its drawbacks. There is an enormous workload, which drains students. There is little time to reflect on larger issues and little time to catch one's breath. Classes are held each day, five days a week, for two years. While other business schools may offer the luxury of Fridays free from classes, Harvard prides itself on the intensity of its program. Even with the recent reduction in workload, Harvard's program remains difficult.

Harvard also places a lot of emphasis on performance, and students are pressured to do well both in class and on exams. The school argues, and justifiably so, that there is a great deal of pressure in business, and that students must become accustomed to it. However, at Harvard, pressure and anxiety take their toll, and many students seek some form of counseling during their two years.

The attitudes of students and professors sometimes leave something to be desired. Students tend to be very aggressive. That is the way Harvard likes them and trains them. Professors can also be very intimidating and demanding. Occasionally, professors go overboard in their criticism of students and are incredibly insensitive. At other times this criticism is a highly effective teaching tool. Aggressiveness can be a strength and a weakness. At Harvard, it is both.

Another criticism can be directed at the grading process. Students go to great lengths to make comments in class because participation counts so heavily in grading. Some comments are highly relevant; too many others are repetitious.

Finally, Harvard trains general managers well, but does only a fair job of training technicians and technical experts. Students who seek technical specialties are advised to apply to other top business schools.

Going to the Harvard Business School is a major investment

in time and money. Is it worth it? After speaking with numerous graduates, the answer is unquestionably yes. Most of those I spoke with said the MBA was a key factor in getting their current job, and provided the basic tools and skills to handle it. Many said the Harvard MBA instilled them with confidence or an intangible feeling of being able to do well in business. This encouraged them to try new areas and take on new management challenges. A Harvard MBA provides more than just a set of skills and credentials: it fosters an attitude that is essential to success. To Harvard Business School graduates, the rewards are well worth the enormous effort it took to get the Harvard MBA.

Chapter 2

STANFORD GRADUATE SCHOOL OF BUSINESS*

THE PROGRAM

« *My first hint of what was in store for me at the Stanford Graduate School of Business came from a second-year student. In a typically friendly fashion, he introduced himself, and then offered me his congratulations and his condolences —congratulations for having gotten into the program and condolences for having to go through the first year!*

When I picked up my syllabi before the first day of classes and realized how much preparation would be required for the first class (accounting), I began to get apprehensive. Once I got there, my apprehensiveness progressed to acute anxiety when the guy next to me mentioned that he was a CPA and had failed the exemption exam. (If a CPA was not able to get out of taking accounting, how could I, an undergraduate liberal arts major, even expect to pass the course itself?) By the end of the class, after my classmates had expounded articulately on shareholders' equity (not an affirmative action program), LIFO and FIFO (not trendy names for dogs), goodwill (not the stuff

* BY PAT HUDSON, MBA, STANFORD

28

that is passed out at Christmas along with peace), and 10-K's (not an inferior quality of gold), I was no longer anxious—I was in a state of shock. »

The Stanford Graduate School of Business offers an MBA program of unsurpassed quality, marked by a devotion to "balanced excellence." At Stanford, that phrase is used repeatedly to describe all aspects of the program: courses that blend theory and practical experience; professors who must be both excellent teachers and academic leaders; and students with a staggering array of previous experience, who are both serious and fun-loving, motivated and supportive, analytical and creative. The Stanford GSB is committed to preparing students to become effective, professional, high-level general managers. It is this commitment to excellence that allows the Stanford Graduate School of Business to maintain its leadership position among graduate business schools.

The Stanford MBA program is designed to be flexible and responsive. As part of its main goal to develop general managers, the program:

- fosters innovative thinking and creative problem-solving;
- provides basic analytic skills;
- develops expertise in applying analytic skills;
- strengthens interpersonal skills;
- builds self-confidence; and
- encourages a desire for continued learning.

Courses are generally worth 4 units, and the program requires 108 quarter units for graduation, typically 60 units or fifteen courses in the first year and 48 units or twelve courses in the second year. Stanford is on the quarter system, with three ten-week quarters per year. (No summer courses are available at the GSB.) Eleven core courses are required the first year, ten of them generally taken in the first two quarters. Core courses include a heavy dose of the technical and the analytical: Financial Accounting, Cost Accounting, Decision Sciences, Production, Finance, Microeconomics, Macroeconomics, Statistics, Computers and Optimization Models, and (oases for the liberal arts major) Organizational Behavior and Marketing. Strategic Management, also required, is usually taken during the spring quarter of the first year. Business and the Changing Environment is the only required second-year course.

« It was the challenge of my life! Unlike the engineers and science majors in the class, known endearingly as "quant jocks," I hadn't had math since high school. Yet there I was, facing mountains of new materials, learning concepts I'd barely heard of before, and wearing out the batteries on my calculator with amazing regularity. After only four short weeks, we were blitzed by five three-hour midterms. And the intensity continued to build to the end of the ten-week quarter when we had five four-hour finals, all in the same week. I didn't think I'd make it, but my own determination — I'd never failed at anything before—and the unbelievable support of the entire school carried me through. By the end of autumn quarter, I felt like a survivor! »

Students may take exemption exams for any of the core courses. If they pass the exam, they receive no credit but may take electives in place of the core courses they have exempted. Regardless of whether any core courses are exempted, at least part of the first year and most of the second year are devoted to elective courses. Students must complete a minimum of fourteen elective courses in order to receive their MBA. There is no requirement to specialize; a range of about one hundred electives is offered and breadth of coursework is encouraged.

Up to sixteen units (four courses) may be taken in any upper division or graduate-level courses anywhere in the university. Stanford University has an outstanding reputation in all disciplines: medicine, law, engineering, the sciences, and the humanities. For this reason, many GSB students take advantage of the resources of the rest of the university during their time at the Business School.

There are 318 entering students per class at Stanford. Each class tends to be quite diverse, reflecting the diversity of the applicant pool of 4,200. Students come from all regions of the United States and from dozens of other countries. Women make up more than 30 percent of the class and minorities constitute 14 percent. All undergraduate majors are represented: liberal arts (23 percent), economics (20 percent), engineering (31 percent), math/sciences (16 percent), and business (10 percent). Very few students (less than 5 percent) come right out of college. The median age for Stanford students is twenty-seven, although the range is from twenty to forty-five.

Partly because of the small size of each class and partly because of the friendly atmosphere, everybody soon knows everybody else. Even the staff in the library, the registration office, and the placement office, as well as the professors, call the students by their first names (and vice versa). Sections provide a further source of support and camaraderie. Students are randomly divided into five sections of sixty students each for the first quarter's courses. Each section represents a wide variety of personalities, backgrounds, and perspectives. These sixty people get to know each other well and develop lasting friendships.

« *Among the people in my section were CPAs, lawyers, high school teachers, an artist, a submarine officer, a fighter pilot, bankers, engineers, advertising executives, an airline pilot, a*

Peace Corps volunteer, a magazine editor, and a costume designer. I remember my first group project. The four of us had typically diverse backgrounds, with previous employment at a bank, a college drama department, a shipping company, and the navy. There were no "experts" in the group and four very different opinions. The assignment was to develop a marketing strategy for a regional coffee company. I think I learned as much about teamwork as about marketing from that case; organizational skills emerged, brainstorming sessions occurred, and we developed an effective group process. In fact, I can't remember what marketing strategy we recommended, but the lessons I learned about organizing, listening, and managing have stuck with me. »

The group project is one of many teaching methods used at the GSB. Stanford is continually searching for better ways to educate managers, and the school makes extensive use of seminars, field trips, independent research, and projects for local companies. Both case method and lecture are used at Stanford. The proportion within a given class varies depending upon the type of course. The more technical subjects (about two thirds of the required courses) are generally taught via lecture with short cases emphasizing problem-solving as a basis for class discussion.

« *Decision Sciences was one of those courses with short cases and long answers. Decision trees and probability theory do simplify decision-making . . . eventually. They force you to break a problem into all possible actions and uncertainties so that you are playing with a "full deck" when you make the decision. Actually, Decision Sciences gave me some very helpful tools for decision-making but, more importantly, taught me that interpretation of the data is a matter of judgment. Basically, you have several alternatives in using your completed decision tree. You can decide it's a perfect model and should be thoroughly believed. You can consider it imperfect but good enough to be useful. You can view it as providing an interesting perspective but fall back on intuition. You can decide it was a waste of time. Still, you're not a Stanford MBA until you've drawn your first decision tree. »*

In the more qualitative subjects, where answers are not right or wrong, the case method is primarily used. A case presents an actual company experience, brings you in at a critical decision point, and asks you what you would do. For example, should Gillette enter the cassette market? Should Heublein buy Hamm's? How should Southwest Airlines respond to Braniff's price-cutting move? Cases are a good method of teaching a disciplined approach to problem-solving. A case discussion begins with an analysis of a company's current situation: the internal environment, including the company's objectives and resources, and the external environment, especially the consumer and competitive scene. Given the company's situation, alternative courses of action should be considered. The "solution" to the case is the recommended course of action.

« There's no "right" answer waiting to be found. Cases call for the type of reasoning, judgment, and creativity critical in the "Real World." In the Real World, good business management calls for rational thinking plus creative insight. That's why, to me, an MBA plus a liberal arts BA is often a good combination for a general manager. An MBA adds a logical framework to the holistic thought process you gained in college. It provides the analytical tools you need to tackle complex problems, but analysis alone can't replace intuition, creativity, and insight. The best case discussions call upon this unique blend of skills. It is this same blend of analysis and judgment,

so essential to a successful manager, that Stanford strives to develop in all students. »

True to its philosophy of balanced excellence, the Stanford Business School teaches a general management perspective but does not neglect the fundamentals. Courses stress thinking like the president of a company but also understanding enough about technical concepts to appreciate them, to use them and/or manage their use, and not to get "snowed." Assignments, often involving projects for local companies, generally combine the need for a broad perspective with the use of basic techniques.

A few of the more popular elective courses are listed below.

- Marketing Strategy
- Small Business Management
- New Ventures
- Strategic Planning
- Investment Management
- Negotiations

Stanford offers the Public Management Program, which prepares students for positions that involve extensive contact among business, government, public interest groups, and not-for-profit organizations. The Public Management Program, which is fully a part of the MBA program, combines full MBA training with in-depth exposure to public and not-for-profit policy issues and public sector management problems. Between 10 and 15 percent of each entering class opts for the Public Management Program. These students bring a wide range of backgrounds to the school.

« *Some of the most interesting people in our class were in the Public Management Program. These people didn't necessarily*

aspire to be captains of industry, but they were bright, moti-
vated, and added tremendous breadth to the class. One of our
classmates had been a Washington, D.C. cop. After graduat-
ing from a top university, he had chosen police work because he
wanted his life to make a difference. He came to the Business
School to increase his administrative effectiveness, but never
broke his ties with the police force. I remember throughout our
first two quarters, he was flying back and forth to Washington,
D.C. to testify against some of the criminals he had arrested.
Eventually, armed with his MBA, he went back on the beat to
work his way up in the police department. »

Complementing its commitment to providing a first-rate
general management education, Stanford has a well-deserved
reputation for academic excellence in all disciplines. Unlike
other schools, where much research is devoted to chronicling
how companies have been run in the past and developing
cases, Stanford is a leader in introducing new concepts to
business which eventually become generally accepted practice. The courses offered at the Stanford GSB, therefore,
reflect what is going on near the frontiers of research. One half
of the roughly one hundred electives offered are new every five
years, either as entirely new courses or as extensively revised
existing courses. Currently, the school is developing a new
emphasis on political economics. International management
and global issues are also being integrated into the MBA
curriculum. The school now offers eleven elective courses on
international topics, and core courses have grown to reflect the
new emphasis. As a result of this stimulating academic environment, as well as the small size of the school and Stanford's
attractive location, the GSB has been able to recruit a stellar
faculty. Many students choose a broad course of study and
select a particular class as much for the reputation of the
professor as for the subject.

« *I wasn't quite sure what possessed me to take Money and Capital Markets from Professor Van Horne. I fully intended to go into marketing after graduation. Professor Van Horne was legendary for his toughness. I worked my tail off and I've never used the stuff since. But somehow the exhilaration and pride I felt to get "Honors" in that class full of aspiring investment bankers instilled a self-confidence in me that has endured for years. In fact, it gives you a real feeling of pride and achievement to complete your Stanford MBA. I never would have believed, before I started, that I could work so hard, stretch so far, or learn so much. The program is a challenge from beginning to end.* »

GETTING IN

GETTING into the Stanford Business School is not easy. Over 4,200 applications are received each year for the roughly 300 positions in the MBA program. The school is looking for students with high academic aptitude coupled with senior management potential. The criteria the Admissions Committee list as important in selection are: "academic performance, motivation, achievement orientation, capacity for creating and taking advantage of opportunities, maturity, interpersonal and communications skills, assertiveness, self-confidence, and leadership potential."

« *The secret — if you can call it that — to getting in is first to get out in the world and prove you've got what it takes. That's why at the Biz School everyone is special. You know that anyone you choose to strike up a conversation with at a party, for example, will have something unique in his or her background, will have done something to separate him or her from the 4,000* » *applicants who weren't admitted. It's a great pleasure to associate with so many consistently outstanding people.* »

The application procedure is fairly exhaustive. It requires completing and filing the application, essays, summary of experience, recommendations, GMAT scores, and transcripts. Interviews are not required and are granted for information purposes only. The essays, especially, make the applicant think hard about himself, his strengths, weaknesses, skills, successes, failures, and goals. It is best to be totally honest in your application and not try to "psyche out" the Admissions Committee. It is better to get recommendations from people who have worked with you, really know you, and will tend to confirm the things you say about yourself, rather than from big names who will say nothing substantive.

Work experience is not required but is highly recommended; it significantly enhances the student's benefit from and contribution to the program. Diverse students from a variety of educational and cultural backgrounds are sought. The School encourages applications from special groups, including minorities and women, and schools outside the United States. Once having applied, however, members of these groups must meet competition from the entire applicant pool.

« *Getting into Stanford is a real accomplishment. Stanford is the toughest business school to get into: only one in ten is admitted versus one in eight at Harvard and even better odds elsewhere. One of the favorite topics of conversation early in the first year is "why I chose Stanford over Harvard." But despite Harvard's previous years of preeminence, Stanford students are not preoccupied with Harvard, and after the first few days, Harvard is seldom mentioned, except for an occasional refer-*

ence to "The No. 2 Business School" or "a well-known Eastern business school." »

ACADEMIC ENVIRONMENT

GRADES are intentionally deemphasized at the Stanford GSB. Courses are graded on a H (Honors), P (Pass — divided into P+, P, P−), and U (Unsatisfactory) basis. Each professor determines the relative importance of exams, papers, group projects, and classroom participation in awarding grades. A "P" is the standard grade, with + or − granted at the professor's discretion. Typically, no more than 15 percent of the grades given in any course are H's. U's are given only if they are merited, since the GSB has no set failure rate. Thus, an H is fairly difficult to get and a P fairly easy. But grades are not posted. Corporate recruiters are instructed not to ask for grades and students are encouraged not to provide transcripts. Class rankings are not known until graduation day, when the top 10 percent in the class are announced.

« *Grades are not a hot topic of conversation at Stanford. Most students feel there is little correlation between great grades in school and success in the business world. People come to Stanford to learn and to help their own futures, not to compete for grades. To many students, P stands for "Plenty Good Enough." Plus, everybody figures that if you made it through the admissions process, you're already in the top 1 percent of the population — so what do grades prove? A Stanford MBA ought to be sufficient credentials for anyone. I remember one particularly unlikely "scholar" whom I accidentally discovered had made all H's one quarter. He begged me not to tell anyone!* »

The academic environment tends to be supportive, cooperative, and free. There is an honor code in force at Stanford. By registering at the university, students affirm that they will not give or receive aid on exams. Open book exams are common, and in keeping with the spirit of the honor code, professors do not proctor exams. In fact, students can take exams anywhere they please, without supervision. Classroom interactions are generally cordial and friendly. Students do work hard and do strive for excellence, if only because that is the kind of people they were even before they were admitted to the program. They are concerned about their grades, but primarily as a sign of achievement in pursuit of a personal goal.

« *I felt a lot of pressure at Stanford, but it was internal rather than applied by professors or peers. The program is very challenging: the quantity of material covered is awesome, the pace is dizzying, the students are very bright — so there's no time for coasting while the others catch up, like there used to be in college. I was used to being at the top of the class, but so was everyone else. That situation can create enormous pressure and it is to the School's and students' credit that all concerned manage to maintain their sense of humor and balance most of the time.* »

Students rarely flunk out of the Stanford Business School. In fact, less than 3 percent per class fail to receive their MBAs. The School screens students carefully to be sure that anyone admitted to the program has the potential to complete it. Some students do not finish the MBA program, but invariably this seems to be because of a personal shift in priorities or a change in motivation, not a lack of talent or intelligence. It takes a lot of personal commitment and self-discipline to get a Stanford MBA.

« *I really learned time management at the Business School. During the first year, most students spend sixty to one hundred hours per week studying, including twenty hours per week in class. I wasn't at the low end of that range during my first two quarters. I worked much harder than I had at my full-time job before Business School. And still, there is simply too much to do; you can't do it all well. So you have to be clear about your own priorities, in terms of the relative importance of various courses, the trade-off between an H and a P, the value of hearing the president of GM speak versus studying an extra hour for the Accounting midterm. Even more fundamentally, you have to decide consciously on the amount of time you will reserve for your social life or your family life. The Business School can and will take 100 percent of your time — if you let it.* »

SOCIAL LIFE

« *One of the hardest things for a first-year student to get used to at the Stanford Graduate School of Business is the beautiful weather. Temperatures average 60 in winter and 75 degrees in summer, and it seems a shame to be inside studying when it's 70 degrees and sunny outside. Around midterm time — which on a ten-week quarter system comes very quickly — the realization sinks in that going to business school in California isn't going to be quite the holiday one had envisioned. One of the valuable skills a Stanford MBA acquires in two years is the ability to balance the rigorous course load with enough tennis to keep one's sanity!* »

There is an active social life at the GSB and it contributes significantly to the MBA experience. Like most everything else in California, the social life at the Stanford Graduate School of Business tends to be rather informal. There is a comfortable, open feeling at the school. Large patios are an integral part of the facility and are often the gathering place for students, professors, and staff during lunch or between classes. Laughter and animated conversation prevail.

Clubs abound at the Stanford GSB, and provide students with the opportunity to get to know people outside of class and to develop special interests. A few of the most popular clubs include the Black Business Students Association, Women in Management, Business Development Association, New Enterprise and Small Business Association, and Student Association for Public Management. The Business Development Association, for example, is a very active club, which provides free consulting services to hundreds of businesses in the area. The BDA is an excellent opportunity for students to help out a local organization, explore career interests in various fields, and practice applying some of the skills learned in the classroom. Various clubs also sponsor conferences for the students. For instance, a conference on manufacturing bought Lee Iacocca of Chrysler and John Young, CEO of Hewlett Packard, to the school, and provided workshops for students and alumni to discuss their entrepreneurial interests, strategies, and successes. Another popular series is "The View from the Top," which provides students the opportunity to attend talks by prominent CEOs.

Since there are no classes on Wednesdays, Tuesday nights are frequently dedicated to quiet socializing, like grabbing a burger and a beer with a bunch of friends at the Oasis, a local hangout. On Fridays, LPFs (Liquidity Preference Functions) are sponsored by companies recruiting at the GSB, but the students generally stay and chat long after the recruiters have left — until the beer and wine are gone.

Some more-organized social events are also popular. A sizeable GSB contingent attends the Stanford football games in the fall. People go to football games at Stanford as much to get a tan and listen to the band as to watch football. A football game at Stanford is a pretty "mellow" affair — a most relaxing way to spend an afternoon away from the books.

Each fall, the Biz School sponsors a Bay Cruise, an evening of dancing on a cruise ship that slowly makes its way around San Francisco Bay. Each spring, GSB students host business students from other major West Coast universities for the Challenge of Charity, a weekend of dances, picnics, and sporting events that raises money for the Special Olympics for handicapped youngsters. Another social event of note is an annual show which has skits and songs lampooning the Business School and the business world in general.

« I remember a particularly outrageous skit a bunch of second-year students put on during my first quarter at Stanford. The situation revolved around the marriage of "Gary Embiay" to "Job." The wedding ceremony began with a slight variation on the traditional:

"Dearly Beloved . . . We are gathered here today in the sight of the efficient market and in the face of the SEC, to join together this MBA and this firm in holy synergy; which is an honorable estate, instituted of profits, returns and rising growth rates . . ."

The skit had us howling from beginning to end as we watched Gary Embiay handing over his tennis racquet, Coors can, and cut-offs in exchange for the Tie. The program concluded with a hysterically irreverent Chairman's Prayer:

"Ar Jay,† who Art in Biz School
Salary Maximization be thy game.
Let top recruiters come,

* REPRINTED WITH PERMISSION FROM *THE REPORTER*, STANFORD GSB NEWSPAPER.
†ARJAY MILLER WAS THEN DEAN OF THE STANFORD GRADUATE SCHOOL OF BUSINESS.

And our praises be sung,
In the Real World as they are at Stanford.
Give us this day our starting salary
And forgive us our P minuses
As we forgive them that taught us accounting.
Bleed us not with taxation
but deliver us our rebates.
For ours is the income
The power and the glory
For ever and ever and ever,
Exponentially.

A JOB"   »

Needless to say, the social life at the Business School revolves around the Business School. Conversation relates
largely to course assignments, professors, classmates, and, in
the second year, jobs. Nonstudents, therefore, often find it
difficult to appreciate the jargon, inside jokes, and hot topics
at a Biz School social event. A spouse's inability to share the
MBA experience, either socially or academically, as well as the
tremendous time demands of the program, makes these two
years somewhat trying for most marriages. However, groups
such as the Biz Partners Club offer programs to help include
the nonstudent in life at the Business School. It is a little easier
to be single, as long as you are prepared to stay single. Finding
the time to develop a meaningful relationship is difficult,
especially with someone from outside the Business School
who will probably have no understanding of or patience with
the time requirements of the program. Even romance between
classmates is a difficult undertaking. Nevertheless, two or three
MBA marriages seem to emerge from every class. Dual career
planning has become an important concern in the past few
years. Each fall, current and alumni couples participate in a
panel discussion sharing their dual career concerns and dis-
coveries.

Living in California is a social event in itself. While the quarter system does require three sets of final exams each year, it also permits a Christmas break and a spring break completely free of studies. Many Business School students spend that time enjoying San Francisco, just thirty-five miles north of campus, or the many natural wonders of the state, including the Pacific coastline, wine country, Lake Tahoe, and Yosemite National Park.

RECRUITING AND JOB SEARCH

« *It's a culture shock! Suddenly the beards are gone, the hair is trimmed, and there are navy blue suits everywhere. Recruiting season has begun. Actually, you get to build up to it gradually. It starts off innocuously enough: just a BBL here and there in the fall quarter. That's a forty-five minute opportunity for a recruiter to tell a classroom full of students (munching their brown bag lunches, hence BBL) why his company is just the place for them. BBLs are well attended, since a large proportion of students come to the Business School to change careers and to broaden the job options open to them. BBLs are an incredible opportunity to learn about different industries and companies in an informal setting. On any day, there are three to five taking place and the inevitable trade-offs must be made: Which one do I go to or what else should I be doing?* »

First-year students begin interviewing for summer jobs in February. Most students have a summer job between years at the Business School, and many use this job as an opportunity to explore a new industry. Alumni contacts and on-campus recruiting help students locate such jobs.

The job search in the second year is a much longer and more concentrated effort. Every second-year student's résumé must be submitted for the Résumé Book soon after returning to school in the fall. The Résumé Book contains the three hundred résumés of the graduating class and is indexed according to job objective, academic degree, and home states or countries. It is published in early November and sold to recruiting companies for $150 per copy. Career recruiting begins the first week in November; no evaluative interviews are permitted before then. All recruiting companies must interview through the Placement Office, where students sign up for one of the fourteen half-hour on-campus interview slots on each recruiter's daily schedule. Students can sign up for any interview/company on a first-come, first-serve basis. Most are easily accommodated.

« *It's like another full-time course! During the height of recruiting season, it seems like there's a cocktail party every night. These can be pretty stuffy affairs, but provide a chance to ask some questions of the sponsoring firms. As you progress past the first on-campus interviews, follow-up interviews occur over dinner or during a full day at the company. Winter quarter of the second year finds many students on "flybacks" to visit prospective employers. It takes a lot of time out of an already busy schedule, but the job search is serious business.* »

The Career Management Center is an excellent resource for students. Each year, the staff offers a five-week noncredit career planning course focusing on self-assessment, skills identification, priority setting, and life-style options. The office also sponsors workshops on such topics as résumé writing and salary negotiations. Mock interviews are videotaped so that students can refine their skills. About two thirds of the graduating class ultimately accept a job for which the initial contact was made through the Career Management Center. The remainder largely accept jobs they scouted out themselves (often using alumni contacts) or from previous employers.

Roughly eight hundred different companies (over two hundred fifty on campus and an additional six hundred via written communication), representing all kinds of industries, geographic locations, sizes, and jobs, recruit at the Stanford Business School. The spectrum is so broad because Stanford trains its students for a wide range of positions. Fundamentally, the Business School teaches the tools and the outlook that will continue to serve an MBA throughout his or her career. A successful career in business means moving into higher levels of management where the job becomes progressively less defined. Basically, a general manager is responsible for guiding his or her company through a changing environment with a constantly shifting set of challenges that he or she cannot readily predict. A Stanford business education aims to provide students with the analytical and technical skills they need to excel at their first jobs, as well as the management perspective they need to become the corporate leaders of tomorrow.

Stanford's placement record is excellent. Most students have several offers to choose from, three or four on average. Consulting positions have attracted 18 percent of the graduating class in recent years. Finance draws 30 percent of the class, with 23 percent of those going to investment banks. Marketing is the next most popular area, attracting about 9 percent of the class. About 60 percent of the students join companies with 5,000 or fewer employees. Roughly one third of the class stays in the West and another third accept jobs in the eastern states, particularly New York City (25 percent). The midwestern states generally attract about 8 percent.

A recent trend at Stanford has been the popularity of small "high tech" firms among graduating MBAs. Being in the backyard of "Silicon Valley" exposes students to career opportunities in the venture capital industry, high-technology companies, and entrepreneurial ventures. In large part because of the proximity of this exciting industry, Stanford MBAs have a tendency toward entrepreneurship and risk-taking, and high expectations for growth and success.

« *Of course, every interview doesn't turn into an offer. We all got our share of "bullets" or reject letters. In fact, in a brave display of gallows humor, the best bullets were posted on the "Bullet Board" in the student lounge. But, in general, it's a seller's market, and the biggest problem most students have is deciding which position to accept. Your opportunities are pretty much unlimited, which can be mind-boggling. There are lots of decision criteria: degree of challenge, size of responsibility, flexibility, future opportunity, fit with the corporate culture, and money. Actually, money is by no means the most important of these: 50 percent of my class did not accept their highest salary offer. It is critical that you define your perfect job. It's easy to be swayed by classmates' opinions and values, but they'll only be around for another few months. Your job will last much longer — if you choose wisely.* »

ON THE JOB — FIRST YEARS OUT

A Stanford MBA provides excellent preparation for most entry-level jobs in terms of the specific skills acquired, the analytical thought process learned, and the capacity for learning — and for plain old hard work — developed during the two-year program. Almost equally important is the self-confidence the program inspires in those who meet the challenge and earn the credential.

An MBA is expected to be able to use certain "tools of the trade": decision trees, PERT charts, probability theory, statistics, financial ratio analysis, present value analysis, variance analysis, cash flow analysis, data analysis, regression analysis, risk analysis. Which of the tools are utilized most depends on whether the first job is, for example, assistant product manager for a marketing company or associate in an investment bank. But the tools one learns in the Stanford MBA program are quite useful in the first year on just about any job in business.

« *The MBA program taught me the language of business and introduced me to a whole range of analytical techniques. Of course, like any new language, you aren't really fluent until you have to use it every day. When it was my own business being analyzed, I suddenly began to appreciate cost accounting and statistics like I never did in Business School. I learned a lot my first year out, from my boss and from the other MBAs in the company. I remembered some wry advice one of our professors had given us at Stanford: Don't go to a company where you are the only MBA because they may try to prove that an MBA isn't worth it — and use you as the example! I felt my degree was worth it and knew that others in the company shared that feeling.* »

MBAs are notorious job-switchers, and many do switch jobs after a year or two. Some MBAs take a job with one of the large companies that have the reputation as "training companies," such as IBM or General Foods, or at a top consulting firm, with the intention of moving on after a couple of years. They call this work experience their "second MBA." Others leave their first job because it does not meet their expectations, either in terms of being too demanding on their personal life or in terms of their enjoyment of the work itself. It is possible that these switchers did not adequately do their homework in order to understand the company and the job before they took it, but it is equally possible that the first job was unintentionally misrepresented by the company in the fierce competition for top business school talent. Some change firms for higher salaries, although most Stanford MBAs are quite satisfied with their salaries their first year out. And the average Stanford MBA has doubled his salary after five years.

« *One important way to avoid being disappointed in your first job is to keep your sense of perspective during recruiting. You have to keep reminding yourself: This is not the Real World! In the flurry of competition among firms for the graduating class of MBAs, you may have been royally wined and dined. But don't be surprised if the VP who took you out to dinner at school doesn't recognize you when he passes you in the hall at work. And don't expect them to hand the business to you when you walk in the door. You'll have to work hard to prove yourself and to earn their trust and respect. A Stanford business education will be a great help, but the easiest way to fail in your first job is to have the idea that an MBA automatically guarantees success.* »

SUMMARY OVERVIEW

THE Stanford Graduate School of Business is an excellent institution, well deserving of its reputation for unsurpassed quality. The strengths of the Stanford Business School are manifold.

- The caliber of education is outstanding. The professors at Stanford are at the forefront of their fields. The course-work exposes students to the latest techniques and challenges students to stretch and learn at their utmost capacity.
- The students at the Stanford GSB are exceptional. Their intelligence, motivation, and breadth of previous working experience greatly enrich the overall education.

- The environment at Stanford is conducive to excellence. It is supportive, cooperative, friendly, and (both figuratively and literally) warm.
- The Career Management Center is a valuable resource in finding a job. The staff performs a public relations role of sorts with the business community, maintaining cordial contacts with all the top recruiters. They assist students with job-hunting skills. They deftly handle the logistics of putting prospective employee in touch with prospective employer.

The MBA Program at Stanford is not perfect, however.

- Most students complain that too much material is covered in too little time, so that sometimes the pressure is intense.
- The first two quarters, especially, are quite quantitative, which can be very difficult for students without technical backgrounds.
- The Business School is such a cooperative and supportive environment that some MBAs have a period of adjustment in rejoining the corporate world, which may tend to be somewhat anonymous, competitive, and political.
- The Stanford Graduate School of Business is very expensive. Living in the Palo Alto area is expensive. Giving up one's job for two years is very expensive. Going back to Business School can be quite a sacrifice.

« But I'm glad I did it. For me, it was definitely the right decision, and I know that the great majority of my classmates would say the same. Cynics have claimed that the real strength of the MBA program is the admissions process: Stanford knows how to pick the winners and then doesn't mess them up too badly in two years. The cynics say most of the students would have been winners in any case, with or without an MBA. I can't agree with that. Stanford does admit high-potential candidates, but the program clearly improves one's chances of *reaching that potential. My Stanford MBA gave me the tools and perspective I know I'll need to be successful. It broadened my opportunities; the jobs I've held since graduation have been essentially open to MBAs from the top schools only. It raised my personal standards by showing me what real excellence is. It increased my self-confidence and confirmed my general management ambitions. I believe I may be a CEO someday, and I doubt that I would ever have lifted my sights so high without my Stanford MBA. »*

Chapter 3

THE WHARTON SCHOOL*
(UNIVERSITY OF PENNSYLVANIA)

THE PROGRAM

THE Wharton School is part of the University of Pennsylvania. It is located on a campus deep in the heart of West Philadelphia. Every year roughly 750 new MBAs graduate from there and venture out into the business world.

What is so special about these novices that they can command starting salaries higher than some of the people they will start working for? They all have a Wharton MBA. They are the fortunate few selected from roughly 6,000 applications and 45,000 inquiries. They survived two years of rigorous curriculum, social life, and job search. Now they are entering positions where they are expected to perform well and learn quickly. If they do not move up, they'll be moved out. They're on the fast track.

The average class profile shows that an entering Wharton student is likely to be slightly over twenty-six years old, and has had about four years of professional experience. Beyond that,

* BY MICHAEL DUGAN, MBA, WHARTON

52

the similarities stop. About 83 percent are American, 73 percent male, and they are scattered evenly among geographical and undergraduate backgrounds. In two years, however, they will all have one thing in common: an MBA from Wharton.

In the continuing debate over whether the case method is better than the lecture method, the Wharton School decided to take the middle ground. At Wharton you get both. The goal of Wharton's program is to teach you to think and analyze problems so that it becomes instinctual. Curriculum handles about half of this job, and group interaction, teachers, and exposure to the professional world handle the rest.

The curriculum consists of a core of eight subjects, plus business policy, five electives, four major requirements, and an Advanced Study Project. In all, you need nineteen course units to graduate and most courses are worth one unit.

Interaction with teachers, other students, and professionals is heartily encouraged. Wharton is designed to facilitate co-operation rather than competition among students. All students take all of their first semester core courses together through a cohort system. There is no class rank or cumulative average. This lack of measurable comparisons between your fellow students fosters a camaraderie that produces many long-lasting friendships.

Every program has its ups and downs and its easy and impossible courses. Wharton is no exception. You need at least nineteen credits to graduate, and at the beginning, they seem a long way off. If you have not dealt with calculus or long division since high school, you might wonder if you'll ever make it through.

The core is probably the most frightening. These are the required courses, and they are also the least likely to drive you wild with enthusiasm. As a marketing major, I was hardly excited by debits, credits, and long-term annuities, and I'm sure the converse was true for the accounting and finance majors. Of course, no one in his right mind was turned on by statistics. But, all in all, the core is survivable. The rest of the curriculum is likely to be far more interesting, since those are the subjects you wanted to study in the first place.

The key to remember is if you have gotten into Wharton, you can handle the curriculum. The hard part is getting in. Sometime within the first week, after being intimidated by someone's awesome credentials, you will probably look around and ask yourself, "Why me?" No, it was not a mistake. If you got in, you deserve it. Two years later most of your class (about 95 percent) will be leaving with an MBA.

During the two years at Wharton, you'll be very busy. There are nine required courses designed to strengthen your business aptitude: Accounting, Finance, Marketing, Management, Microeconomics, Macroeconomics, Quantitative Methods, Statistics, and a Business Policy course. Almost any of these courses can be waived by either a test or departmental permission. If you waive the course, you get no credit for it; you substitute it with an elective.

Accounting is basic accounting. It can be a nightmare or a breeze depending on whether as an undergraduate you were a philosophy or music major or a corporate tax planning major. Extra help and tutoring are available. And if necessary, you can take the course twice.

Management and Marketing will probably be your first exposure to the case method. Although it is time-consuming, analyzing cases is an excellent way to learn the fundamentals of managerial decision-making. Both courses will incorporate business ethics and may also require group projects and formal presentations.

« I remember walking into my first management class. There were about forty students intently watching this professor who walked, talked, and acted like Inspector Clouseau from the

Pink Panther. He was difficult to understand at first. He explained in his Italian accent that we do not study management to teach "minkeys" to respond to a banana, but rather we are here to learn to design incentives so that people will want to do the task we need them to. He taught management from an Italian perspective. Since you cannot fire people in Italy, we were not allowed to use firing as alternatives to solving our cases. Some teachers would let you fire the entire company if you thought that would solve the case. The perspective of any course depended entirely on the instructor's background and opinions. I happened to prefer the humanistic Italian viewpoint; others did not. »

Microeconomics can be pretty tough. You may now begin to see where Wharton earns its reputation as a "numbers" school. There is a considerable amount of math. Don't worry; you are all in it together and help is always easy to find.

Macroeconomics is one of those subjects you cannot clarify. Obviously there are no right or wrong answers; if there were, the world would never be plummeted into the recessions, depressions, slowdowns, or other vagaries that periodically afflict it. Your course will reflect the particular view of your teacher who will make brilliant arguments demonstrating how easily the economy could be righted if only world leaders would follow a few simple rules. It's never that simple. But regardless of the argued position, the course does give you a better understanding of the complexities and intricacies of any economy.

Quantitative Methods is probably the single course most responsible for giving MBAs a bad reputation in industry. This course attempts to break many problems into formulas no one will even understand. These formulas can be very helpful. But when you get your job, use them in secret and do not, I repeat do not, try to explain them to anyone who has been making decisions "their way" for over ten years. Tell these people you are just a good guesser.

« *During my summer job I noticed people's reluctance to deal with numbers and formulas. I was working at a national magazine, which had the most archaic system of deciding how many copies to send each distribution chain. One man had been doing it on judgment alone for over twenty years and was indispensable to the organization. Unfortunately, the man was getting slower and slower over the years.*

Having successfully completed my coursework in quantitative methods, I suggested that we develop a formula to distribute the magazine based on prior issue performance, performance a year ago, and a few other easily calculated criteria. With that formula, they could have allocated distribution more accurately and more quickly in five minutes than it took this one man two weeks to do.

Welcome to the world of reality. My suggestion was not exactly greeted with open arms. The man immediately decided that I was trying to get rid of his job. I was told that computer services did not have the capacity to provide such a formula, and basically, I got the message that I was summer help and had no right to go around trying to reorganize a successful operation.

Now when I look back on it, I can surely see that I rushed into that recommendation assuming that everyone at the magazine was as eager as Wharton School students are to streamline operations. In fact, what they wanted to do was survive. The magazine had just been acquired by a much larger conglomerate, and they saw my formula as an extension of that control. The new management had already "cleaned house" of the obvious deadwood and it was only a matter of time before they would initiate programs to streamline the operation. No one wanted the summer help accelerating the process.

It was my mistake and not an unusual one for an MBA. I had made profit and efficiency my goals and objectives. In reality, that is not always what people want in a corporation. Sometimes preserving the status quo is a far more realizable objective for lower or middle management, and in this case, they had nothing to gain by my improvement. Quantitative Methods has very little capacity to deal with the informal human goals. I cannot blame them for resisting. »

Statistics is the same course you probably tried to avoid in college. It has now caught up with you. You have to bite the bullet and dive into probability, regression, hypothesis testing, and student-t distributions. If those terms are unfamiliar, just wait and see what else Statistics has in store for you. I got lost after the coin flipping and black jack examples.

Finally, there is Business Policy. You should take this course in your second or third semester because it integrates much of what you've learned in the core into a strategic framework. Business Policy stresses top-down, executive-level decision-making and analysis of the corporate entity. The outstanding reputations of Wharton graduates probably stem, in part, from their skill in problem analysis and solution methods, acquired through these courses.

« *There was one particular teacher who was known for his consulting and a problem-solving matrix that had been named after him. He taught my Policy and Planning class. He also modestly billed himself as the "world's greatest consultant." Very few of us doubted that he had earned his title. For example, he stated that his work could have been a major factor in the Westernization of the Moslem world, and a catalyst for upheaval in the entire Middle East. He developed a plan that led to the first tractors being sold to Turkey, which in turn completely restructured the country's economic and cultural*

57

foundation. The effects of this soon spread to the entire Middle East.

Sound improbable? It is not. Within several years, Turkey was transformed from a country that was operating at barely subsistence levels to one that was a major grain exporter. Suddenly, its entire social, cultural, and religious heritage was invaded by the Western World. This is the basis of the undercurrents of rebellion and violence that are proliferating in many of the Moslem lands today.

The most important thing we learned from this example is that a person cannot look at one deal as an isolated event that has no repercussions outside of it. The problem must be considered completely and in absolute detail to arrive at the best solution. There are other instructors at Wharton with stories that can rival his. Some are overexaggerated and others are understated. No matter what, there is a collection of some of the world's finest analysts at Wharton, and you can be exposed to their methods and thinking in a number of Policy and Planning courses. »

Additional noncredit courses are required, such as Introduction to Computing, Mathematics for Business Analysis, and Management Communication. The computer course emphasizes personal computer literacy and software applications that will be relevant at Wharton and after graduation. Both the computer and math requirements can be waived by passing tests. Oral and written communication requirements are handled through a required semester-long course.

That is it for the core. Everyone has to survive it and almost everyone will. Despite all the complaints, the courses give a broad base to your understanding of the economy, business, and individual corporations. The core is also a common nemesis that links everyone together.

By the end of the second semester, you must declare your

major. There are majors in Accounting, Decision Sciences, Finance, Health Care Management, Insurance and Actuarial Science, Public Policy and Management, Management, Real Estate, Marketing, and Transportation. If none of these particularly appeal to your interests, you can design your own major.

The requirements are the same for all majors. You must take four courses in your area of specialization and complete an Advanced Study Project (ASP). Hopefully, your major will be compatible with your interests, and you will find these courses enjoyable and instructive.

You may feel a little differently about the ASP, which is a semester-long research project quite similar to a thesis. Just like a thesis, it is often the victim of procrastination. ASPs are usually done in the last semester when job interviewing is at its peak. It's very likely that you could be in two or three different cities during any week. That makes it very difficult to keep up with standard courses, and even harder to start an independent research project. The best advice is to try to get your ASP done in the first semester of your last year, if possible.

« *Every program in every university in the world has its barriers like an ASP. It is the final hurdle to jump before the degree is yours. Some people buried themselves for two weeks before graduation trying to complete it. Others were up well into the night before graduation completing the opus. Finally, others gave up completely and did not finish the project until all of their colleagues had left campus. They decided that rather than rush it, they would hand it in after graduation. ASPs make for a lousy summer vacation, so bite the bullet and try to finish it before your last semester. It makes the entire experience less frantic and more enjoyable.* »

Some majors offer special seminars as an alternative to the traditional ASP. These can be ideal if you anticipate an extremely difficult semester with little time for independent research. The seminars are also good if you are a procrastinator by nature and function better with a little structure. If, on the other hand, you prefer independent research, you have the option of doing a thesis over two semesters.

Finally, we reach the electives. You have an unlimited range of possibilities with these subjects. Entrepreneurial and Venture Initiation, Multinational Management, Speculative Markets, Leadership, and Business Responsibility and Population Ethics are just a few of the popular choices. You can choose to specialize further in your major or you can expand your coursework to any of the graduate schools at the University of Pennsylvania. This is your chance to get back to art history, philosophy, or any of the other subjects you felt you left behind as an undergraduate. In addition to Wharton, the University of Pennsylvania has some of the best graduate programs in the country. The School of Engineering, Medical School, Law School, and Annenberg School of Communications have excellent reputations. Taking a course at any of these schools broadens your education and your base of friends and contacts.

Electives are what you make of them. You can use them to pad your schedule, or for something fun, interesting, and enjoyable without guilt. My personal advice is to save them for the last two semesters. In the last semester your zeal for studying has long since faded as a result of "senior slump," exhaustive interviews, or an overdue ASP. Your electives can be a refreshing change from the fairly intense grind of the previous year and a half. Luckily, there are teacher ratings done by students and published by the Wharton Graduate Association that provide guidance to picking easy and difficult courses.

« *During my last semester, I decided to take a class in business ethics. I thought it would be fairly easy and that the time demands would not be so great. I really had little intention of learning anything applicable to business, and I had no question about my morals or ethics. Yet, I was shocked by some of my own decisions and my positions during role-playing assignments.*

Within several weeks, my conscience had gotten the better of me and I was working harder on that course than on some of the others. I was also very surprised to find that out of all the courses I took, this one turned out to be one of the most important. I pursued it as a lark, and yet it significantly shaped my attitudes and approach to business.

Years later, when I was an advertising account executive, I fell back on the rules and personal codes I had made for myself in this course. I was working on the Rely Tampon account during the final days before the decision was made to withdraw them from the market. I am not sure how I would have acted without the course, but looking back on it, I am happy about the courses of action I recommended. I feel I made the right decisions, and I stuck by my guns even when upper management was not always in agreement with me.

The point is, electives can be very helpful, often unexpectedly. Take what you want and do not feel guilty about choosing a course that may be less taxing. A course's usefulness has nothing to do with its level of difficulty. »

You now know what is required to get a Wharton MBA, but what are all these courses like? How are they taught? How hard are they? Let's take a closer look.

MBAs have a well-deserved reputation of being aggressive overachievers. That is probably the major thread that winds through everyone's credentials. If they weren't superaggressive then they probably wouldn't have applied to and gotten into Wharton in the first place. People at Wharton are NOT mellow or laid back. There is a great deal of energy, hyperactivity, or whatever you want to call it. At first, this gets directed toward the classroom. In later semesters, it is focused on the job hunt, extracurriculars, and partying.

In the early stages of the first semester, there's a tendency to overstudy and overprepare. Students are hyped-up and ready to attack the program. That sets the stage for your first classes. Chances are it is one of the core courses. There will probably be a lot of anxiety as you begin the program. It will culminate with the first set of exams, but by the end of the semester you will have a much better sense of your academic priorities.

The size of the classes vary. There can be as many as one hundred students or as few as two. It all depends on the course, the department, and the teacher. Unlike Harvard, not everything is done with case method. Therefore, even the structure of the courses vary infinitely. Some use case method, some lecture, some depend on class discussion, and others base everything on a final paper or exam.

Overall, Wharton has a strong finance reputation. There is an emphasis on numerical analysis and almost no major has escaped the disciplines of linear programming, model building, or statistical analysis. Don't let that scare you away. If you fear math like the plague, there are many ways around the numbers, and in some majors you can escape fairly math-free. Naturally, you are likely to get a heavy dose in Finance or Accounting. In other majors that are less quantitative, however, you can take electives that focus more on qualitative analysis than on math. Of course, if you happen to like formulas and quantitative methods, you have found nirvana. You can have as much math as you want; there is plenty available.

Until 1971, the Wharton School was known as the Wharton School of Finance. With a name like that, it is of little wonder Wharton had the reputation of focusing primarily on finance. That reputation is probably deserved. Roughly half of the students are finance majors and a great number of the alumni are in financial positions in industry.

In many ways, however, the reputation is no longer appropriate. The school has made a serious commitment to other fields. The programs in Health Care Management, Marketing, Decision Sciences, International Management, Entrepreneurship, and Real Estate are among the best in the country. The faculty consists of scholars who are world-renowned practitioners in their particular industry. Almost all of them are still very much involved with private corporations, primarily as consultants.

While Wharton's reputation is still very strong as a financial training ground, its other departments deserve equal recognition. As more and more alumni have distinguished themselves as entrepreneurs, international managers, and marketing mavens, the fine Wharton name now stands for a more broad-based spectrum of excellence.

GETTING IN

THE key to a Wharton MBA is getting in. If you get in, chances are that you will graduate. The question is then, "How do you get in?"

There is no easy way to answer this question. Wharton has no admissions formula. Rather, Wharton is interested in looking at candidates from a global perspective. They are interested in applicants who have both a solid record of academic achievement and show the potential for management success. In this regard they evaluate everything from transcripts, GMAT scores, and professional or academic recommendations to other evidence of leadership and management experience and ability. Since the school receives so many applications for the limited number of spots, they can afford to

be very selective. Therefore, it is important to carefully artic-
ulate why you want to get an MBA and why you want to do it
at Wharton.

« *It is very hard to identify much of the rhyme or reason
behind the admissions committee's acceptances. In my class,
there was a medical doctor, several lawyers, a woman who had
been in charge of some factories in Afghanistan for over ten
years until she was expelled by the Communists, and a large
assortment of other people with just as varied and sensational
achievements.*

*I was fresh out of college with a couple of summer jobs, some
good board scores, a decent GPA, and lots of energy. Why did
they pick me or why did they pick them? I have no idea. I was
a little intimidated by my classmates' achievements and they
were a little intimidated by the fact that I was used to the grind
and rigors of a full-time scholastic program. But, we all helped
each other. They taught me about real life, and I showed them
how to get used to the demands of studying full time.* »

There is a "rolling admissions" policy, which means that
applications are evaluated in roughly the order in which they
arrive. That system makes it pretty important to get your
application in early.

Wharton looks for students who are mature and committed
to getting their MBA, and who show through their applications that they have direction and a sense of purpose. They
usually interpret professional experience and strong extracurriculars as favorable indicators.

Evaluative interviews are used at Wharton, with almost
three quarters of the entering class being interviewed. The
school offers group sessions where you can ask questions and
find out more information about the program, meet students,
and visit classes. If you feel you have something to offer, but

your numbers do not look good on paper, don't hesitate to go see someone. Like any top business school, Wharton wants good people and if you can convince them you will be an asset, you have a chance of getting in. Unfortunately, there are no easy paths. You have to be creative, persistent, and capable of selling yourself.

ACADEMIC ENVIRONMENT

As I mentioned in the previous pages, Wharton tries to de-emphasize competition. There is no class rank, and grades are based on a Distinguished, High Pass, Pass, or No Credit system. This fosters a spirit of cooperation and promotes a fertile, interactive environment.

If you can get into Wharton, the chances are very high that you will successfully complete the program. Wharton spends a great deal of time selecting students who can meet the requirements and then gives them every opportunity to get through. Flunking out is possible, but it is rare.

There are some extremely difficult courses and the general workload is pretty rigorous. But most of the pressure at Wharton is internal. The motivation to go for a Distinguished rather than a Pass grade comes from the students. You create your own level of expectations.

« Like many of my other colleagues, I decided in my first semester that I would have to get Distinguished marks in all my courses. I spent night after night in the library and received all D's except for one High Pass. My elation was soon tempered when summer job interviewing started. Not one company asked me what courses I was taking, what my grades were, or if I could read or write. They assumed I was smart since I was at Wharton, and all they wanted to know was that I could get along with them.

After my initial disillusionment wore off, I decided that maybe it was time to extend my life beyond the doors of the library. I discovered the MBA house, Thursday Happy Hours, and began to notice that some of my fellow students were pretty interesting people. I eventually ran for treasurer of the Wharton Graduate Association and entered a world where coursework is something you did in undergraduate school.

I honestly feel that my education really started at the beginning of my second semester when I began to enjoy and participate in the other activities that Wharton has to offer. Corporations are not particularly interested in bookworms. They are more interested in people who can relate to others. Wharton offers you plenty of opportunities for that. »

SOCIAL LIFE

ONE of Wharton's best features is its social life. There is a tremendous amount of socializing, which is done on both a formal and informal basis. For example, every Thursday afternoon there is a Happy Hour that is attended by a large number of first- and second-year students. Wharton does not hold classes on Friday, so these evenings often carry over long into the night.

The major social organizer is the Wharton Graduate Association (WGA). This is the student government and it is subdivided into clubs: academic, professional, and social, including the Wharton Journal, Intramurals, International Student Groups, and others. Each of these clubs has special events and speakers for either socializing or learning more about an industry or company. The WGA also organizes other social events like Casino Night, The Walnut Walk, and The Follies.

You will never have a problem finding something to do, but

you may have a problem finding the time to do it. The workload is heavy and often it seems it will never let up. Somehow, everyone seems to be organized well enough to get in a good amount of socializing.

The social times that you spend are very important, as well as enjoyable, because your fellow Wharton students will probably be the basis of your professional network in later years. There were some people who opted not to participate socially, but I feel they missed a very valuable part of the education.

« *The social life can sometimes be more grueling than the actual coursework. Each semester there is a "Walnut Walk." This is an event that is famous in Philadelphia. All the Wharton students dress in formal attire and tennis shoes and gather at a bar down on the waterfront. This motley crew proceeds to walk up Wanut Street and through about twenty bars on the way back to the campus.*

It is a pretty funny sight to see two hundred people pour into a quaint little tavern in formal clothes with tennis shoes on. It is even funnier at about the twentieth bar where these people arrive completely intoxicated. The crowd is normally very rowdy and quite out of character for future leaders of Corporate America.

On the weekend of my last Walnut Walk, I had to reach to my limits for stamina. I had drawn up the agenda of bars for the event, so of course, I felt obligated to visit every one. After arriving back at my apartment at around 6:30 A.M., I had just enough time to grab two hours sleep before running in a five-mile race at 9:00 A.M. Needless to say, my performance in the race was something less than spectacular. My performance in an intramural softball game in the afternoon was even worse.

I had to be on a flight to St. Louis that evening for a Monday morning interview. But actually I was lucky — otherwise I would have had to attend a steering committee meeting and then someone's engagement party. Walnut Walk weekends are particularly rough, but they are not much different from many others. »

The specific time demands of the program are dependent on the type of courses, the professors, the style, and method of teaching. Case method courses require more hours of daily work because you have to be prepared for each class. In general, the workload is heavy, but the beauty of the program is that you can set your workload to your needs. Different people have different priorities. To some students it is more important to meet the Chairman of Citibank at a club function than to get a Distinguished in Finance. The amount of time you spend studying is up to you.

Going to any school while you are married can be very difficult. Wharton is no exception. It can demand valuable time away from your spouse. The Wharton Graduate Association tries to remedy this in some ways and invites spouses and partners to all its events. Most importantly, however, WGA tries to encourage involvement and friendship and to provide a place for partners and spouses in the Wharton experience. It has established a club, called The Wharton Partners (for married couples or people who are living together), that sponsors numerous get-togethers and discussions.

There is little hardship in being single at Wharton. There is a great deal of socializing, and relationships form on every level. There are even marriages that start at Wharton. Basically, it is similar to the social situation in undergraduate school, except the people are a little older and sometimes a little more mature.

Housing for graduate students is a mixed bag. Campus housing is pretty functional. The apartments are fairly expensive but they are relatively safe, comfortable, and convenient.

On the other hand, if you live off campus, close to the university, the apartments are generally older and less expensive. Good apartments and good landlords are scarce. But still you can usually find fairly reasonable accommodations.

« *I was visiting one friend who lived off campus and her apartment was so old it still had a Murphy bed. The place was well maintained, but it was just old like many parts of West Philadelphia. She happened to be very lucky. The hot water, electricity, and heat worked. In fact, the place was even more cockroach-free than the University's housing.* »

The other alternative is to live in Center City or another better area of Philadelphia, where living is more scenic, but less convenient.

Thus, housing is what you make of it. Most MBA students, especially first year, prefer to live on campus. After that more move off. In either case, the housing is certainly livable and most students enjoy it.

RECRUITING AND JOB SEARCH

AFTER you put in two years, complete nineteen credits, and go to countless interviews, you are now ready for your new career. What has Wharton trained you for? It probably has not trained you for any one particular job. Your new company will take care of that. Wharton has given you an approach to problem-solving, and a working proficiency with industry language and techniques. Basically, Wharton has trained you to learn and learn quickly.

Your training is not confined, however, to the classroom. Rather, it is continued by the Office of Career Development and Placement. During your two-year stay at Wharton, you have the opportunity to participate in a wide range of activities which will help you identify the skills, attributes, values, and preferences you seek in a career. The focus then shifts to identifying opportunities in the marketplace. Speakers, ranging from entry level MBAs to middle managers to CEOs, provide insights into various industries and functions. Having targeted specific areas of career interest, you can take advantage of training in job-search techniques. Seminars are held on such issues as developing a résumé, interviewing effectively, and generating off-campus opportunities. Students are encouraged to work individually with a counselor in developing job-search strategies.

The benefits of the career development process become very evident when you begin interviewing on campus. Over 400 companies recruit at Wharton. Recruiting begins in October of the second year and continues until late spring or until you accept an offer. Initial interviews are conducted on campus. They are relatively short and informative, and provide a good indication of compatibility. If there is a mutual interest, then the company will arrange for you to visit them for a second, more in-depth interview. It can get pretty hectic, especially if you are exploring different industries scattered all over the country. One week I had to be in St. Louis; Elkhart, Indiana; New York; and Morristown, New Jersey. Needless to say, your coursework can suffer if you have not planned your schedule well. Try to get as much coursework out of the way as possible before the last semester.

By the end of their second year, students will have had, on average, twenty-five initial interviews and received three job offers. Major areas pursued by Wharton grads include investment services, product marketing, management consulting, real estate, and corporate finance.

In recent years, more students have expressed interest in and secured positions with smaller firms. While much of the on-campus recruiting is done by larger firms, Career Development and Placement actively encourages correspondent listings from smaller firms.

The process for securing summer jobs between the first and second years is similar. There are not as many companies with available summer positions, and the supply of summer positions usually depends on the economy. Most students do get very good summer jobs, using a combination of on-campus interviewing, correspondent opportunities, and their own initiative. The beauty of a summer job is that you can get a good look at an industry without making a long-term commitment. This can be a very useful opportunity, particularly if you are undecided or unsure as to which field you would prefer.

ON THE JOB — FIRST YEARS OUT

« *I was out of school for about a year. It was ten o'clock at night and I had just come in the door from work, when the phone rang. The caller said, "Hello, I'm Jack Thompson, second year at Wharton, and I'm sitting here in Vance Hall tonight with some alumni and other students. We're calling some of our New York alumni tonight trying to raise money for the Wharton Fund and we would really appreciate it if you could donate."*

Did I give or not?

I looked around me. I was living in an overpriced condominium that was too far away from the office. I had spent all day worrying about whether or not the FDA would approve the withdrawal announcements for my account, Rely Tampons. The headline of the front page of the newspaper announced there had been another death from toxic shock syndrome, believed to have been caused by Rely Tampons. I had not had a day off or even a date in three months. How did I get myself into this?

Wharton. For some reason, I gave. »

An MBA, even a Wharton MBA, cannot prepare you for a specific job or situation. It really does not give you anything magical. To get in you had to be bright, aggressive, and capable. With those traits, you could do very well at any job with or without an MBA. However, Wharton does refine your ability to focus on and identify a problem. It also helps you structure your logic for creative problem-solving. Armed with your natural abilities and an understanding of Wharton's problem-solving techniques, you are ready for most any job. The most important value of the MBA, however, is that it opens the door for that job.

There are many smart, competent people in this world and they may be capable of doing your job. The Wharton MBA gives you something that indicates you will be successful. With the degree, you are eligible to compete for a handful of top jobs against a much smaller, elite group.

The MBA is very useful on the job, and you will utilize the discipline and techniques you learned at Wharton. The situations and circumstances may be different, but the concepts are similar.

People with MBAs from top schools are sought after by many companies. Obviously, there is a great deal of job switching that occurs after the first year. Some people are lured away by more money, some switch industries altogether, and others find that the match they thought was there does not exist. Often you can get more rewards by moving than staying loyal to a company. When that's the case, it's time to change jobs.

« *A close friend of mine originally took a job with a corporation in Washington, D.C. After about one year, he saw that he could not go farther very quickly, so he was persuaded to accept a consulting job in New York. After about eighteen months in New York, he got another and still better offer from a consulting firm in Philadelphia. Now he is back in Philadelphia. This is his third job in about three years, but all of his moves were smart career and financial decisions.*

This is not just one isolated case. Alumni reunions are a must if you want to keep track of everyone. It seems as if almost everybody in my class has changed jobs once or twice since graduating in '79. About every six months I clean out my phone book. I always have more than one card for people and cannot remember which company was their old one and which is their current one.

Headhunters also play a big role in this. My first headhunter called me three months after I was out. I had not even found the men's room and someone was looking for a person "with my experience." The day they pulled Rely Tampons off the market I had calls from at least six headhunters who thought I would be fired.

Headhunters can be a valuable resource. Do not be afraid to talk to them, because sometimes they can have very tempting offers, and some day you might need them in a hurry. »

The average salary for a Wharton MBA is about the same as for Harvard, Stanford, and the other schools in this book. But, average salaries can be misleading. I had in my class a medical doctor, several lawyers, and other professional people who got offers above $80,000. That distorts an average. A Wharton MBA will add handsomely to your expected salary, whatever your level of experience.

Generally, I am very glad I got an MBA. It opened the door and gave me access to an industry at a level I might not have attained otherwise. It has given me a credential that is respected and will continue to open doors for me wherever I go.

Most importantly, it gave me a chance to make some very close friends who, within a few short years, are very likely to be leaders in their industries.

SUMMARY OVERVIEW

A Wharton MBA makes sense financially and personally. There are, of course, several strengths and weaknesses to the program.

Three major strengths distinguish Wharton as one of the top business schools in the world. The first is the people; the second is the interactive climate; and the third is the career placement. Each of these components build on each other to give the program its strong reputation.

The people are by far Wharton's greatest asset. There are world-renowned instructors in every department who are dedicated to teaching. And, a high-quality faculty is naturally going to design a program just as good.

The students are just as exceptional. They are selected from the top applicants in the world, and about 98 percent have at least two years of professional experience. They are of various ages and represent many countries and professions. When you combine this diversity of background with the energy and intelligence of the students themselves, you get a population that few programs can rival.

Wharton also acts as a catalyst to stimulate the interaction of these groups. The grading system reduces the outward measures of competition to facilitate cooperation between students and faculty. No matter how intelligent, students who are so competitive that they do not share ideas learn nothing from each other. It is also easier to seek advice from faculty members when your grades or class rank is not at stake.

The general feeling is that there is enough of the pie out

there for all of us. We would rather share it with a friend and help each other. This attitude creates tremendous bonds that last long after graduation.

Let's face it. We seek an MBA so that we can get a better job than we could without one. Obviously then, career placement should be examined as one of the most important elements of the program.

Wharton's career placement program is outstanding. From day one, they begin to groom you for the time you will leave. Almost all of the Fortune 500 companies come to campus recruiting each year.

In the first year, you begin to prepare for the summer job search in October or November. The actual interviews start in February. Wharton can be a great help with summer jobs and internships, but it's an even bigger help with permanent placement. With a Wharton MBA, your choices are unlimited. You can go to any part of the world, and into almost any industry that is remotely related to your major. Even better, you start out at a salary that puts you in the upper 15 percent of the population.

In fact, there are almost too many options. You can very easily have interviews in three different cities during any given week. Since so many companies visit Wharton, however, you can examine a wide range without ever having to leave Philadelphia. If you want to pursue them further, and they you, be prepared to travel.

Although the program is very strong, there is one flaw worth mentioning. This is the emphasis Wharton places on the large corporation. Wharton, like other schools in the top ten, feeds Fortune 500 companies. Most of its courses are taught in a manner that prepares you for those organizations. Obviously, some skills can translate very easily to smaller firms, while others can't. However, as more and more students express interest in small business, Wharton is making a greater effort

75

in this area. More courses related to entrepreneurship are being offered and a Small Business Development Center has been set up. There are many fortunes to be made in small firms, and a good MBA can sometimes shine more quickly and easily there than in a large corporation with many MBAs.

In summary, Wharton has an excellent program. It is people oriented and encourages interaction through a deemphasis of competition among students. The social life here is probably the best among the business schools. Wharton's career placement center is unsurpassed and presents you with more career opportunities than you can examine.

I'm very glad I went to Wharton. I feel that its program is among the finest, and there is probably nothing better for your earning power.

Chapter 4

CHICAGO BUSINESS SCHOOL*

THE PROGRAM

« *"For the first few months at Chicago you will probably wonder, 'How did I get in here? I don't belong here.' But you do belong here! You may not think you belong here, and you certainly may not know what you're doing here, but you do belong here. That decision was made for you."*

Such were the words of a professor during Orientation week. Almost everybody at one of the top business schools feels that way when they first arrive. This is largely because of the variety and wealth of knowledge and experience spread among your classmates. Within a couple of months, the terrifying doubts and insecurities are gone and you can actually begin to enjoy your B School experience. The only mistake I made in "going" to Chicago was choosing the wrong way to drive to the campus. As I drove toward the university through the South Side of Chicago, renditions of "Bad, Bad Leroy Brown" went through my head and I wondered if I would "survive" for two years at the university. Though the area outside of and surrounding the

* BY MARK SLAVEN, MBA, CHICAGO

university is not the most pleasant, Hyde Park, where the school is actually located, is a pretty and relatively safe community. The university's ivy towers and Gothic architecture are very impressive. A pleasant blend of old and new architecture amplify the beauty of the campus. There are plenty of trees and lots of grass which make for very comfortable and attractive surroundings. But before you can enjoy the beauty of the campus, you have to get through the curriculum. »

Each year approximately 500 new students enter the Business School at the University of Chicago. While the mix of students and diversity of backgrounds are tremendous, the demographics of each entering class are quite similar. Approximately 28 percent of the class are women, and 16 percent are minorities. Eighty-seven percent of the admitted students have had full-time work experience. The average age of the entering student is twenty-six. About one-half the students were either economics or business majors, one-quarter were science or engineering majors, and the final quarter pursued either social sciences or the liberal arts in their undergraduate institutions.

« I was most impressed (and somewhat intimidated) by my classmates. I soon became friendly with people who had been managers in oil companies, vice presidents of major banks, steel industry consultants, nuclear submarine captains, and several budding entrepreneurs. One person, who owned his own business since high school, had arranged several creative financing and marketing plans for his company and has been interviewed on talk shows across the country. I really wondered how a "lowly engineer" like myself could compete against people with such business knowledge. »

Such diverse and extensive knowledge among the students makes the University of Chicago a competitive place. How-

78

ever, several skills are important to succeed at Chicago and good business knowledge is only one of them. Fortunately for myself, ability in quantitative methods is another important skill.

Chicago is known for its strength in finance. In part, this stems from its extensive course offerings, its pioneering research work in this field, and from its heavy application of quantitative methods and models. There are many facets of finance at Chicago. A sampling of the course offerings and research work reveal the breadth and scope of expertise within the finance area: capital market efficiency, the capital asset pricing model, portfolio theory, capital budgeting, capital structure (debt policy and dividend policy are examples), and personal financial planning. Chicago is "at the leading edge of technology" in many of these areas. Regardless of which school you attend, you'll be reading many of the research articles done by some of the great finance professors at Chicago; names like Fama, Miller, Hamada, and Lorie (the finance faculty is unbelievable).

It's incredibly exciting to learn about the latest theories and ideas on finance from the people who are actually doing the work. You'll find that quantitative methods and models are applied in areas you never would have conceived.

But the frontier courses and research work don't stop with finance. Similar courses and work have begun in accounting, although it's still somewhat in the infancy stage. It wouldn't be surprising if over the next ten to twenty years Chicago plays a leading role in shaping thought in this arena as well. Who would've thought that theories and models could be applied to the accounting process? If they can be, Chicago will find the way.

Modeling and quantitative techniques aren't restricted to "numbers" type courses at Chicago. There is another area of work that's receiving more emphasis, and that's in modeling human judgment and decision-making. Imagine building and applying quantitative models to the way people make decisions and then finding that the models work better than the actual people in making future decisions.

If you are beginning to think that Chicago is fairly quantitative, you're right. Most of the courses at Chicago tend to be somewhat quantitative in nature. In many of these courses you'll apply specific models to a variety of problems. Some models are readily accepted as useful and scientifically correct tools. Other models are applied to a situation in a theoretical context and are helpful in training your mind to think in a different way than it's accustomed to thinking. In any case, you will see models developed and applied to many different situations, from modeling capital asset prices to modeling human behavior.

Despite its quantitative nature, which makes it very demanding, Chicago's program is exceptionally flexible. This allows students from diverse backgrounds to structure a curriculum to meet individual needs and desires, gives the program a much broader focus, and underscores the new emphasis the school is placing on general management, marketing, and small business. No one particular course is required at Chicago. However, there are three cores of topics from which each student must choose a total of eleven courses. These cores are as follows:

Concepts and Methods Core:
    Microeconomics
    Macroeconomics
    Managerial Accounting
    Statistics
    Management Science
    Behavioral Science

Applications Core:
    Financial Management
    Industrial Relations and Human Resource Management
    Marketing Management
    Production and Operations Management

Policy Studies Core:
    Business Policy
    Policy Problems in the Management of Governmental
    and Non-Profit Organizations
    The Firm in International Management
    Health Care Management Policies

Students have a great deal of flexibility, and need only choose one course from each topic in the Concepts and Methods Core. But within each topic there are several approved courses that the student may choose from. In the Applications Core, a student has to choose only one course from three of the four topics. And finally in the Policy Studies Core, a student chooses only one course from the four topics.

It is easy to see that even for the "required" courses, the student has the freedom to choose which topics to cover in each core and which course to take for each topic. The student is then left with nine free electives to build the program he or she desires. Credit may also be received for certain courses taken in other graduate branches of the university. Students may choose to "concentrate" in a particular field (probably similar to a "minor" in college) or may seek to go further and "specialize" in a particular topic (similar to a "major" in college). Many people take advantage of Chicago's strength in finance and concentrate or specialize in an area of finance. The curriculum is so broad that a student can take almost as many courses as he or she would like in a multitude of areas. Most courses are quantitative and/or theoretical in nature, but some escape can be found through a careful selection of alternatives. Don't be too concerned about your ability to handle differential equations and calculus in your first-quarter economics course. Most students are in the same boat.

« I remember my first economics course on the first day of classes. As the teacher began writing equations and drawing curves on the board, people begain gasping, moaning and looking around the room in disbelief. Because we're all supposed to be so bright, the teachers sometimes assume we have more knowledge than we do. But most professors quickly adjust to the level of students' comprehension. »

The rationale for allowing flexibility in the program is apparent. Students entering the program have a tremendous variety of experience, knowledge, and skills. It would be wasteful for someone to take basic courses in a field in which he or she is already proficient. For example, an economist is not required to take a basic economics course, and can choose among advanced economics courses to satisfy the core requirement. Many students prefer to take the basic entry-level course. They may not feel secure enough to take a higher-level course, or they may think their background is not strong enough. The severity of the program will vary, depending on the curriculum you establish for yourself and how well you want to do. Most students are smart enough to receive a steady diet of B's and C's with a modest effort. For those aspiring to be consultants or investment bankers, or who want to do well for other reasons, a B+ or better average requires a strong commitment and a lot of work.

The program also allows for flexibility in scheduling. Classes usually meet twice a week for an hour and twenty minutes. There are generally no Friday classes, and you may be fortunate enough to have a couple of mornings, afternoons, or even days free of classes. It may sound easy, but if you want to do well it becomes very difficult. And Chicago is on the quarter system. You usually start the quarter off one week behind, since you have two classes' worth of assignments due for the second class. Most courses have a midterm and a final in addition to extra projects, papers, or cases; there's little time to slough off. If you decide to take it slow the first week, you can literally spend the rest of the quarter (ten weeks of classes and one week of exams) trying to catch up. The amount of material covered in one quarter is approximately equivalent to the amount you'd cover in a semester at many schools.

Most classes are taught by lecture, although cases are used to varying degrees in some courses. There is a lot less in-class pressure with the lecture method. You can plan an occasional partying night for the middle of the week without fear of being embarrassed or ill prepared in class the following day. However, don't expect all classes to be easy, laid back, passive experiences. Some professors are very difficult.

« *Unfortunately, (or so it seemed at the time) I had the most demanding and intimidating professor during my first quarter. This was no accident. This professor deliberately teaches new students precisely because they are more easily intimidated. You had better be prepared for his class or you'll feel like crawling out on your belly by the time he's through with you. I put the greatest amount of effort into his class and yet received my lowest grade in Business School from him. (Chicago uses the basic alpha grading system. It basically consists of A, B, C, D, or F. No pluses or minuses.) I spent forty hours a week preparing for his class, and I studied for his final for a solid two weeks.*

I was so nervous for the final (it was my first one in B School), that I spent a sleepless night before the exam. I remember the sick feeling I had in my stomach as I walked to his final at 7:30 A.M. on a gray, misty morning in December. I remember feeling even sicker when I couldn't do the first four problems on the exam. I thought this guy was going to end up nailing me despite all the work I'd put into his course. I wanted to shoot him and walk out of the room.

However, I didn't shoot him or walk out of the room, and in retrospect, having this teacher in my first quarter was one of the best things that could have happened to me at Chicago. I had expected Business School to be tough and this professor's course exceeded my expectations. But I learned quickly that I would have to work hard to survive at Chicago, and I learned to be prepared for each class. I learned to study each night as if I had a final exam the following day. It is not absolutely necessary to go to such extremes to do well. But this professor forced me into a routine that I continued to use throughout Business School, and it was probably the key factor to my success in the program. »

Most of the professors at the university are excellent. They're very bright and many are renowned experts in their field. The caliber of research work is extremely high. But as with any school, there are professors who cause you to wonder, "How did *they* get in?" The quality of a course is directly related to the professor, and so choosing a professor can be very important. Fortunately, the student has some freedom in making this choice. Since the good professors are always in high demand, students are not guaranteed their first choice of courses every quarter. The university uses a bidding system designed to assist students in planning and scheduling their courses. The students conduct quarterly ratings of professors to provide useful course information such as an overall evaluation of the professor, the average number of hours spent per week in preparing for the course, and the value and amount of material studied. The university also provides a biography of each professor and a synopsis of his/her teaching method and the material that will be covered and work required in the course. All this is quite helpful when you are selecting professors and courses.

Each quarter you'll find yourself in classes that range in size from twenty to one hundred and twenty (depending on the popularity of the course and room capacity). This arrangement provides the student with maximum exposure to the rest of the class without necessarily inhibiting the development of close friendships. In some classes you will work closely in a group with three or four other students. There are also numerous social activities (to be discussed later) where you'll have ample opportunity to establish new friendships.

In addition, there are numerous, almost daily, presentations and discussions sponsored by the many "groups" in the Business School (e.g., Management Consulting Group, Asian Business Group, Women's Group, Black MBA Group). Each group arranges to have representatives and leaders in business come to campus to discuss career opportunities for students and to cover major issues of concern in their field. These presentations are open to all B School students and should be taken advantage of to complement the curriculum.

The university has a tremendous reputation in the business community as evidenced by the extensive corporate recruiting on campus and the rapid advancement of Chicago grads in corporations. Based on my experience with the university, that reputation is well deserved. An MBA from Chicago carries clout in the business world.

GETTING IN

EACH year Chicago admits approximately 540 students into the Business School from a pool of about 3,300 applicants. And each year the competition becomes even stiffer. Almost all applicants have strong credentials and have excelled in at least one area. However, don't let the quantity of qualified applicants deter you from applying to a top school. It is difficult to say what the admissions committee will look at as a deciding criterion, but it may be just the thing that you have. I am living proof that a person does not have to be in the top tier of his college class or ace the GMAT to get into Chicago and do well.

Though there are no specific quotas, the composition of each entering class is fairly similar. Most of the top business schools will accept only a small percentage of applicants with no prior work experience. It wasn't long ago that Chicago had roughly a 50–50 split between students with and without work experience. However, this has been changing in recent years, and Chicago now accepts many more students with previous experience (87 percent). People who have work experience probably bring more insight and knowledge into group and classroom discussions (at least those people with experience think they do), and personally, I feel that people with work experience will get more out of the program.

« *However, do not let a lack of work experience deter you from applying to Chicago or any other business school. A friend of mine at Chicago felt uneasy about his lack of work experience. During orientation it seemed to him that almost everyone had work experience. He had been offered a nice job by a law firm and he was seeking advice on whether to stay or get work experience before returning to business school. The general consensus was that work experience was a good thing to have, but since he had already been admitted to Chicago it did not seem to make sense to leave. He stayed, did well, and was able to parlay his MBA into an excellent job. The point is, work experience provides some leverage for getting into business school. But if you do not need it to get in, do not pursue it for the sake of it.* »

Chicago also seems to be looking for students who have a technical background. From what I observed, these people tend to do very well at Chicago, which is generally theoretical and quantitative in its teaching approach. Comfort with numbers and mathematical manipulations can be a big plus.

Now that I have scared away all people without a technical background, I would like to add something of a disclaimer. There are many different skills that allow you to do well at Chicago or any other top business school. Quantitative skills are not necessarily the most important at Chicago. Many courses do have a quantitative slant, but classes are still geared toward the large percentage who have no technical background. The quantitative stuff may tend to be much easier for those with technical backgrounds, but anyone at Chicago can handle it.

Letters of recommendation also play a fairly significant role in the application process. Good reference letters from teachers, coaches, and employers are very important. Great letters of recommendation from uncles, brothers, and fathers, even if they happen to be important executives, carry little weight. Reference letters provide the admissions committee with an opportunity to find out more about you as a person and whether or not you're likely to succeed in the program. If a school requests three or four letters of recommendation, I strongly advise against sending in seven to ten letters. I don't think the committee will be impressed. You can send in one or two above what is required if you feel it is necessary, but you might want to state in writing why you are doing so. For example, if you had two previous jobs, and several employers, and had played sports in college, you might want to send in more than the three required letters. Since interviews are not required, these recommendations take on even more importance.

« When I was applying to Chicago I was told by Business School friends that almost every applicant had at least one

significant accomplishment to report. In my case I felt that no one achievement stood out as superior. But there were a variety of accomplishments that I could mention. I took advantage of my diverse background by drawing references from my associations with coaches, professors, and past employers. I had been told by a friend on the admissions committee that letters of recommendation are examined very carefully. I think they may have been the reason I was accepted into the Chicago program. »

Chicago is looking for students who they feel will do well and contribute to the program. As I've mentioned, the backgrounds of the students are diverse and the quality of applicants outstanding. Thus, it is inevitable that a certain amount of luck may be involved in getting admitted. If you aren't admitted the first time you apply, you might consider getting more work experience, retaking the GMAT, or doing whatever else you feel might help your situation. A first rejection doesn't mean you won't get in if you apply again later. You might get "lucky" the second time around.

ACADEMIC ENVIRONMENT

ONE of the things about Chicago Business School that impressed me most was the extremely friendly academic climate. Not only isn't the overall environment "cutthroat," but there is a tremendous willingness among the student body to help other students solve their academic or personal problems. If you miss a class or don't understand something, you can always find an abundant source of students willing to lend their notes or an explanation.

« During the heavy interviewing season my second year, I traveled quite a bit and missed a lot of classes. I would return

home late at night halfway into the week and call up a friend to ask, "What happened in class today? What is the assignment? Can I copy your notes tomorrow?" The assistance I got was truly remarkable. Friends would not only let me copy their notes and answer questions, but they would sit down with me for an hour and fully explain all that had happened in class. It was always a pleasure to return the favor. »

Most classes are taught by lecture, so there is less pressure to be prepared to participate in class. However, the extent of participation varies. In some classes, participation is purely voluntary. In others, you damn well better be prepared to speak on any and every day. Some classes require group or individual presentations. Though these may sound threatening, sufficient notice is almost always given and they can even be fun, once you overcome your nervousness. After presenting a case, a group will then have to field questions from the class. There are always one or two students who think they know everything and who tend to be outspoken. You don't have to worry about them. If the class doesn't put those individuals in their place, the teacher probably will. (Be wary if you're "one of them.")

The University of Chicago does not feel compelled to fail a certain number of students. In fact, it's pretty difficult to flunk out of Chicago. This is another way in which the university reduces pressure. Occasionally, there might be someone who just isn't capable of doing the work. But this is very rare. It's more likely that the student who flunks just doesn't want to put much effort into the program. And, even that is very rare. The overall attrition rate is only about one percent.

Now if you think Chicago sounds like a breeze, let me set the record straight. It's difficult to get excellent grades (a lot of A's) at Chicago. The biggest reason is that competition for the top grades is very keen. If you're satisfied with B's and C's, you can relieve yourself of much of the competitive pressure.

« *During the second half of the second year, most of my friends were telling me not to study so hard. "You already have a job so what the hell are you studying so hard for? Grades don't matter anymore." But they did matter to me. It was the internal pressure that drove me to study so hard. Good grades are there to be had for those who are willing to work for them. For most people, this will require a few more hours at the library and a few less hours at the bar.* »

The program is demanding, but it is not regimented and won't make you feel like you're in grammar school. Presumably you're at Chicago because you're smart enough to want to learn. No one is going to check your attendance every day. There are no gold stars for perfect attendance. Everyone is mature enough to know that they'll get proportionally (maybe exponentially?) as much out of the program as they put into it. There are no demerits for missing class. It's your loss. Perhaps because everyone is treated as a responsible adult, the student body responds better to the professors. One easily gets the impression that the professors actually enjoy teaching at Chicago.

The opportunities for learning are not limited to the classroom. Daily lectures and discussions sponsored by the many groups and organizations in the Business School are an integral part of the academic environment. Top executives from all industries are brought in either to lecture on a special topic of interest, or to field questions from students on subjects important to MBAs. There are constant opportunities to rub elbows with these people at luncheons or small social gatherings. These seminars are an important part of your education at Chicago; take advantage of them. You'll be glad you did.

The hallways and student lounge at Chicago are always buzzing with people and excitement. Students come out of class, congregate in the hallways, and talk about the crazy financial models that finance professors Fama or Hamada just went through in class. There is talk of statistics, economics, and finance, finance, finance. Students discuss the best and worst teachers, the Miller article they read the night before, the party this coming weekend, and the companies recruiting on campus. They gather in groups to talk about assignments, cases, and exams. And they queue up at the Xerox machine to make copies of notes from classes they have missed. The "grapevine" at Chicago is the most informal yet comprehensive source and network of information.

Chicago is an exciting, vibrant, challenging place to learn. The overall academic environment is outstanding and may be characterized as relatively unpressured, friendly, and perhaps unmatched in opportunity.

SOCIAL LIFE

Now for the good part. The social life in Hyde Park itself is pretty dull. If you are looking for something to do on an off night and you want to stay in Hyde Park (actually, no one "wants" to stay in Hyde Park, but if you have to), there are a couple of fairly sedate, nondescript bars that students frequent. Other than that, there is not exactly a plethora of social activity in Hyde Park.

Fortunately, the social life is not limited to the opportunities in Hyde Park. The Business School sponsors a sufficient number and variety of activities to satisfy most students. The most frequent and perhaps the most popular social events at the Business School are the weekly, and sometimes semiweekly, LPFs (liquidity preference functions). First a presentation is made by a company that discusses the opportunities for MBAs within their firm. This is followed by massive beer consumption, socializing, brown-nosing, and eating. (Food ranges from

Doritos and Enchalada dip to cold cut buffets, wine and cheese platters, and imported beer, depending on the sponsoring company's generosity.) The LPFs take place most frequently on Thursday afternoons and evenings and sometimes on Tuesdays as well. The presentations generally last no more than an hour but the beer drinking sometimes continues through the following Monday. Many students will go to the LPFs (actually skipping the presentations!) and plan to have one or two beers before a serious night of studying economic models. But eight hours and twenty beers later they may find themselves in a lively bar downtown. Not only does this destroy Thursday night's study plan, but it wreaks havoc on Friday, the day most people think they will use to get caught up with their work.

There is a variety of organizations on campus, but the main body is the Business Students Association (BSA). This group consists of five students who are chosen by the class, and who act as student representatives to the administration. They also sponsor and schedule several social activities worth mentioning. The main event in the fall is a dinner-dance for Business School students. This is generally held at a posh downtown hotel and is complete with bar, dinner, and dancing. This is a most memorable event and often marks the beginning of some long-lasting friendships.

« My wife and I met a couple at this dinner-dance who became our closest friends at school. The nice part was that we shared many enjoyable evenings together exploring Chicago. The bad part was that my wife and the other guy's wife spent many enjoyable days together shopping and spending our student loans. They now live half a country away, but we keep in close contact and plan to see them soon. »

The major event in the winter, and a very popular one, is the Broomball Tournament, which is held annually in the middle of February. Broomball is an outdoor game that may be compared with hockey, since both are played on ice. But the similarity ends there. Substitute sneakers for skates, brooms for hockey sticks, and a soccerball for a puck, and you have Broomball. With eight people on the ice for each team, you can imagine it's a pretty wild time. Hot chocolate, coffee, donuts, and beer are in abundant supply throughout the tournament. This helps you withstand the freezing temperatures.

The main spring event is a "Booze Cruize" on Lake Michigan. This is definitely a must. Picture a boat packed with booze and business scholars cruising Lake Michigan along the shores of Chicago. Viewed from the lake, Chicago looks beautiful and spectacular. The cruise is one of the most memorable (or forgetful?) events in Business School. The boat is usually just the beginning of the much longer night. The partying would continue back at a friend's apartment or at some club downtown.

If you get bored, or tire of the activities on campus, you can always shoot downtown. By bus, car, or train you can be anywhere downtown in twenty minutes. Chicago is a dynamic city by day, and fantastic by night. The nightclub area is densely populated with bars and people. Most bars have no cover charge and you can reach just about every bar by foot. And probably the thing you have to be most wary of downtown is yourself. Chicago is also known for holding numerous festivals and ethnic celebrations in which many city restaurants sponsor booths where you can sample their fine foods and drink.

If it is just a pizza you want, then Chicago's deep-dish pizza is a must. It's a full meal in itself. We spent many Friday nights consuming massive quantities of pizza and beer. There are two outstanding pizza places within walking distance from campus. And you can also find a number of local delis, and small, fine places for eating Mexican, Chinese, and Italian food.

You can determine your own level of social activity. Once you overcome the first-quarter jitters (if you have them), there will be ample opportunity to socialize. You don't have to be single to participate in the social activities. Spouses are welcomed and encouraged to attend. There are many married couples in the Business School, and there are even functions that are specifically for married couples. These special events provide an outlet for couples (particularly those with children) who do not often find the time to participate in other activities. Couples also socialize off campus and team up to take advantage of all the cultural and social activities Chicago has to offer.

Many couples develop long-lasting friendships born out of common and shared problems at Chicago. On one hand, being married places demands on your time that may take away from your academic or social involvement with Business School peers. (It often provides a good excuse not to work on a Friday night, though.) On the other hand, you may tend to commit yourself more to your studies and find it easier to do so. After all, there is a good chance that your spouse is supporting you while you are in Business School, and the last thing your spouse wants you doing is slacking off when you probably should be studying. But it takes an understanding and supportive spouse to work all week and then watch you study on a Friday or Saturday night.

« A routine weekly exchange between my wife and I would go something like this:
What are we going to do Friday night?
I have to study.
You can study all day Friday. I want to go out.
We'll see.
Friday: O.K. let's go out.
No, never mind. I want you to study.

So sometimes we would go out together or with another married couple. Sometimes my wife would go out with the wife of a friend while her husband and I studied. »

The quantity and quality of housing at Chicago is quite good, and overall the housing facilities are generally very satisfactory. Married couples are usually put in married student housing, which allows greater opportunity for meeting other married couples. The School provides these couples with apartments in high-rise buildings, security is seldom if ever a problem, and all housing is fairly close to campus. Most single students live in university housing for at least their first year. Again, most of the housing is in high-rises. One or two of the larger housing units are more reminiscent of college dormitory life. Many students will move out of university housing and rent their own apartments for the second year. There are plenty of very adequate, and often large, rental units available in Hyde Park at very reasonable rates. There are also a number of available rental units and condominiums downtown and in the near North Side of Chicago, if you can afford them and do not mind the commute.

All in all, housing and social events are in bountiful supply at Chicago. Those who take advantage of what Chicago, the school and the city, has to offer, will not be disappointed. Once you find the time, there is not a better or more enjoyable place to go to school.

RECRUITING AND JOB SEARCH

EACH year, literally hundreds of companies interview students on campus, and hundreds provide the school with information on job openings and availabilities. Recruiting for full-time positions begins in late October and runs through March. The interviewing process can consume an incredible amount of time. You may find yourself being interviewed by companies on campus, and then traveling all over the country for on-site interviews.

Since recruiting is the name of the game, Chicago has recently upgraded its resources to include a new Career Resource Center and a new placement facility. In addition, the school does an excellent job of getting companies to come to the school, and of placing students. Each week the school posts a list of all the companies that will be interviewing on campus during the following two weeks. There is a description of the available position, and a list of requirements or special qualifications that the company may be seeking. Students bid for available interview slots on a computer (Chicago's free market system). Each quarter, students are allotted a quota of non-transferable bidding points. Since the companies can see only so many people, not everyone will get the schedule he or she wants. This usually isn't a big problem; there are often other ways to see the company representatives while they are on campus. I have never heard of anyone missing out on a desired job because they could not get on an interviewer's list.

« *Many companies will sponsor an informal presentation and cocktail hour with hors d'oeuvres, a day or week before they are scheduled to interview on campus. These get-togethers provide students with the opportunity to learn more about the firm and to rub elbows with some of the company's representatives. These festivities can also provide the opportunity for a free meal. While other students were clinging to corporate skirts and jackets, I was gorging myself on shrimp cocktail. After all, no one ever got a job at one of these presentations. But many people went home hungry.* »

All kidding aside, these presentations are a very valuable source of information. It enables you to gain some insight into the personality of the company, and many people make a decision on whether or not to interview with these companies based on these presentations.

For most first-year students, interviews for summer positions are held during the spring of the first year. Only a limited number of companies recruit on campus for summer positions. But there are other channels to pursue. Students may end up going to school during the summer, and graduating one quarter early. Students graduating a quarter early are often able to get a good jump on their classmates in getting jobs.

For those really serious about landing summer jobs, the search should begin early and should not be restricted to the opportunities the school provides. Many jobs are obtained by pursuing the opportunities that are posted on the bulletin boards at the Business School. In fact, that is how I obtained my summer job.

« *A job description had been posted on the bulletin board for an operations consultant at a major Chicago bank. I had no strong banking interest, but I had considered consulting as a possible career choice. I called the bank to set up an interview. I had about a half-day of interviews with several consultants at the bank and ended up with an offer, which I accepted.* »

For second-year students seeking full-time employment, the opportunities are tremendous. But again, the job search should not necessarily be restricted to the companies interviewing on campus. Virtually all students have a job lined up by the time they graduate and most of these are obtained through the school. But it never hurts to pursue opportunities on your own, at least as an insurance measure. It may be helpful to land a summer job with a firm you feel you might be very happy with on a permanent basis. If you do a good job for them, you may end up with an offer to return full time. This relieves a lot of pressure and provides a safety net to fall back on.

ON THE JOB — FIRST YEARS OUT

MANY people begin a new job (and for many it is their first full-time job) with some apprehension. But the apprehension and doubts are different from the ones you had upon entering Chicago. An MBA from the Chicago program, particularly if you have done well, is a tremendous confidence booster. During your career at Chicago, you will have heard about past Chicago grads who are doing well in various fields, and you will have heard many positive things about Chicago's reputation. You are confident that you can and will do well. Chicago has prepared you well for your new job. You may not find yourself using the same specific quantitative tools to solve problems, but you have learned how to apply analytical skills toward the solutions of a variety of new problems.

« *Since I have been employed, I have had the opportunity to work with a number of MBAs from several of the top ten schools. I have felt as confident and as well prepared as the others to handle the various problems to which I have been exposed. On the other hand, I have been the recipient of some "grief" from other workers for my "Chicago" approach. That is, I have had a tendency to want to quantify everything, model every problem, and do analyses in a statistically valid way. On a recent assignment with a consulting firm, I wanted to take a random sample of products that a company was buying and evaluate how these products were procured. From the sample I would be able to make inferences about the whole population of products they bought. For many reasons it became impossible to collect the data in the form I wanted. My boss said that the need for so many data points was a clear sign that I was a new associate. When I get to his level I will be able to draw lines and show trends with only one data point. At the highest level in the firm, I will not need any data points to make inferences. »*

You soon find out the rest of the world does not necessarily think in the quantitative way that Chicago teaches, so you have to adapt. But it is usually easy to do because Chicago also teaches you to conceptualize and to think analytically.

The Chicago MBA is a ticket to a fast track and will usually land you a position with a lot of exposure. Once you are in such a position it is up to you what you do with it. Chicago will prepare you to communicate with anyone in the business world (you will learn the "Chicagoese" language), and will equip you to move quickly up the corporate ladder.

The MBA is certainly key to high starting salaries, a high-visibility job, and great opportunity. With average starting salaries now over $45,000, almost everyone's salary expectations will be met, if not surpassed. If you choose a career in investment banking or consulting, your starting salary is likely to be beyond your wildest expectations (the number of hours you will work may also be beyond your wildest expectations).

« Since I quit a job where I was earning in the mid-twenties to go back to school full time, I feel pretty well qualified to assess whether getting the MBA was the right decision. The answer is an unequivocal yes. The decision to go after an MBA full time is not always an easy decision to make. If you are faced with leaving a well-paying job and you consider only the short term, then it does not look like a worthwhile decision financially. But you have to consider the long-term picture. It may take a few years after graduation to get where you would have been financially if you have not gone back to school. But that break-even point will come a lot sooner than you think,

and after that it is all gravy. The potential for making a very high future income increases tremendously with an MBA. »

SUMMARY OVERVIEW

CHICAGO has a lot to offer an individual, and in terms of academics, social activities, cultural events, and career opportunities, Chicago may be unparalleled.

The academic program is consistently strong in all areas, particularly finance. Some of the professors whose names you hear at any business school, Fama, Miller, Ibbotson, et al., teach MBA students at Chicago. If you have the opportunity to take a course from one of these people, you should do it. They are incredible instructors with great minds. They will teach finance from capital budgeting to capital asset pricing model to corporate finance with expertise and insight that you cannot find anywhere else. However, demand for the top professors exceeds the supply. You will no doubt have to settle for "second-best" for several of your courses.

The camaraderie among the students is tremendous. Not only will you find assistance from your classmates, but also from counselors who are available to aid you in selecting an appropriate program and to make sure you get the most out of the program. Generally the professors are also very willing to help students outside the classroom when they can. The problem is they are just not available as often as you might like.

Socially, the opportunities and activities at the school and in Chicago are exceptional. The big drawback is that Hyde Park has little to offer by way of exciting night life. If you want more than pizza or a few beers, you will have to go downtown. But, culturally, Chicago is tough to beat. Museums, theaters, and art are all in abundant supply. In two years at Chicago you will have just begun to scratch the surface. The only difficulty may be finding the time to take advantage of it all.

Career opportunities with a Chicago MBA are tremendous. One need only compare our average starting salary with other schools to appreciate that.

At Chicago, there also are a couple of drawbacks. First, the formal curriculum does not aid in development of oral communication skills, since most courses don't require oral presentations or participation. There is a class in communication skills, but it is optional. Second, although the school has added a new administration/placement facility, it is several city blocks from the main business school building. This makes it a bit of a "commute" from the classroom to job interviews. Chicago, lacking an auditorium, also is short of space for conferences and special events. Finally, one last warning is that it may take time for most of you to adjust to living in Hyde Park, which is in the South Side of Chicago. It's not as bad as some stories might lead you to believe, but it's definitely an adjustment, and some students should expect to be never totally happy living there.

In summary, going to the University of Chicago was the best "move" I made in my life. Together the university and the city provide opportunities that are difficult to match anywhere else. An MBA from Chicago is definitely worth the time and effort it takes to get it.

Chapter 5

SLOAN SCHOOL OF MANAGEMENT*
(MIT)

THE PROGRAM

« *The first day of school. And here I was, bravely heading out without my mother to see me off. No pencil box. No new shoes. No promise of a graham cracker recess. What was I doing? Thirty-year-olds aren't supposed to have first days of school. Not for themselves, at any rate.*

As I crossed the salt and pepper bridge to Cambridge, I mustered my resources to convince myself that I would not be the only reborn business school student at Sloan. I have been, in the not too distant past, a sociology-major Durgin Park waitress. Sure, I could carry six prime ribs at once; but could I carry six courses at MIT?

While I had read, avidly and with relief, the student profiles which assured me that there were all sorts of people at Sloan, I envisioned a goodly proportion of techified nerds who could never bring themselves to leave "The Institute" (did all MIT students still wear black pants and white socks, or had that gone the way of the slide rule?), of hard-core business types

* BY MAUREEN ROGERS, MS IN MANAGEMENT, MIT

who'd put in their two requisite post-college years as bank trainees, of wunderkinder born with the perfect knowledge that their life work would be a career in business.

Quant jocks all, who had mastered the most arcane and abstruse forms of mathematics, of which I had never heard and could only feebly imagine.

And, of course, myself. The token low-tech type. Admitted under some weird affirmative action program for exradical waitresses. Admitted on the whim of some dean with a perverse sense of humor. Admitted by mistake. I, who had taken my first (and only) calculus course at the age of twenty-eight. An experience which, as one repatriated classics major who had undergone a similar epiphany told it, was almost as grand and profound a revelation as sex.

My most dire suspicions and fears were confirmed when the first person I met turned out to be a twenty-year-old economics-math wizard. I considered running home to practice balancing tea cups. Perhaps there was an opening for a girl with experience at Durgin.

But later that night, I was much relieved to meet my orientation group. Here we had not only two of the child prodigies I had feared (as to the ark, one M, one F) — who turned out to be good Sloan friends — but an updated version of those cliché-ridden WWII bomber squadrons that likely existed only in lousy movies. One reflective, serious-minded Ivy Leaguer. One Japanese industrialist. One 1960s City College radical. One black engineer-athlete. One preppy with no first name and three last names who seemed to have detoured on his way to "the business school across the river." One Latin charmer.

All engaging, intelligent, motivated, interesting people. Bringing my own analytical abilities to the fore, I determined that the likelihood that the only good people in the class had landed in my orientation group was minimal.

Things were beginning to look up. »

Sloan does attract a diverse group, a "normal distribution" of business students. The class numbers approximately 185 students of whom 21 percent are women. The median age is twenty-six, some 8 percent are under twenty-three, and 17 percent are over twenty-nine. Sloan students come from all over the United States, with the largest number, 31 percent, hailing from New England. The international presence is a commanding 30 percent. Finally, as would be expected, a great number of students have a technical or scientific background with 39 percent majoring in engineering and 16 percent concentrating in physical sciences in their undergraduate colleges. Surprisingly, though, about a third of the class (32 percent) majored in the social sciences or the humanities. It's clear that Sloan looks for diversity in its students coming in and for uniformly well-trained and disciplined managers going out.

Life at Sloan begins, horrifyingly enough, with calculus and economics tests. While this is certainly not the way to start a beautiful relationship, it is useful in ensuring that everyone is prepared to tackle the core curriculum. The threat of performing poorly on these screening exams is a powerful incentive to rework some of those economic and math fundamentals. Passing familiarity with human nature would seem to indicate that most people would let the preschool reviewing slide if there were no mechanism for checking up on them.

« I sat down a month or two prior to entering Sloan and "psyched out" exactly what would be on these screening tests. Since I was going to business school, not "real" school, I figured the level of calculus they were interested in was enough to get you through microeconomics. I thus reviewed only the most simpleminded calculus stuff, blithely and pointedly ignoring the more difficult matters, like trigonometry. On the other hand, I reasoned that, since the core economics course assumed *intermediate-level economics training, I had best be prepared for an intermediate micro-macro exam.*

Neither one of my anticipations was met, the result being that I was able to breeze through both tests in record time: I spent ten minutes (of the allotted hour) on the calculus test because I was only able to answer two questions; rather than sit there and frustrate myself with my total and undeniable inability to integrate a trigonometric function (I was lucky to recognize a trigonometric function), I left.

I handled the economics sections with equal dispatch, albeit more successfully, for I had totally and undeniably overprepared. To pass the economics screen, one had to remember which way the supply and demand curves headed. But, while the test was long and covered a lot of territory, the level of economic sophistication required was generally not far beyond that stage.

For my efforts, I was: (a) delivered a note declaring my knowledge of calculus marginal (which I already knew) and the suggestion that I take the informal refresher course given by a fellow student (which I did); (b) easily able to cope with the core economics workload, having already prepped a good deal of the material covered in it. One caveat to anyone who would consider coming in "cold" to Sloan: failure to pass the economics screen results in having to take a remedial, not-for-credit introductory economics course in either Micro- or Macroeconomics, or both, adding to the time required to obtain the Sloan degree. »

Applied Economics I (Micro) and Applied Economics II (Macro and International) are just two parts of the core, which is the fundamental basis of the Sloan curriculum. The core, which is generally "done with" during the first two semesters is comprised of thirteen courses. Six of the core subjects, for which classes meet twice a week for a full semester, are Applied Economics I (Micro); Applied Economics II (Macro and International); Accounting and Finance I (Accounting); Managerial Behavior in Organizations; Decision Support Systems II (Statistics); and Decision Support Systems III (Decision Models). The other seven core subjects, for which classes meet three times a week for half a semester, include Accounting and Finance II (Financial Management); Communication for Managers; Industrial Relations and Human Resource Management; Strategic Management; Decision Support Systems I (Information Systems); Introduction to Operations Management; and Introduction to Marketing Management.

As intended, the core is a pretty good sampler of what you "need to know" in order to claim to be a bona fide MBA (or, in the case of Sloan, an SM: the degree granted is a Master of Science in Management). The core is also fairly well balanced between the relatively rigorous and the relatively simple. There are fairly straightforward ways to waive out of most of the core requirements, and a number of students with economics or mathematics backgrounds manage to complete the program in three semesters.

As expected, Sloan makes substantial use of personal computers in its core curriculum. Many of the subjects in the core have been revamped to take advantage of Project Athena, a campus-wide commitment at MIT to increased computing availability and utilization. Sloan is a modern business environment with — at last count — 220 IBM PC/XT/ATs, 25 Xerox workstations, 20 Macintosh SEs, 15 Macintosh 512Es, 3 AT&T 3B2s, 2 IBM RT PCs, an IBM 4341 mainframe, and a Prime 850 Minicomputer. Two computer laboratories exist for students to use for course work and research.

While it is during the last semester of the master's program that the greatest "real" pressure is on, the academic workload and pressure is intense during the first semester. This is when most people take the core courses that involve the most number crunching and grinding work: Economics I, Statistics, Accounting. Although much of this work is not difficult in any conceptual sense, there always seems to be an awful lot of work hanging over you. There are homework problems in a number of courses. Even if they aren't counted toward the final grade, it is usually best to keep up with them — otherwise there's the risk of falling behind in class or doing poorly on those tests which assume you've done your homework.

One thing that greatly contributes to alleviating the stress and strain of the first few months at Sloan is the study groups. First-term study groups, formed in the interest of sanity and survival in coping with Economics and, to a lesser degree, Statistics problem sets, are generally an off-shoot of the orientation groups. After spending a few intense days getting to know your orientation buddies, and competing as a team with them in a survival game, it is only natural to turn to them when presented with your first problem set and problem set deadline. A good amount of academic work at Sloan occurs in groups, which, in a sense, simulates a good many business environments and problem-solving situations. When work is expected to be individual and original, faculty members let it be known. Overall, the "work as a group" attitude prevails at Sloan.

The work/orientation group is generally the nucleus of your first social group as well. As time goes on, and people drop in and out of your group, an interactive process occurs. By the end of the second year at Sloan, things have so evolved that, rather than your work group being your social group, your social group is likely your work group for any class project that comes along.

Once the core curriculum is completed, the workload is dramatically altered, and the emphasis shifts from problem sets/examinations to projects/presentations. Not only are the time demands different, but the nature of the work has shifted: it is generally more interesting and a closer approximation of what one would be doing in the outside world.

In terms of size, Sloan classes vary from one hundred or more students in a few of the core courses, which are, for the most part, open to the rest of the MIT community (i.e., there will be undergraduates around), to relatively intimate classes of ten or so students in postcore, somewhat specialized subjects. Tossing out the outlying observations (it's amazing what an even quasi-quantitative education can do for you!), the average class at Sloan is likely to contain in the range of twenty to thirty students.

Classes are principally lecture and discussion. Most professors are open to questions from the audience at any time, and even the most inane and seemingly foolish questions will not be ridiculed, except, perhaps, by fellow classmates. Rarely are students called on in class. Sloan does not have the pervasive tension and intensity that comes from always having to be prepared. Many smaller classes require presentations, and students prepare carefully for these, if only to spare themselves the humiliation of looking ridiculous in front of their fellow Sloanies. One quarter of the courses rely, in part, on the case method, which provides a nice break — since anything that smacks of realism is a welcome relief from theory and number-crunching. These tend to be the more advanced subjects, mirroring Sloan's belief in establishing a solid theoretical grounding before challenging students to apply concepts.

One unique and somewhat controversial feature of the Sloan program is the requirement of a thesis. While the thesis is not expected to be of the length, depth, breadth, or, frankly, quality, of a doctoral dissertation (it is more along the lines of a major paper), it is regarded by a number of Sloan students as the foremost hassle of their Business School career, particularly since it comes during the final-semester job search.

In defense of the thesis (not to imply that a formal defense à la Ph.D. is required: it's not), many students actually enjoy the opportunity by choosing a thesis topic that is more applied than theoretical — leading to the development of contacts in the outside business world — or to dabble in an area of interest. And of course, many students just prefer to churn out one major effort, rather than to take on two or three extra courses. The overall academic orientation at Sloan is, not surprisingly, quantitative. This reputation is both well deserved and overblown. Some quantitative background and ability is absolutely essential. This means that incoming Sloanies should not have severe number phobia. Some calculus is an official entrance requirement. What this translates into, realistically, is that it is requisite to be able to differentiate an algebraic equation. You can safely ignore the integral sign on those few occasions when it rears its beastly head. The less quantitative students can easily avoid those electives which are more math-intensive.

Sloan's academic forte is finance, which is "state of the art," "on the leading edge," etc. There are a goodly number of "name brand" financial economists on the Sloan faculty. While it is somewhat unlikely that Sloan graduates use theoretical finance in the conduct of their quotidian business lives, the finance concentration at Sloan is an impressive credential. And it is surely useful for those in finance positions, in consulting, and in banking, to have some formal analytical grounding underlying the intuitive wit to "buy sheep and sell deer." Also, you can impress your friends and acquaintances at cocktail parties by discussing the CAP-M or whether dividends do indeed matter.

Applied economics is also quite strong, and it is possible, given Sloan's close proximity to the MIT Economics Department, to see household words like Paul Samuelson and Bob Solow (both Nobel laureates) in the hallways. MIS (Management Information Systems) is another "big" concentration at Sloan. In fact, some outsiders suffer the misconception that everyone at Sloan is, at least tangentially, a computer science/systems maven of sorts. Not so.

Students are allowed to take courses in other departments of MIT, and there is a new cross-disciplinary engineering-management program, but there is certainly sufficient diversity and offerings at Sloan itself, and most students do not feel particularly compelled to look elsewhere.

Declaration and completion of a concentration area is required at Sloan. This generally means taking two or three courses beyond the core. Given overlapping requirements for concentrations (Applied Econometrics and Forecasting for Management, for instance, can be applied toward Marketing and Economics), most students end up with at least two concentrations (and often multiple versions of their résumés, depending on what they want stressed). The thesis is generally, but not always and necessarily, written in the area of one's concentration.

Despite MIT's reputation as a grind factory, despite the academic rigor (for Business School, that is), despite the pressures to do well/buy a conservative enough suit/finish the thesis on time and within the correct margins/find a job that will pay at least what you made before entering Sloan, the atmosphere at Sloan is surprisingly relaxed and congenial.

The overarching ethos at Sloan is that of working cooperatively. Most informal practice and implicit policy encourage group endeavor and class solidarity. There are pressures; there is competition. But even here, teamwork tends to generalize and "thin out" the feelings of pressure; and most official competition is among groups.

One stimulating academic competition is the labor-management game, which occurs, for the majority of Sloan students, in their second semester. Each class section is divided into a number of teams, which pair off — one side labor, one management. The groups are then presented with a case: labor gets one side of the story, management gets the other. Teams have three days to decide the terms of a collective bargaining agreement; any team that fails to reach a settlement and winds up with a strike is required to write a paper explaining exactly how negotiations broke down.

While the bargaining game starts out as a sort of fun exercise, some teams really get into the role-playing aspects of it — showing up wearing labor or management "costumes" (hard hats and overalls; three-piece suits), for instance — and feelings can run pretty high.

« *I was on the management squad for our group, and, while we were not hard-core role-players, or even that serious at the outset, our labor counterparts were in dead earnest. There was a good deal of personal attack and name calling from them during our first joint session. Their deliberate aggression and hostility (they figured we'd cave in to avoid a strike and having to write a paper) resulted in an immediate breakdown of negotiations.*

In any case, our side refused to back down, so we ended up with the only striking union. This really turned out to be pretty interesting and beneficial for the entire class. A faculty member with a long history of negotiation and arbitration experience was brought in to analyze the case, and to present his feelings, based on our position papers.

We in management were relieved when we were found to have bargained in good faith. Even if we had not been vindicated, the experience was very revealing and useful. Afterwards, labor and management declared a truce and made certain that the hard feelings that developed in the course of the bargaining game would not spill over into the rest of our lives at Sloan. »

Students also develop "group consciousness" in the core Managerial Behavior in Organizations course. Again, the class is divided into subsections, and there are a number of activities, often of a fairly ridiculous and simpleminded nature (group poetry writing, games reminiscent of playing telephone, etc.), which are made into competitions. Their principal purpose is to develop awareness of group dynamics, communications flows, and other useful things for people to be on the lookout for throughout their business careers.

In Advanced Marketing Management, a software package comprises the heart of the course. Students organize into teams — firms — and compete against each other through the semester in a complex game with many variables: pricing, packaging, promotion, distribution, new product development. The game controls the environment, and success or failure depends on how well each firm responds to other firms' actions and the changing environment.

Overall, while the image of MIT may be somewhat forbidding, the fundamental, salient features of the Sloan School are its academic excellence, its quantitative orientation, its informality, and the cooperative and friendly spirit among its students. And the pride Sloan people hold in the ever-distinguishing feature of being the best, albeit only, business school of Cambridge, Massachusetts.

GETTING IN

LIKE, presumably, other business schools of note, Sloan is looking for intelligence, achievement, and ambition. While all applicants may feel themselves possessed of these attributes, and while it would be nice to run life on the honor system and take people at their words, there should be some objective evidence to demonstrate that applicants are, indeed, bright, accomplished, and ambitious. Candidates to Sloan are also required to have taken (or plan to take prior to attendance) calculus and introductory courses in micro- and macroeconomics. While there are not-infrequent exceptions made to these requirements, they are pretty much Sloan guidelines.

Students without these courses may start out with something of a handicap in the core courses, and find themselves taking pre- or plus-core courses to get up to speed.

Someone lacking rudimentary knowledge of economics and calculus would be uncomfortable at Sloan. The core economics course absolutely presume familiarity with the fundamentals of economic analysis. It also necessitates mustering up enough math to solve the intersection of the supply and demand curves, perform marginal analysis, etc.

The "average" Sloan student comes out of a fairly well-known undergraduate program, got fairly good grades (a B average in Physics is given more weight and respect than an A in Phys Ed, however), and scored in the mid-600s on the GMAT exam. There are no hard and fast rules here, however. There is no magic cutoff point for the business boards. While good boards help, low boards don't automatically lead to rejection. Sloan is looking for a diverse and well-rounded class, and therefore grades and boards are only part of the story. The reputation of your undergraduate institution also is not necessarily the determining factor. You can graduate from the most obscure college in America and still get into Sloan. (Having come out of one of them, I am living proof of this fact.) You can offer up a straight A average from Princeton and get rejected.

Overall, Sloan is looking for people who have done something interesting, imaginative, and creative, as well as those whose prior careers and lives are slightly more mainstream. All bagpipe players are not automatically accepted. The classes at Sloan are generally rather eclectic bunches. Mine included an astrophysicist, a white water guide, a psychiatric nurse, a professional photographer, a brownstone rehabber, a Jane Austen scholar, and a fellow who ran a toy company while picking up a simultaneous degree from Harvard Law School. It also included engineers, commercial bank loan officers, math teachers, and systems analysts. The students went a long way toward making Sloan a diverse and interesting place.

When I was at Sloan, students served as readers on applications, along with faculty members and administrators. In most cases, a "no" from one of the three readers meant a turndown. One outcome of this student participation was that the incoming classes at Sloan tended to be mirror images of the class that accepted them. This was quite an interesting phenomenon. The two classes at Sloan at any given time tended to have fairly distinct and opposite personalities. My class was considered fairly eccentric and extraordinarily social. The classes on either side of us were more conservative and generally more serious. Alas, Sloan has abandoned the practice of having students help process applications. I suspect this practice was a victim of Sloan's modest expansion in the mid-1980s, which make it less wieldy, and less feasible to have student readers.

« Having served as a reader, I can guarantee that three things will make a favorable impression on the reader. One is a well-written essay. Second is a demonstrated interest in business. Some applicants clearly come across as people who are on lifelong fishing expeditions. Some appear to be professional students: "After completing my doctorate in Astrakhan art, I would like to attend business school, prior to applying to medical school so that I will feel, by the age of forty-six, that I am truly a well-rounded person." If any place encourages career change, it is Sloan. Points are given and not taken away for having had a past nonroutine business life. But there are extreme cases, and they generally won't pass the admissions screen at Sloan. Third, and most important, some expression of true knowledge of Sloan and its program, and a strong interest in it, is essential. Applicants should not imply, by default, that the reason they want to attend Sloan is because it's there.

What attracted me to Sloan was its small size (while the

school has grown, it's still smaller than most of the top-ranked business schools), the applied economics concentration, and the fact that Sloan was a short walk from my home on Beacon Hill. I was wise enough to include two of these three reasons in my application. »

Given that Sloan is at MIT, there has been an historic association with engineering, and, indeed, Sloan was, for a long time, primarily a management school for MIT types. Although some people still perceive of Sloan in this way (in fact, one former employer asked me why I wanted to go to school with "a bunch of engineers"), it cannot be overemphasized that Sloan has gone a long way toward distancing itself from this image. Applicants should believe that Latin majors and English teachers are welcome, as are MEs, CEs, and EEs.

In fact, for someone making the change from some sort of "liberal arts" career (teaching, editing, social work) into management, a Sloan education can be of real advantage in the transition. In many businesses' eyes, it seems that one has to atone for those frittered away years, and the "high-powered" MIT management degree may be just the right compensation.

ACADEMIC ENVIRONMENT

THE most obvious feature of academic life at Sloan is that, while hard work and commitment are an absolute necessity, there is a marked absence of the sort of cutthroat competition for which professional schools are often noted. This is not to say that there is no grade-grubbing: there is. But there is no such animal as class ranking. Grades, if posted, are done so anonymously. People rarely flunk out.

Grading at MIT is on an A, B, C, D, F basis (for GPA purposes, an A is a 5, B a 4, etc.). Grading is highly dependent on subject and professor. Some courses give blanket A's. Others are quite stringent in awarding A's (or even B's for that matter). Since there are no uniform grading policies or standards, students are quite aware that the rank and GPA have little meaning.

Courses vary considerably in degree of difficulty. This was readily apparent on one exam day during first-year finals. The morning exam was statistics, a fairly difficult enterprise for anyone who had never taken statistics before; the afternoon final was labor relations, during which people kept taking breaks to chat, have coffee, etc. It was somewhat akin to going from the ozone layer to ground zero in about three seconds.

In terms of the types of coursework required for grading, more core courses have midterms and finals. Many have problem sets or brief case analyses. Postcore courses rely more heavily on presentations and papers.

Students are expected to maintain a 4.0 (B) average, and this is monitored and warnings are given out. Students with low GPAs after the completion of core can choose their electives with an eye toward picking up their average.

I was not aware of any official flunk-out policy. I only knew of two people who left Sloan while I was there. One decided he despised the entire world of business and had only gone to school to please his family (and I have since heard that he was dropping back in again). Another failed a core course on two occasions and voluntarily left rather than face it again.

Sloan is by no means Pollyanna Academy, but the academic environment is just not set up to guarantee that some students will be made to feel like failures. (Thus Sloan fails to parallel real life.) Students are encouraged to work together, and a number of classes are graded on the basis of group projects and presentations. Cooperative effort is something of a Sloan byword.

« *I found the students competitive at Sloan, but not competitive at the expense of others. People wouldn't come to Sloan*

in the first place if they had no competitive spirit in their souls.
But most people wanted to get good grades because they were in
the habit of getting good grades, or because they wanted to do
better than last time, or because they wanted to do better than
students they felt were particularly obnoxious. I suppose this is
not really different than any other place, but at Sloan, there
was really no competitive aura. »

At Sloan, if you're good enough to get in, you're good
enough to get out. There are some awards for academic
accomplishment: best thesis, best accounting student, best
all-around student, and so on. But students don't really
compete for these prizes, and I suspect that, as in my case,
most people aren't even aware of these awards until after
they're awarded.

Since competition is limited, for the most part pressure is
also minimized. In the first semester there is some pressure,
but in many ways it is more collective than personal. In
a number of core subjects, group work on problem sets is
encouraged (not to mention, given the constraint of the
twenty-four-hour day, necessary).

Students should expect to put in full-time study nights, at
least through first semester, but there should seldom if ever be
the need for a consistent string of working till 2 A.M. or
all-nighters. If you do your studying at the Dewey Library,
there are always people around to ask for help, gossip with, or
go with to Steve's Ice Cream. Sometimes there are queuing
problems in the computer terminal rooms, which is a waste of
time and a true annoyance if you're under deadline pressure.
But supper is usually a good time to catch a free terminal, as
are weekend mornings. With a minor amount of diligence and
care, it is quite possible to plan your life so that class requirements do not consume all of your time and haunt every
waking or sleeping hour.

SOCIAL LIFE

HAVING lived in Boston for twelve years, I entered Sloan with my social life pretty well in place. I did not come to Sloan intending to meet new friends or to party, but there were plenty of opportunities to do both. Although my participation level was less frequent and energetic than that of the younger students, I made a number of friends and attended a number of parties. Sloan does have quite an involved social scene for anyone interested, although I am told that the level of social activity is somewhat dependent on the class. My classmates apparently rank among the more socially oriented in Sloan legend.

There is a weekly "Consumption Function" — a beer, wine, and munchies party to celebrate the end of classes for the week.

« *For me, the Consumption Function was not so much a wind-down as it was an event that served an unintended academic purpose. Somewhere along the line, I developed a total mental block against linear programming. At one of the consumption functions, a fellow LP sufferer confessed that he was never able to "pivot" correctly unless he had had a few beers. I took his advice, and found that I had a much easier time grinding out my LP homework under the influence of two Lites!* »

The Consumption Functions are sponsored by the Graduate Management Society, which is the three- or four-person student-elected social steering committee for Sloan. GMS also sponsors end and beginning of semester off-campus "real" parties. My class's farewell dinner was held at the New England Aquarium, which led us all to develop a certain degree of compassion for the seals and penguins that had to put up with us for a few hours. While the Consumption Functions are meant for those who are attending Sloan, the outside parties are for spouses/spouse equivalents/significant others, as well.

Because Sloan is relatively small, many party-givers feel that they can invite everyone in the class. This largesse is clearly based on the assumption that not everyone will go. (Think of the landlord.) The point is that social opportunities do exist.

A lot of informal socializing goes on between classes. Sloan's early 1980s renovations have created several student lounges, one with an adjacent cafeteria, which provide attractive space for group meetings and casual studying and relaxation. Kendall Square, once a gloomy subway stop, is well under way with a $250 million redevelopment program, which includes a first-rate hotel, the MIT Coop and Bookstore, many office buildings, and a host of new restaurants attracted to the area by this exciting new complex. If the sun is out and it's over forty-five degrees, students congregate on the front steps of the Sloan Building or on Hermann Plaza, which has recently been resurfaced and decorated with planters in which flowers bloom from late spring through most of the fall.

Almost all of Sloan's facilities have undergone extensive renovation since 1980, making for an attractive and functional business campus.

With the exception of the most hermitlike, indifferent, or overextended individuals, it is difficult to leave Sloan without having had at least one (however perfunctory) conversation with each of your classmates. Everyone has at least a nodding acquaintance with everyone else, although, after orientation, there is no enforced camaraderie.

Those with families clearly have less time to sit around in bull sessions, and they are often the ones found in the libraries snatching study time between classes. There were more men than women with children in my class, but people can easily extend their Sloan careers beyond the usual two years, and I know of several women with small children who have done just that.

For single men, there are far fewer women at Sloan (and at MIT in general) than there are men, but there is certainly no dearth of either single, young non-Sloan males or females in the Boston area. While women, blessedly, no longer go to school to earn their MRS degrees, there are a number of couples who met in my class who went on to "dual careers." Several entrepreneurial types also made friendships which they carried over into small businesses which they set up after leaving Sloan.

There is housing available for graduate students, both single and married, on the MIT campus, but it's not in bountiful supply, and some of it is a bit of a hike from the Sloan School. MIT also maintains apartment listings and a roommate service. For those who prefer to fend for themselves, student budget housing in Cambridge and Boston is scarce. Both Boston and Cambridge have had their housing problems exacerbated by rent control, condominium conversion, and, not incidentally, the existence of a large student population. Affordable housing is not likely to be found within walking distance of Sloan, but MIT is on the "best" Boston rapid transit line, expanding housing possibilities even for those who do not own a car.

Boston and Cambridge are fairly congenial towns for students. Not only is the area loaded with students, but proximity to ocean and mountains makes weekend getaways feasible, if you have the urge to escape from the hordes of students.

RECRUITING AND JOB SEARCH

SLOAN trains people for both staff and line positions in management. A typical Sloanie goes into a Fortune 500, strategic planning consulting, management information systems, technology management, or, increasingly, investment banking firm. Roughly 10 percent of each class ends up in a small or start-up company.

Sloan's placement record is quite strong, particularly for the mainstream student (one who is not saddled with the checkered career that likely got him or her accepted to Sloan in the first place; or one who does not have a less than usual career interest or geographic preference).

Even though Sloan is a small school, a relatively large number of companies (163 in 1987) recruit on campus. Another 300 or so write to Sloan announcing opportunities for graduates.

The students who are most successful in the Sloan placement process are those within two standard deviations from the mean student in terms of age, education, and past experience. The more outré, by whoever's standards, students are less well served. It is harder to find a job if you're over thirty; if you have never worked in the private sector; if you absolutely have to live in Oregon. Depending on their own personal demographics, or on geographic or career preference, some Sloan students are effectively on their own, although there are a number of ways other than on-site recruiting in which the placement office supports job-hunting students.

The placement office prepares and sells first- and second-year résumé books. It maintains a large correspondence file containing information on job opportunities in firms that are unable or unwilling to mount a large scale interviewing effort on campus. The jobs listed in the correspondence files are often more defined, and more interesting, than those coming out of the interviewing mill. Sloan also maintains a frequently updated computerized listing of Sloan grads. This file is cross-referenced by industry and geographic location. Most Sloan grads are willing to help out the newly minted, at least by coming through with a few names or suggestions. Sloan is in the midst of developing a stronger old boy/old girl network, and strengthening alumni ties in general. The new glossy

SLOAN magazine is part of this effort. Faculty members (most consult) are another good source of job leads.

Still, the majority of Sloan students find their first full-time position through the campus interviewing process. Interviewing schedules are a combination of "closed" (by company invitation) and "open" (any interested student meeting the job specs). Interview slots on "open" schedules are assigned through a priority card system. Some firms select all open schedules, seeing everyone who signs up as long as there are open slots. Others will choose closed schedules or interview students off campus. (Look for invitations to the Marriott at Kendall Square or the Hyatt Regency, which is just across the river from the Harvard Business School.)

First-year schedules are generally "closed." Recruiting firms select from the résumés and cover letters submitted by students, and those with a less "silver spoon" résumé can make a case for themselves in writing. Unfilled "closed" slots are opened up to the entire class.

"Closed" schedules may seem a brutal policy, but many firms hold strong convictions about the type of employees they are looking for, and closing the schedule may merely mean that you're spared the inevitable turndown. (And some rejection letters will come so fast that you would swear they were typed before the interview!)

While most of us know how to cope with elation, coping with rejection is more difficult. Most people at Sloan have never had to deal with rejection before, and the vast majority of students will receive turndowns that strike them as arbitrary, feckless or heartless. Maintaining your sense of perspective, humor, and equanimity during the whole process is essential. (Even companies that invite you to interview may have a bullet with your name on it awaiting you when you walk out the door.) Students tend to be very supportive of each other during the job search, trading horror stories, interview tips, job leads, and outright good old moral support. (There are, of course, a few insensitive idiots who, for the life of themselves, just can't understand why *you* have only received one offer — from your father's insurance agency — while *they* just can't make up their minds about which of their two dozen $50K offers to accept. But they are in the distinct minority and can be easily avoided.)

« *One fellow in the class ahead of mine received an intensely flattering letter from one Blue Chip firm urging him to sign up for an interview. When he failed to respond, they followed up with a telegram or two, so he decided to sign up for a slot. The day before the interview, someone from Blue Chip's recruiting office called to make sure he wouldn't forget his appointment. At this point, he began writing his imaginary ticket to first-job paradise, and was debating whether to ask for four or five weeks of vacation. Unfortunately, he received his "Dear John" letter within hours of his interview — the letter stressing that some folks just didn't have the background to fit in at good old Blue Chip. Fortunately, he did have the good humor to post the love letters and telegrams for the rest of us to share.* »

The bulk of students have offers in place, and have made their acceptances, by graduation; but "special" students may still be looking throughout the summer after graduation. There are generally happy endings all around: as far as I know, even the most seemingly employment-resistant member of my class had a job within a few months after leaving Sloan. But there are really no guarantees.

Sloan graduates demand and get the going rate for top-of-the-line MBAs. While the "Rolls-Royce" consultancy and investment-banking offers inflate the mean salary, Sloan graduates are competitive with those of top schools.

For the most recent graduating class, the mean starting salary was $50,000. Those with technical undergraduate degrees average slightly better than the nontechnical. Salaries range from $24,000 to $80,000, with consulting and investment banking leading, and accounting and commercial banking lagging in the salary sweepstakes. Twenty-eight percent of the class went into manufacturing; the other 72 percent to a variety of positions in nonmanufacturing firms, with consulting, financial services, and investment banking accounting for the majority of these jobs.

ON THE JOB — FIRST YEARS OUT

« *The Sloan degree was certainly adequate preparation for the first year on the job as far as I was concerned. While I seldom use a specific skill or piece of information picked up at Sloan, I consider the degree my union card. Since I work in a company that is sometimes referred to by insiders as a Sloan ghetto, there is no doubt in my mind that the Sloan degree landed me the job. I suspect this is true of most business school graduates. Sure, a firm is hiring you, but they're also in great part hiring your degree and your school.* »

Post–B School success is an artifact of performance, politics, and luck. The Sloan degree provides a solid foundation on which to base that performance. The analytical, technical, and group problem-solving skills acquired at Sloan can and do give Sloan graduates a performance edge. Performance is not always measurable in bottom-line terms; much of it is based on perception. It generally helps your case if you are perceived as bright: Sloan grads are.

The Sloan skills are handy too. It is an increasingly quantitative world and computers are to today what calculators were to the past. The Sloan numbers emphasis with its strong analytical grounding make the transition to the wonderful world of business that much easier. As a result, Sloan MBAs tend to do very well on their first job.

Nevertheless, finding perfect job satisfaction is difficult; it is highly unlikely that it even exists. This is certainly true of the first job out of business school. A number of people that I know of have switched jobs during their first year out. I've even heard of one first-month switch. This occurs particularly when the job was over- or misrepresented, if the person over- or misrepresented himself or herself, or if the person was unclear about his or her true career objectives.

« *One Sloan MBA friend was obsessed with landing a prestigious and lucrative job. It was absolutely essential to him that he get the sort of job that everyone else in the class at least thought he should want. He spent the better part of his two years in Business School cultivating the top consulting firms and investment banks. His MBA was a true platinum passport, and he received a number of top-echelon offers. Unfortunately, some of the time spent grooming himself for the "biggies" should have been spent asking himself whether this sort of job was what he really wanted. It took him about three months to realize that investment banking was not what he wanted, and the next three years deciding to quit. When last I heard, he was living off his accumulated bonuses and "finding himself."* »

Assuming you are in the right job, the next step is climbing the corporate ladder. Generally, Sloan MBAs move rapidly. Sloan does not have an extensive old boy network in all industries across the board, but where Sloan graduates are found they do well and help their own. The Sloan degree is a well-respected credential, which, like the American Express Gold Card, brings instant respect and says more about yourself than almost anything else you have done starting out in the business world.

SUMMARY OVERVIEW

PERSONALLY, I am an enthusiastic advocate of the Sloan School, and overall, my experience there was far happier and more fruitful than I had anticipated. The students were friendly, the atmosphere congenial and supportive, the coursework — at least a good part of the time — interesting and stimulating. The outcome, for me, was fine: I wanted to work in a relaxed, open, informal environment, easily commutable and fairly well-paid. There were trade-offs, of course, and the inevitable organizational pitfalls cannot be avoided (yes, kids, politics and bureaucracy occur everywhere). But on the whole, I am satisfied, and the Sloan people I talk with are generally satisfied, as well.

On the downside, Sloan is still in the process of overcoming its reputation as a "tech" school, which does not yield students as polished as those graduating from other top schools. One Stanford MBA acquaintance was "surprised" that so many Sloan grads went into investment banking and consulting, since these were fields in which style and image seemed so important. He supposed, like a lot of people do, that all Sloan grads wear high-water pants and talk in machine code (when they're not playing video games).

In truth, most Sloan students look just as good in gray flannel as anyone else; perhaps better, for two years at MIT seem to lend everyone a tolerance of, if not an outright affinity for, the color gray.

Sloan/MIT is not the world's most attractive or inviting campus, although Sloan facilities have been upgraded and renovated recently. Still, anyone who absolutely needs to be surrounded by red brick, ivy, trees, and duck ponds had best avoid MIT. The buildings at "The Institute" have numbers, not names. While this may be fine for those fully attuned to postverbal society, it is somewhat disconcerting for those of us still somewhat enamored of language. After two years, I was still unsure why Building 10 was called Building 10. Nor was I convinced that all corridors in Building 39 eventually lead to Building 38.

On the upside — and it certainly outweighs the downside — I suspect that the academic content and quality of courses is higher at Sloan than it is at a number of B schools. The "rigor" of the Sloan program renders the Sloan degree a somewhat satisfying attainment — sort of like Haagen Daaz ice cream rather than Dairy Queen. At Sloan, people learn how to "do" something: solve a problem, find an answer, perform an analysis. They may never be called on to do it, but they sure know how.

The atmosphere at Sloan is congenial, relaxed, conducive to learning (if that's what you want to do) as well as to developing friendships. The students at Sloan are very bright, they are very interesting, they are very friendly. Which is not to say that all Sloan students are bright/interesting/friendly, but the overall aura is. Sloan's small size makes it possible to get a good deal of "customized" attention — academically and personally. It is really much like a small town, in the best sense of small town: tolerant, rather than parochial and insular; friendly, but not overbearingly or obnoxiously so — no one is going to force his/her attentions on you, and no one will ever have to tell you to "Have a nice day." There is also a somewhat pervasive self-deprecating humor throughout the place: high marks for that.

I found Sloan a very fine place to go to business school. For what it is worth — and it's worth a lot to me — I give it my highest endorsement.

Chapter 6

KELLOGG SCHOOL OF MANAGEMENT* (NORTHWESTERN UNIVERSITY)

THE PROGRAM

« *Thinking about moving to Chicago, the largest midwestern city, was a little intimidating to someone from a small town on the East Coast. Especially after driving through large industrial towns like Gary, Indiana, on the way. As I drove out of Chicago toward the Northwestern campus, my fears disappeared. The graduate school was set in a lush, green campus in the heart of a beautiful Chicago suburb. What a great place for a business school, I thought.* »

The Northwestern University campus is located in Evanston, Illinois (infamous home of the Women's Christian Temperance Union . . . more about that later). This beautiful Chicago suburb is located just twelve miles north of the "Windy City." The graduate school of business is located in the center of the campus in Nathaniel Leverone Hall, a structure built specifically for graduate business study. Looking out some of the

---

* BY CHARLESANNA DAILY ECKER AND BILL ECKER, MMS, NORTHWESTERN

windows in Leverone Hall, one is struck by the true beauty of the campus: from the school's private beach along Lake Michigan to the widely varied architecture on campus. The location provides the best of both worlds: a peaceful suburban location, with easy access to the city of Chicago.

Within this rather idyllic setting is Northwestern's graduate school of business (known officially since 1979 as the J. L. Kellogg Graduate School of Management). While Northwestern is viewed as an upstart by some and a school of longstanding reputation by others, it is increasingly being recognized as one of the finest graduate schools of management in the country. In any list of business schools, Northwestern is invariably listed among the top five programs in the country.

Like all top ten business schools, Northwestern has strong programs and faculty in each area of study, but marketing is where the school has made its reputation. The Kellogg School's Marketing Department is considered by many to be the finest program available in the country. The department houses the well-known marketing "gurus" Phillip Kotler, Sidney Levy, and Louis Stern, as well as a host of up-and-coming marketing professors of national reputation. Their leading-edge research ranges from qualitative brand imagery to analysis of distribution channels. In addition, the school offers more than fifteen marketing courses covering everything from the basics of marketing to the finer points of consumer behavior, market research, and modeling techniques for marketing.

In many ways, the development of such a strong marketing program represents a shrewd piece of marketing on the part of the school itself. By demonstrating an expertise in marketing education (an area where there wasn't significant competition among other top schools) Northwestern has built its reputation as a top school for business education. Since that time, the other functional areas have been strengthened considerably, so that they too are consistent with Northwestern's first-class reputation. Today, a business student at Kellogg can major in any functional area and receive an excellent education.

The degree offered by the Kellogg School is called the Master of Management (MM) — as opposed to the MBA offered by almost every other school of management. The philosophy behind this name is that Northwestern is concerned with developing general *managers* who may choose to practice their craft in any sector of the economy, rather than just exclusively in the private sector. This is one of the things that sets Northwestern apart — it has a variety of programs to meet the needs of a diverse group of students. The Kellogg School offers four institutional specialties within the Master of Management program (all utilizing the same basic management skills):

- Business Management
- Hospital and Health Services Management
- Public and Not-for-Profit Management
- Transportation Management

The Business Management specialty is chosen by approximately 85 percent of the student body and it's the equivalent of the MBA offered by other business schools. As this represents the largest portion of the school, I've concentrated on this specialty. The other areas, however, are high-quality programs and represent an excellent and somewhat unique opportunity for potential management students who have decided to pursue careers in these other fields.

When the Management School opens in September, the first week is devoted to CIM — Conceptual Issues in Management. CIM is an orientation week composed of lectures, a computer simulation game, and informal discussions with faculty and business leaders from the Chicago area. The week also provides a good overview of the management program, and offers an opportunity to meet faculty and other students in an informal setting before formal classes begin.

« *Like most of the other students at Kellogg, I had gradu-*
ated near the top of my class in undergraduate school. How-
ever, like many of my classmates at Kellogg, undergraduate
school never forced me to spend all of my time studying to get
good grades. It seemed that I always had extra time to do what
I wanted, whether it be sports or partying or whatever.

Early on at Kellogg, I realized that my undergraduate rou-
tine would not cut it. I quickly realized that, unlike undergrad
school, everyone at Kellogg was as smart as I and coasting
through would not be possible. My first few weeks were spent
studying every waking hour, and I later found out that most of
my classmates were doing the same thing. But as time went on,
I guess we all became more efficient because we all found time
to do all of those extracurricular things we did in undergrad-
uate school. »

Candidates for the Master of Management degree must
complete six quarters of classes to graduate. There are twelve
introductory courses regardless of institutional area. The first
year is primarily devoted to nine required core courses. These
include: Accounting, Management, Organization Behavior,
Quantitative Methods, Economics, Statistics, Operations
Management, Finance, and Marketing. Because the subjects
are unfamiliar to most of the student body and the courses tend
toward the quantitative, the core courses usually require the
most intense study time for new students. But, the core courses
are valuable. They provide exposure to a broad range of management topics and give the student the necessary background
to begin choosing an area (or areas) of concentration. During
the first year there are three electives, and during the second
year all of the courses are electives. Students can specialize in
Accounting and Information Systems, Decision Sciences,
Economic Development, Finance, Human Resources, Industrial Relations, International Business, Management Informa-

tion Systems, Managerial Economics, Marketing, Operations Management, Organization Behavior, and Policy and Environment.

Northwestern offers a program generally not available at other top schools: a four-quarter (twelve-month) program. This program is available to graduates of accredited undergraduate business programs, and it grants students the same degree as their six-quarter counterparts. The program is designed to minimize the repetition of coursework for undergraduate business majors who want to get their masters in management. Enrollment is extremely limited; only 64 people per year are admitted (compared to 410–420 for the six-quarter program). The four-quarter program is a great opportunity for the undergraduate business major to get his or her MM in one year, and can represent a net savings of $60,000 to $70,000 over the two-year program (one year less of school, and one more year of earnings). However, in this program, the student has only one year to choose and pursue both a major(s) and a career. Therefore, it is recommended only for students who know what they wish to specialize in before entering graduate school.

Students in the four-quarter program begin the management program in June with four courses: Economic Analysis for Management, Quantitative Models for Management, Management of Processing Systems, and Management of Enterprise. These courses are designed to supplement undergraduate business courses and insure that the four-quarter class is prepared to join their six-quarter counterparts in advanced elective courses during the fall quarter. It is assumed that four-quarter students have a strong business background, and the courses cover a large quantity of material (often equivalent to two quarters' worth of material) in a short period of time. Those students without a strong, well-rounded business education will find the summer schedule extremely grueling, but for most it's both a review of familiar material and an exploration of more advanced business topics.

Kellogg has approximately 900 full-time students. (Close to 1,200 more are enrolled in the part-time evening program.) Of these, 840 are enrolled in the six-quarter program (420 per class) and about 60 students are enrolled in the four-quarter (one-year) program. The size of the student body is similar to many of the other top business schools. As with other top programs, 35 percent of each class are women, 10 percent are minority, and 12 percent are foreign students. The average age of entering students is 26, and 98 percent have had prior full-time work experience. In contrast to the more technically oriented student bodies at some other top schools, approximately 60 percent of Northwestern's class majored in humanities or the social sciences.

The "typical" student at Kellogg is a bright liberal arts major with two or three years of work experience. However, within this typical class are interesting individuals with a personal story to tell. Students at Kellogg may have spent two years in the Peace Corps, time traveling abroad, or a few years working for a large corporation.

Classes at Kellogg are seldom over sixty people and are often in the twenty to thirty range. Generally, the more advanced a course is, the smaller it is.

« *Before I went to graduate school, friends asked me whether Northwestern was "case" or "theory." Truthfully, before I got there, I didn't know the difference. Before first-quarter classes started, I took my book list and went to the bookstore to get the required materials. When I got home from the bookstore (about an hour and a half and fifty dollars later), I sat at my desk and looked at the materials that I had bought. There was one "theory" book for finance, one "case" book for policy, a notebook of selected articles from journals for economics, etc. . . . I then realized that Kellogg was both a "case" school and a "theory" school.* »

The best word to describe Northwestern's teaching method is diversity. Teaching methods vary according to the subject and teacher. In general (if one can generalize), introductory quantitative courses are taught theoretically, and as a greater level of expertise is gained, case work and group discussions are used more often. However, by the time of graduation, a student has had courses that use the case, lecture, theory, group project, and individual project methods. Clearly, Northwestern's philosophy is "it all depends," and just as clearly, it works. The school does not have a preoccupation with the ongoing debate of case versus theory that is so frequently heard in the business school community. The school does not advocate any one specific teaching method, but supports whatever method is appropriate to communicate the most information in the most useful way.

GETTING IN

« *I really don't know what got me in to Kellogg. It could have been that I worked my way through undergraduate school, or that my grades put me up near the top of my class. Or, it could have been my work experience as a manager with the school newspaper. I guess I can't pin it on one thing, but probably one without the other wouldn't have gotten me in.* »

Each entering class at Kellogg is a combination of different people from diverse backgrounds. Kellogg draws students from over two hundred undergraduate institutions and from almost every state in the union. There are approximately eight applicants for every acceptance, a figure on par with other top ten business schools.

The school does not have any absolute academic requirements for admission to the six-quarter program. However, the school does recommend that students get some undergraduate coursework in calculus, economics, and speech or debate. Most students find that taking some or all of these courses before going to Kellogg does help. In contrast to the six-quarter program, the four-quarter option requires an undergraduate degree in business from an accredited undergraduate business program.

When screening applicants, the school states that it looks primarily for one thing: potential for a career in management. To determine acceptance, the school uses information found in the application, and the interview. All information is used to measure the intangibles of experience, maturity, and potential (the "X" factor). The application is very important; it serves as the first and most difficult hurdle to overcome in the entire process. The Northwestern application combines data questions with essay questions to determine whether the applicant has the potential to succeed in business. It should be noted that admission decisions are based primarily on the information presented in the application, so one should be extremely careful in its completion.

The second hurdle is the interview. Interviews are now required and can take place either on or off campus. In fact, interviews are given full weight along with GPA/GMAT scores, essay questions on the application, and meaningful and successful work experience before business school.

There are no sure-fire ways to gain admission to any business school, and Northwestern is no exception. Admissions "quotas" are not readily apparent if they exist at all. Whatever criteria they use seem to work; the vast majority of the people admitted to the program are bright, young, and have a strong potential for a career in management.

ACADEMIC ENVIRONMENT

« *It didn't take me very long to realize that the atmosphere at KGSM was different from what I had expected. I was having some trouble with an introductory statistics course when the professor (who I wasn't sure knew my name) stopped me after class. I was expecting a lecture on how I should study harder or something like that. But he handed me another statistics book and told me to read a chapter and come to his office to discuss it the next day. Many graduate schools threaten to flunk a certain number of students, and set policies that require that a certain number of A's and F's be given out in each class, but I realized then that Northwestern's faculty makes it clear that you will graduate and that they are there to help you become the best possible manager when you do.* »

Although the coursework at KGSM is demanding, the assumption is made that if you were good enough to be accepted, then you are bright enough to graduate. The faculty tries to help and encourage you to succeed, rather than threaten you with failure (provided of course that you apply yourself — passing grades are not given to those that don't try). The same helpful, encouraging attitude exists throughout most of the student body. Although KGSM students are by nature achievement oriented and competitive (they wouldn't be there if they weren't), they aren't cutthroat. Because the school provides an opportunity for all students to succeed, there's no need for one student to succeed at the expense of another. It's very common for students to take time to assist fellow students who may be having a hard time with a particular subject.

« *The night of my first quantitative methods exam I was studying late into the night in my room when someone knocked at my door. I was surprised. I had been in school only a few weeks and certainly wasn't expecting any visitors. My late-night visitor was a fellow student who explained that he had a strong mathematical background and had seen my light while returning from the library, and so he had stopped to help me prepare for the test. I soon learned that this sort of occurrence was not unusual — classmates would often help each other study, or offer to type papers for those who had an unusually tough period. »*

Grading methods at the Kellogg School are as diverse as the teaching methods. Some professors never give A's, some give a lot of A's — there is no established grade curve. The basis for grades varies from class to class as well. Grades may be based on weekly tests, class participation, a major paper or presentation, or any combination thereof. In marketing courses particularly, there are many group projects, papers, and presentations, and therefore a student's grade may not be entirely in his or her control. This can be very frustrating, but it provides an excellent experience for the "real world," where an employee seldom carries out a project on his or her own. This method teaches group dynamics, delegation, negotiation, and leadership — all important skills in a working environment. The emphasis on group work also reinforces the esprit de corps mentioned earlier — you can't afford to be "cut-throat" toward classmates when your grade may depend on their willingness to cooperate with you the following quarter.

The quality of the teaching also makes the academic environment at Kellogg special. The school administration apparently fosters this positive teaching/learning environment by placing as high a priority on the professor's ability to communicate as effectively in the classroom as on his or her research and publishing. Professors (especially in marketing) bring into the classroom a mixture of state-of-the-art theory along with practical business sense, and students leave school with a realistic picture of what they will encounter in the business world and how best to deal with it.

The proximity of the school to the city of Chicago also provides additional opportunities for learning. Chicago is second only to New York as a center for industry, and the school maintains close ties with many Chicago business leaders. Chicago-area executives often speak to classes at Northwestern in evening panel discussions. In addition, Careers is a program in which career options are outlined by alumni executives, students, and the Placement Office. Another program is Corporate Connections, which gives summer interns in Chicago and nationwide an opportunity to attend receptions at work locations. One of the most rewarding results of the close ties between the Kellogg School and the Chicago business community is the frequent opportunity to work on long-term projects with Chicago-area businesses. This experience certainly adds depth to the prospective manager's business education.

« *During one quarter, I took a New Products Marketing course as an elective and had an opportunity to work with a major Chicago consumer goods company in a "consulting" capacity. I had never worked before attending business school (I mean really worked) and found it fascinating to get a peek into the real business world. My career interests were in marketing, and this company had a top-notch new products area.*

We were asked by this well-known package goods giant to do some market research. We sat down, looked at the problem in a typical business school fashion, analyzed it thoroughly, and recommended that some sophisticated market research be done. While the company very nicely said that they felt the research would be useful, they also stated it certainly wouldn't be worth the money it would take to get it. Hence, we quickly learned the power of the bottom line in marketing and business in general. Needless to say, I probably learned more in that quarter than any other at Business School. After school, I got a job offer from that company, and I have worked with them since graduation. »

SOCIAL LIFE

« *Before I got to Northwestern, I thought my future KGSM classmates would be unbearably dull and serious. But I decided that I would tolerate a lack of social life in exchange for a first-rate business education. What I found instead was a group of bright, well-rounded people who were interested in a full, rewarding social life as well as a successful business career. KGSM students are certainly serious about succeeding, but they lack the humorless intensity for which top business schools are famous. Nothing exemplifies the special spirit of the student body better than "The Special K Revue," a comedy/variety no-holds-barred production that the KGSM student body writes, directs, and stars in each year.* »

The KGSM student body is truly a social group. The class size and frequent group assignments make it both necessary and easy to meet people. Additionally, the Graduate Management Association (the Kellogg student government) sponsors such activities as the TGIF keg parties, which are held every Friday afternoon in the student lounge. As in many graduate programs where scholastic pressure is a way of life, the common experiences and shared goals foster friendships that are often strong and long-lasting.

One of the most popular times for KGSM students to relax is Tuesday nights. Although the workload at Northwestern is demanding, it is made much more manageable by the very civilized practice of having classes only four days a week. There are no classes on Wednesdays, and this provides both a day to catch up on studies and a perfect excuse to party on Tuesday nights.

« One of the ways we found to fill the Tuesday night void was to set up a bartending course. We hired a professional bartender and gathered once a week for six weeks to broaden and sometimes blur our horizons. Forty people signed up and attendance was almost perfect. We learned how to make everything from martinis to Singapore Slings. Of course, liquidating our product was half the fun. This bartending course turned out to be one of the most enjoyable courses I had at Business School and the one from which I learned the true definition of liquidity. »

Northwestern is located in Evanston, which is the home of the Women's Christian Temperance Union. Although once a dry town, alcoholic beverages may now be purchased in Evanston, which offers a number of fine restaurants and other pleasant gathering places in a suburban location only a short distance from Chicago. Howard Street, the dividing line between Evanston and Chicago, is fifteen minutes away, and the "dives" here provide a Tuesday-night haven for many Northwestern students. In addition, downtown Chicago is only thirty minutes away. The Windy City has all the excitement of any major city — museums, theaters, great restaurants (Chicago has more four-star restaurants than New York City), great shopping, and some attractions that are uniquely Chicago, including the Second City Improvisational comedy theater and Rush Street — an area lined with bars that attract much of the young professional community of Chicago.

Northwestern's lack of successful athletic teams is legendary. Fortunately, for those who like to experience a winning season, there are the Northwestern University intramural athletics and KGSM sports leagues. During the winter months, cross-country skiing is popular and the shores of Lake Michigan provide many scenic trails. Because of the bitter cold of many Chicago winters, much of the social activity in the winter takes place indoors. For those who live in graduate housing, social life centers around the dorm. Impromptu parties spring up regularly, and it's possible to have an active social life without braving the blizzards outdoors.

In the warmer months, extracurricular activity moves outside. There's a private beach for Northwestern students and many lovely locations along the Lake Michigan side of the campus. Winter or summer, the campus is beautiful, and it provides an ideal setting for all sorts of outdoor activities.

The social life at Northwestern is not strictly for single students. Married students often find that their spouses become an integral part of the social scene at the school, as they are readily accepted by the student body. On the other hand, students' spouses sometimes gravitate toward one another as they share common experiences and interests such as supporting their spouse through graduate school and raising families. Overall, married students have a wide range of options! They can enjoy Kellogg and Chicago on their own; or center their social lives around the school.

As for housing, Kellogg has its own modern, refurbished apartment building on the south end of campus. One third of the student body resides in the Living-Learning Center. Additionally, many students choose to live off campus in apartment buildings or one of the many homes for rent.

RECRUITING AND JOB SEARCH

« *After majoring in Advertising in undergraduate school, I struggled to find job offers from small ad agencies for $10–12,000 a year. When the recruiting season began at Kellogg, I* *realized how the tables had turned. Here were several major ad agencies offering me better jobs at almost three times the salary they had been offering me only two short years before!"* »

The job search is an experience that most students never forget. Throughout the recruiting season at Kellogg, the focus turns from academics to the job search. The halls of Leverone Hall fill with talk of the job hunt as friends receive offers from prospective employers. It seems that this intensity and excitement would carry on forever if the graduation ceremony didn't call an end to it all.

The placement office at Kellogg occupies a large piece of Leverone Hall. The school places a high degree of importance on finding the right job — and not just any job. To this end, the placement office has several programs designed to meet the needs of job-seeking students. These programs range from group discussions on effective résumés and interviewing, to individual guidance counseling for students who need assistance in deciding on a career choice. However, it is important to remember that the placement office at any school can only provide the information to help the student make more informed decisions, and cannot make decisions for them. The fact is that the placement office at Kellogg takes their prescribed role very seriously, and does their job very well.

Kellogg's placement office excels in two areas: maximizing the number of visiting companies and interviews granted, and personalizing the entire recruiting process to whatever extent possible. Each year, over three hundred companies visit Northwestern and grant over eleven thousand individual interviews. This offers each student at KGSM the opportunity to have an average of twenty-five interviews during the recruiting season. This astonishing figure is certainly higher than at most schools, and more than enough to let each student explore numerous employment opportunities. Interviews at Northwestern are doled out on a "bidding" system, which is used in some form at most of the top schools. The system gives each student a certain number of points that he or she can "bid" to get interviews. This usually assures that a student can interview with companies on the top of his or her list, and won't get shut out of important interviews by other students taking practice or warm-up interviews.

« *The morning of my first interview, I got up and nervously leafed through the information I had gathered about the company. I guess because it was my first interview, and I really wanted to work for the company, I took my preparation very seriously. I had read whatever I could find about the company, and had attended the company's cocktail party a few days before. As I put on my suit I kept thinking of the questions they might ask, and responses ran through my head in rapid-fire succession. I also put together a list of questions to ask the interviewer to show that I was serious. I walked to Leverone Hall and my mouth got drier, my palms moister. I sat in the waiting room reading the company's latest annual report, listening for my name to be called by the interviewer. When I heard my name and looked up, there stood a familiar face. Not only had I seen my interviewer at the cocktail party a few nights before, but he and I had hoisted a few beers together. At that point my nervousness disappeared. I assume that the interview went well because one week later I was invited to visit the company for a follow-up interview.* »

Northwestern does a very good job of "personalizing" the entire job search experience. The school encourages companies to have as much informal contact with the student body as possible. One common practice among companies is to have a cocktail party a few nights before their interview day. Additionally, the school encourages prospective employers to have KGSM graduates/employees visit classrooms to talk about their work experience. This too helps to take some of the "nervous edge" off the interview day.

Northwestern's placement record in recent years, like that of all top business schools, has been outstanding. Students attending Northwestern can expect upon graduation to be presented with job and salary offers comparable to those received by students at any of the top ten schools. Starting salaries in the $45,000 to $55,000 range are not uncommon. Differences in average starting salaries among the top schools most often reflect the mix of accepted jobs rather than discrepancies among salaries.

Kellogg graduates pursue jobs in all functional areas. The top three employers according to industry are investment banking (22 percent), brand management (21 percent), and consulting (15 percent). Other industries that recruit in lesser numbers are financial analysis, financial services, advertising, and lending. Northwestern graduates can choose from a wide range of job options.

There is also recruiting for summer employment. Contrary to what any school says, good summer experiences are significantly harder to find than good full-time jobs. Fewer companies have summer employment programs. Therefore, although Kellogg's summer placement program is felt to be on par with other top schools, there are few cakewalks to good summer jobs. Some students will get good summer jobs through the school, but many students will have to seek their own employment opportunities. This, however, is likely to happen at any school.

ON THE JOB — FIRST YEARS OUT

« My first week on the job, we received a call from the plant telling us that our packaging was "out-of-spec." Immediately,

I was told to drive to the plant and "fix it." After driving for about an hour I realized that I didn't even know what "out-of-spec" meant. My nervousness increased. As I walked into the meeting room, I was greeted by twelve people and twelve different sides of the same story. Slowly but surely, I was able to sort the story out and fix the problem. I realized on the way home that night that I had really come a long way. Two years earlier, I probably would have fallen apart under the same circumstances. I think that my B School training with its problem-solving orientation enabled me to handle a very tough situation without panic. »

Along with the facts and theories taught at most schools, the Kellogg School takes a "real world" approach and teaches practical problem-solving techniques and other specific skills. Kellogg students usually find that they are well prepared to move into the business community. They are knowledgeable about the functional area they have chosen; they know how to conduct a meeting, make a presentation, organize a project, and effectively manage the resources around them. In short, KGSM graduates not only know how to analyze a problem and recommend a solution, but they also have many of the skills necessary to execute that solution effectively.

One year later, most KGSM grads find that both their salary and status in their organization is near the top compared with the other MBAs who joined the company at the same time. Although there is little job switching in the first year after graduation, it is not uncommon for graduates from all top business schools to start moving two or three years after graduation. The Northwestern degree, along with good postgraduate work experience, provides an entry to many other interesting career opportunities, and some students do avail themselves of these opportunities. The ability to move is enhanced by Northwestern's strong and active alumni organization. These alumni are often important contacts that can provide information and help you secure a job. (Kellogg, founded in 1908, has more than 25,000 alumni worldwide.) Today, Kellogg is represented in almost every major company by an alumnus.

« *Looking back at the time I spent at Northwestern, I firmly believe it was one of the best things I ever did for myself. When I compare where I am today to where I probably would have been if I hadn't attended KGSM the differences are astounding. I have a job several layers higher, in a far better company, with four or five times the earning power than I would have had. In addition, there is certainly more future potential for rapid advancement in both salary and status.* »

SUMMARY OVERVIEW

NORTHWESTERN has worked hard during the last decade to earn its rightful place among the top ten graduate schools of management. Once only a school with a strong regional reputation, Kellogg now has a strong national reputation that grows each year. One can safely assume that the Kellogg degree will only get more valuable over time as more and more people acknowledge the school's top-notch quality. Kellogg's growth as a leading management school was recently recognized in a nationwide survey designed to determine how corporate recruiters from leading manufacturing and service companies view graduates of the top MBA programs. Those responding ranked Kellogg as the best in training managers, and Kellogg graduates as leaders in knowledge of marketing, ability to work as part of a team, and overall value to employers. Kellogg graduates were also ranked most likely to stay with a company.

If one attempts to describe Kellogg in one word, that word

would be diversity. This diversity can be found in the backgrounds of the entering students, in the teaching methods, and the grading methods. Unlike some of the other top schools, academic truisms are the exception rather than the rule. Additionally, the suburban Chicago location offers students many diverse settings in which to spend their free time.

Scholastically, the school's recognized strength is in marketing, where it is considered by many to be the very best in the nation. However, KGSM students will receive a solid foundation in all of the business basics prior to graduation. A marketing major, for example, will not be just a trained marketer, but will be a general manager with strong marketing training. Also, it should be noted that the school has not developed a superior marketing program at the expense of other functional areas. Many of Kellogg's programs rival any of the other top ten schools.

Kellogg also has several other strengths that set it apart. First it has three concentrations — Hospital and Health Services Management, Public and Nonprofit Management, and Transportation Management — that allow students to develop an expertise in areas not traditionally covered by most of the top business schools. In addition, the four-quarter program is a real opportunity for undergraduate business majors to eliminate the academic duplication that occurs in a conventional program.

Kellogg, like other top schools, has its points of weakness. Two of the most persistent, however, appear to be diminishing as problems. First, because of the school's long-standing association with the Chicago business community, job opportunities for graduates tend to be concentrated in that area. However, as the school's national reputation has grown in the past decade, recruiters are coming from all over. In fact, 48 percent of those recently graduated stayed in the midwest (usually by choice) to work, and 33 percent are employed in the northeast. The reputation of the school has also grown on the west coast. Kellogg today has alumni in all fifty states and in more than one hundred twenty foreign countries around the world. Second, Kellogg's strength in marketing tended to overshadow other areas of strength at the school. That, too, is changing; since 1980, in particular, there has been increasing interest in graduates on the part of consulting firms, investment banks, and real estate services, among others.

All in all, the Kellogg program is outstanding. The flexibility of the program, the strength of the marketing and other departments, and the sociable student body make Northwestern a great choice for anyone who wants a well-rounded, balanced, high-quality MBA program.

Chapter 7

THE UNIVERSITY OF MICHIGAN BUSINESS SCHOOL*

THE PROGRAM

« The Michigan Graduate School of Business is located in the heart of one of the nation's largest and best academic bastions, The University of Michigan at Ann Arbor. In one sense, the MBA program is a part of and influenced by all that surrounds it. One can't help but notice the flavor of Big Ten football as the almost religious, campuswide pilgrimage of fans winds by the Business School on the way to the stadium. And the evening air is often permeated by the boisterous antics of frat houses and sororities that line the street across from the school. Too, there is the electricity of student demonstrations and the hustling and bustling of a thousand organizations, parties and events throughout the expansive campus.

But bottom line, this graduate school at The University of Michigan is a highly specialized, self-contained community that means serious business. Its purpose is to train business leaders. For two years, MBA candidates eat, sleep and breathe business in a very tough, demanding program. With a yearly

---

* BY LEN SAVOIE, MBA, MICHIGAN

graduation crop of less than 400, and bonded together by a rigorous schedule that never lets up, MBA candidates at the Business School quickly become a close-knit group. Students have to work together to survive the rigors of the program. By being tough and industrious, Michigan has developed a top-flight MBA program within the heartland of football, parties, and a fine public institution. »

Although the program at Michigan is very demanding, it is also balanced and flexible. It spans two full academic years and is comprised of twenty courses taken over four semesters. Of these twenty courses, students must take ten that are specifically prescribed as the core curriculum. Most core courses must be taken in the first two semesters, and these provide a solid grounding in the basics. Areas covered in the first year include Accounting (financial and managerial), Organizational Behavior, Computers, Statistics, Finance, Marketing, Applied Microeconomics, and Operations Management. At the beginning of the program, students may take placement exams for these courses, and if they demonstrate previously acquired expertise they become entitled to take electives instead. In the second year of the program, there are no waivers for the remaining core course, Corporate Strategy. This last course affords students an opportunity to integrate the accumulated learning of the entire program.

The remainder of the program is comprised of electives with minimal constraints as to their selection. With fully half the courses at the student's discretion, the program becomes highly flexible in meeting individual needs while maintaining a strong balance of fundamental groundwork. Many students also tap into the greater resources of the university to tailor the MBA program to their own specific career desires. MBA candidates may take three or four graduate courses (up to ten credit hours) outside the Business School in Michigan's schools of art, music, international study, communication, and many others.

Michigan demonstrates additional flexibility by offering an evening MBA program. This gives students the opportunity to hold full-time jobs while they spread the traditional two years over a longer period of time. It is also possible to transfer from the evening to the day program or vice versa. About one hundred students (in addition to the 375 in the day program) graduate from the evening program each year. However, many feel that the day program, with its concentrated approach, is clearly the preferred way to get the most out of your Michigan MBA. Neverthless, the evening program provides a nice alternative, if necessary.

There are 375 MBAs in each class in the day program, which is about the average size vis-à-vis the other top business schools. During the first year, students are divided into six randomly selected sections, each comprised of about sixty-five students. Students in each section take most but not all courses together during the first year. In this way, they get to know each other fairly well.

Each core course has about sixty-five students. First-year electives are generally smaller, averaging thirty-five to sixty-five students. Seminars are limited to twenty to thirty members. Not only do these course sizes provide excellent opportunities for student participation in class, but also for students to know each other and the faculty on a personal basis. In the second year, students from all sections become integrated in the elective courses.

The overall academic environment at the Michigan Business School is a roll-up-the-shirtsleeves, no-nonsense approach. While some of the other top business schools tend to skew to the theoretical or quantitative side, Michigan is more balanced. It's quantitative when it has to be, which is often. It covers all the important theory in the core courses, but with some well-placed restraint. For example, some business school spend almost half of the introductory statistics class delving into the depths of Bayesian decision theory. While it is important to understand this aspect of conditional probability, realistically it is only a tool that the general manager should be aware of so an expert can be called in when the theory needs to be applied. For students seeking further detail, more advanced statistics courses are available.

The introductory marketing course provides another example of this practical approach. By maintaining a balanced perspective on quantitative methods and theoretical depth, the school is able to highlight the practical realities which must be understood for effective decision-making.

« *The case for one marketing class was Fisher-Price toys. The professor had arranged on his desk an assortment of the company's brightly colored products. He began the class by asking what the consumer would identify as the key qualities of Fisher-Price toys. Students responded with answers they had prepared the night before when they read the case. There were mentions of high quality, safety, variety, and value. The professor shook his head, obviously discouraged. Without saying a word he started picking up the toys, one by one, and tossed them over his head. Fairly large plastic dump trucks, dolls, musical instruments, etc. fell full force against the carpet but appeared to be unscathed. The class was amused, but more than that, perplexed. "What the hell is he doing?" He then began to repeat the exercise, and his intent suddenly became apparent. Finally, he asked, "Well class, so what is it that we're selling here?" The class responded as one: "Durability!"*

This was an effective little lesson in getting to the heart of the matter, and it set a precedent for the cases that would follow. »

The teaching method used at Michigan includes both cases and lectures, depending on the subject matter and the objectives of each course. For some courses, a combination of both approaches is utilized. What is important here is that Michigan is not tied to any particular teaching method. It uses whichever it feels is most appropriate for the subject matter.

In the first semester of the program, which focuses on analytical foundations, the traditional textbook/lecture discussion approach is used. When the subject matter is as quantitative and complicated as it is in statistics, accounting, and computers, the straightforward lecture method provides a solid foundation. This foundation then can be expanded upon and developed via the case method in the advanced courses that follow. But with a more dynamic subject matter like marketing, even the introductory course relies heavily on the case method. Human behavior uses a hybrid method (cases and lectures). The teaching method of both core courses and electives generally follows these guidelines.

The overall academic orientation at Michigan stresses general management. Since the school's beginning, its credo has remained to help students "master the techniques of any business career." The required core curriculum is consistent with this objective, as it covers all the basic functional areas of business in the context of an overall management perspective. The process used in class to develop preparation for general management is focused on identifying problems, devising solutions, and implementing decisions in a dynamic business, political, social, and economic environment. This process is also used in elective courses, but obviously the subject matter becomes more specialized and relevant to specific career paths.

Within the context of this strong general management approach, the school enjoys an exceptionally strong reputation in certain academic areas. These include marketing, accounting, information systems, operations management, corporate strategy, and finance. For example, Michigan has an outstanding marketing program as evidenced by its faculty, course offerings, and placement. Many of the marketing professors are actively involved in outside consulting, which provides good hands-on experience to round out the academic side of instruction. The program also offers a wide range of marketing courses in areas such as marketing management, distribution, strategic planning, sales, promotion, retail, international, industrial, research, new product development, and several more specific seminars on varying topics. Michigan's prowess in this field is acknowledged by the fact that the world's premier marketer, Procter and Gamble, considers the school a very valuable source from which to fill its product management ranks and has hired many Michigan MBAs over the years.

Accounting is also an area of particular strength at Michigan. It has a very modern, separate physical plant, the Paton Accounting Center, and is known for its outstanding research, which is often commisssioned by top firms and professional bodies. The accounting department also offers a unique tax specialty concentration. Overall, accounting students at the school come out of the program ready to hit the beach running. Fifty percent of all the accounting students at Michigan (MBAs and BBAs) successfully complete all four parts of the CPA exam at the first sitting, which is one of the highest rates in the nation.

The graduate business program at Michigan attracts students from varied geographic locations, diverse academic backgrounds, and vastly different work experience.

« I remember feeling horribly insecure as I walked into that first social get-together the day before classes started. It's understandable, I thought, for a new MBA candidate to wonder how he got into such a highly touted program. A fluke? A slip in the system? I had spent the last four years as a musician playing in rock bands, so my anxiety level was really hard to

handle. *As the beer began to loosen everyone up a little, however, I soon learned that I was not alone. There were art
students and language majors, geologists, engineers, and what
seemed like everything under the sun, in addition to the CPAs,
bankers, and lawyers one would expect.*

*In the beginning, it was a little more difficult for us non-
traditionalists to compete with the students who had undergraduate degrees in engineering, business, economics, or had
business-related work experience. We were clearly a minority.
But the handicap was only temporary. We were driven by fear
to overcompensate. Moreover, students with artistic backgrounds tend to do better than our more quantitatively oriented
classmates in courses like human behavior and marketing.
Halfway through the second semester it didn't matter anyway,
as previously acquired leverage had faded, and everyone was in
the same boat.* »

The demographic characteristics of the student body at
Michigan have remained quite constant over time. As with
other MBA programs, it is mostly comprised of men (78 percent), with a significant representation of students with undergraduate degrees in business (20 percent), economics (25
percent), and engineering/sciences (26 percent).

Like many other schools, Michigan MBA's are on average
twenty-six years of age with most (88 percent) having a year or
more of full-time work experience. Geographically, more
come from the Midwest (40 percent), with the remainder
coming from the Northeast (28 percent), the South and West
(17 percent) and other countries (15 percent). Michigan does
not keep records of its students' marital status, but on judgment, the majority are single.

In one respect, Michigan is different from most of the other
top ten business schools. It is a public institution. This affects
the composition of its student body, since the school accepts a

greater percentage of in-state students, who subsequently enjoy in-state tuition advantages. However, the overall structure of the program, the quality of its students, and its general management orientation make Michigan very much like the other top ten schools.

The graduate business program at Michigan hails from a long tradition that began in 1924, and provides a quality general management business education usually associated with only private institutions. It also boasts an impressive, modern physical plant that has undergone continuing renovation and has under construction a sizable expansion of library, computer, and classroom facilities.

In summary, the Michigan MBA program is tough and effective. Its students are bright and eager going in, tenacious and driven coming out. The challenges they face during the program provide solid preparation for the business world.

GETTING IN

ADMISSION to the Michigan program is highly competitive, with up to 20,000 inquiries and some 3,000 applications for each entering class of 375. Key sources used to evaluate the academic business potential of each prospective candidate include the applicant's academic record, GMAT scores, work experience, recommendations, and the application itself.

As stated previously, students with a wide variety of backgrounds are admitted into the program. Michigan doesn't really seem to care from what or where you come, just as long as you have established a solid record of achievement that indicates an aptitude and a desire to perform well, both academically and in the real business world. The only nominal requirement for admission is one course in undergraduate calculus.

The essay sections on the application are critical, since all other measurements of future promise are implied from data beyond the applicant's immediate control (e.g., test scores and academic record). In this case, the Michigan application provides three essay opportunities to sell yourself. The first is on personal achievements, the second is on qualities you are looking for in a business school, and the third is on your goals for the next five years.

The catch is that each answer must be limited to only one page. Thus, efficiency, in addition to effectiveness, becomes key. This is the first hint of what you might expect in the MBA program, and is wonderful preparation for the real business world you'll be facing thereafter.

It's undeniably difficult for almost everyone to make a case for their business potential in just one page. This becomes especially challenging if you're straight out of college or have had only nontraditional work experience. Then the essay itself has to work that much harder for you. With only nontraditional work experience, there are just too many things to explain.

« In my situation, the fact that I had spent the last four years playing in rock bands seemed like an overwhelming obstacle. The trick, as I would later learn even more definitively in business school, was to position the problem as an opportunity. After wrestling with it for many hours and hounding every member of my family for advice, I developed a simple outline. First, I drew parallels from my experience to universal business principles. Business, I decided, transcends all fields. In the musical world I functioned as a manager and a partner in a successful business enterprise. I wrote that I was disillusioned with the long-term career prospects and felt I would be better able to contribute and benefit from a more solid traditional profession. I needed the foundation an MBA would provide. Finally, I felt that the creative insight from my musical expe-

rience would make me a unique candidate. The greatest part about this whole approach was that it worked. »

Michigan claims it does not set any type of quotas when selecting its pool of candidates. Michigan residents have a tuition advantage, and so a large number of applications come from the state. But their credentials are as high as nonresidents. Both groups have to have exceptional qualifications.

Interviews are not part of the evaluation process at Michigan but they are granted upon request. They are somewhat helpful in obtaining factual information, but they are best used to get a perceptual net take-away of the school. It's also probably a good idea just to visit the school even before making a decision to apply. Visiting the school provides an opportunity to get a feel for the physical plant, to sit in on actual classes, and to talk with current students, who are probably the best source of advice.

Besides filling out the application and following the rest of the regular admissions procedure, there is very little else that can be done to enhance your chances of getting in. But once you are in, you are golden.

ACADEMIC ENVIRONMENT

« *Everybody always says that the MBA program at The University of Michigan is demanding. But you know this school means business when you see the students coming out of the first accounting exam with those blank stares and pale faces.*

You get your MBA at The University of Michigan the old-fashioned way — as John Houseman would say in his television pitch for Smith Barney, "You earn it." The quality of work required is top notch, and the amount of work is simply overwhelming. In order to survive, one is quickly forced to realize what is important and what can slide. »

The pace of the MBA program at Michigan is very challenging. Four days a week there are grueling classes, and each night enough work to keep the midnight oil burning. Behind this ordeal is the theory that identifying priorities and then working toward achieving them is the best preparation for a successful career in the business world. Sometimes the challenges of Business School can become especially intense, as evidenced by the first Operations Management exam.

« *The professor was known to give brutal exams, but no one was ready for this nightmare. It was scheduled to last three hours, but some students walked out after twenty minutes, unable to answer a single question. The exam consisted of only one short case with seventeen questions, but you had to dig so deep to get the answers — totally incomplete data.*

After the professor called for all the papers, I left with a pit in my stomach. I had answered only seven questions, and half of them, I was sure, were wrong. The next week in class the professor, having heard cries of mutiny in the halls, gave us a little talk. "Yes, the exam was very difficult, perhaps too difficult in retrospect. But you've got to put things in perspective. Most courses use exams that have a median of seventy-five. Half the questions everyone answers correctly. I dispensed with those give-away questions. The median for this exam is thirty-three. You've got to think of how this exam fits into the bigger picture. A year and a half from now your boss may give you an assignment that's twice as difficult. You can't panic." When he handed back the exams, I was ecstatic to have hit the median. I believe I was stronger for the experience, but I'll never forget the agony that went with it. »

Because most students who enter the program are highly motivated and achievement oriented, there is pressure to get good grades. Grading is based on a bell curve with most grades in the A and B range. The median for all core courses and most electives is a B+, and grades above this are difficult to achieve. On the other hand, getting a B in a course is considered very acceptable. The catch is that anything below B is clearly unacceptable, and considered a penalty grade, since you have to maintain at least a B average in order to graduate. Numerical grade averages are computed on each student's "report card," and anonymous deciles are posted publicly to provide everyone with an indication of where they stand vis-à-vis the class.

Class participation often represents 50 percent of a student's grade, and thus the classroom becomes an arena for achievement. Here the tone of the dialogue among students ranges from reasonably competitive to down-right cutthroat.

« *In one core marketing course, a student team was presenting before the class a case that involved a Japanese electronics firm which was considering entering the U.S. television set market. The key assignment was to determine if the firm should build warehouses and develop its own distribution system, or market their products via existing ones. There were a lot of conflicting facts and figures in the case, and, as usual, incomplete data. But the team presented a logical, comprehensive analysis. They identified a break-even point at which proprietary distribution would become cost effective, and recommended using an established distribution system until that point.*

However, the sharks in the class kept badgering the team. "How can you expect to crack something as highly competitive as the U.S. TV market? What the hell kind of assumptions are you making?" This attack went on for several minutes until the professor stepped in. "That's enough. It's not the issue. The assumptions were given in the case. They've answered the questions and did quite well." The student team was battered but relieved. It had survived the academic assault. »

While things can get pretty tough in those classes, outside class most students have the attitude, "Hey, we're all in this together, how are we going to get through it all?" This esprit de corps often leads to voluntary study groups and late-night phone calls to try to flesh out the issues of the day's assignment. This academic camaraderie is by no means considered cheating. Someone who has been relying too heavily on the help of others usually gets burned soon enough on the exam, or more embarrassingly, in class, under the professor's probing questions.

The method of evaluating a student's performance is tough, but fair. Most courses have three exams spread evenly throughout the semester — it's not a Russian roulette–type situation where everything hinges on a single, comprehensive final. Class participation is also obviously evaluated over the entire course, with appropriate acknowledgment for marked improvement.

The professors themselves are generally very supportive. They want each student in the program to perform as well as he or she can, and certainly for everyone to complete the program successfully. As long as a student takes the initiative in seeking help, the faculty will provide additional tutoring during office hours, and arrange time with teaching assistants to supplement this aid. In courses such as introductory accounting and statistics, which most students find bewildering, regular extra-help sessions are scheduled. Many professors also keep old exams on file in the Business School library. These can be invaluable for the scared, neurotic first-year student (such as I was), by providing a feel for the level of difficulty and type of exam that might be expected. A dry run on some of these exams can provide a chilling preview of the real thing and will identify areas of weakness.

The professors are also very willing to counsel students on a variety of subjects — from career guidance to personal problems. Obviously, they also become a key source for job tips and recommendations.

Although it is extremely rare, students can and occasionally do flunk out. Most of the very few who do not complete the program (less than 2 percent), however, leave of their own volition. Some of them may be afraid of failing, but most often they are either unwilling to put in the time and energy required, or find that Business School is not for them after all. Almost everyone who has been admitted to the program and is sufficiently motivated can handle it.

SOCIAL LIFE

SURPRISINGLY, social life does exist at the Business School. When you're working that hard and under such intense pressure on a regular basis, it almost has to. You need the release. And because there is such a short supply of free time, many students skew to the wild and crazy side during their off-duty hours, primarily Saturday night. Michigan business students make up with intensity what they lack in social frequency. Although some students claim to have eschewed all social contact during their two-year tenure in order to concentrate single-mindedly on academic performance and the job hunt, these students were not necessarily the ones that excelled in either. Most students at Michigan subscribe to the philosophy that the best way to succeed during the program is to work hard and play hard.

Clearly, your social life at Business School is what you make of it. There is a plethora of activities to choose from on the Ann Arbor campus, including clubs, parties, movies and sports events. There is also zero pressure to become involved in any of them. There is also nearby Detroit with all its activities and opportunities. The Business School itself is supportive of social activities. The MBA student government sponsors several events each semester, which include dances, group trips to close-by businesses like the Ford plant in Detroit, or get-togethers at a nightclub. MBA candidates also attend the football games together, where they congregate in a special reserved section.

There has been a movement in recent years toward activities that center around the sixty-five-member sections. This change will no doubt further enhance the personal nature of the program during the first year — a time when it is needed most.

There is also a significant amount of entertaining done in student apartments on Saturday nights. These parties are usually open to everyone, and many students feel that they are the best of all times. The saying goes that only MBAs understand, or perhaps are the only ones who can even just "stand," other MBAs, and thus is born the license to let it all hang loose. And when MBAs are in their own element at these parties, they do. There are free-flowing kegs on a pass-the-hat basis, dancing, and unbridled B School gossip, all of which provide a wonderful and much-needed catharsis for the academic pressure that lurks in every classroom and the anxiety that accompanies every job interview.

Professors tend to encourage a balanced perspective between work and play; one teacher even holds informal office hours in a bar on Friday afternoon — a good contrast to the grim grind of daily existence. Faculty members also frequently attend both school-sponsored events and private parties. A few are even known to hold their own parties for the students, and these too can get pretty wild.

Because most Michigan MBAs are single, it seems as though social life revolves around them at the Business School. However, all social activities, both formal and informal, are open to single and married students — it's just come one, come all. There is separate married housing on a total university basis (i.e., not specifically for MBAs). This reflects the need to accommodate and group together students with similar lifestyles within the university community.

Being married at Business School can be a blessing, but it comes with a price. On the positive side, marriage provides a more stable base and a constant companion to help cope with academic and recruitment pressures. Having your spouse share the menial chores of life and earn money is certainly a benefit. On the other hand, the constant pressures that MBAs face can seriously test the relationship. Also, because married students tend to have already established a core of friends outside the Business School, there is less social interaction with single students — and when there is, spouses usually do not attend (married students are sometimes active participants in university-sponsored clubs, however). Finally, when there is so little free time, the married business student tends to spend it alone with his or her spouse. One final disadvantage of being a married MBA is relocating — both to Business School and away from a job or friends and family.

Although rare, some Michigan MBAs end up getting married to other students in the program. If there were more free time, or less single-minded devotion to academic achievement and landing a big job, it probably would happen more often.

All in all, social life at Michigan is active, often wild, and a necessary counterpart to the seriousness of the program. Thinking back on all the social times and events during the program though, there was one get-together that stands out above all others.

« *It was the end of the first semester, and the last exam (Accounting) had just ended. We had survived four grueling months. We walked out of the classroom building into the December snow dazed and stumbling. The exam was exhausting, but we had become numb after an entire semester. A group of ten or fifteen of us headed to the nearest bar, which was around the corner across from the law school. We squished into a dark corner and began ordering pitchers of beer. Beer never tasted so good, and it was only 10:30 in the morning. It was all quiet commiseration at first and then everyone became lively and spirited. We started singing. The law students nursing their coffee were incredulous and asked the waiter what the cause of this madness was. He shook his head and mused, "MBAs."* »

RECRUITING AND JOB SEARCH

« *For most MBA candidates, the anticipation of that final payoff, the big job ticket, begins well before the first day of classes. For many, it starts even before applying to Business School. Once in the program, the high-paying, prestigious position with a top firm becomes the light at the end of the tunnel, the rationale for coping with all the stress and strain. At the beginning of the final semester, the job becomes, in short, the program's raison d'être.* »

Michigan has consistently enjoyed an impressive placement record. In the last several years, classes have averaged over 13,000 interviews with over 400 major firms. The mean number of on-campus interviews per person has been close to twenty, which resulted in an average of three job offers per person.

Moreover, Michigan has taken steps recently to strengthen its placement efforts. As part of the new Kresge Business Administration Library, the Career Resources Center (CRC) maintains extensive career and company information files. These files and videotapes contain recent annual and interim financial reports, press releases, company promotional material, news articles, and a listing of UM alumni who have consented to act as contact people.

Michigan MBAs are as likely to enter the manufacturing sector (45 percent) as they are nonmanufacturing (55 percent), and almost half of all placements are made outside the Midwest region. Finance continues to be the most popular area of functional responsibility (34 percent), followed by marketing (24 percent), and consulting (12 percent). Salaries tend to vary depending on previous work experience, functional responsibility, industry, and location. In 1987, the average starting salary was $42,750.

Over one hundred companies come to campus specifically to recruit first-year students for summer internships. In the summer of 1986, 89 percent of the MBAs worked in internship assignments.

When viewed from the trenches, the job search can be quite a challenge. For many, before the ecstasy of victory comes the agony of many defeats. An MBA from Michigan will not guarantee the best job, a job of your choice, or even a good job. What it will do is provide you with the opportunities to interview with top firms, and a preliminary credibility, which will have to be quickly substantiated. It will also give you the knowledge and confidence necessary to sell yourself, your work experience, academic record, the MBA itself, and your future promise. But it ain't easy.

As they tell us in human behavior classes, most interviewers subconsciously make up their mind to hire a candidate or not within the first five minutes of the interview. Thus despite your grade point average and all the other credentials you can muster, a firm handshake, some appropriate humor, and a little luck can often make you or break you. Because there are so many uncontrollable variables, the interviewing process can be very frustrating and a little disillusioning. You think you've earned the job, but it's yet another hurdle. The bright side is that everyone who makes it through the program gets a job and most of the jobs are excellent. The job hunt is the last lap in the MBA process, the final link to the real business world, and everybody makes it.

ON THE JOB — FIRST YEARS OUT

« *The first day on my advertising job I kept expecting some-one to ask me to define multivariate regression analysis or something equally technical, just as a marine sergeant would order a new recruit to do fifty push-ups for the hell of it. As I met my new boss, my mind was racing to piece together for-mulas and remember business principles verbatim, but all the details they had pushed down my throat at Michigan kept eluding me. So what did I really learn, what did I spend two years dying for? It turns out that nobody actually asked me a question like that the first day, or any day since, but the fear I was experiencing left a bad taste in my mouth for the MBA I had been led to believe was so valuable.*

It wasn't until about six months into the job, in the context of a late-night client crisis, that I realized in a very literal sense what my MBA had taught me: namely, how to think through a problem; how to deal with various personalities and support groups in the context of the problem; how to cope; and how to endure. I realized that knowing all the details at Michigan was what helped internalize the concepts that would remain long after the details themselves were forgotten; that learning the details cold at Business School would help confront details in the real world. And you know, that Michigan MBA felt pretty good right then. »

Most MBA graduates find the degree very useful, but as the preceding anecdote illustrates, the returns on your degree may not be immediately apparent. In fact, it's only over the long term that its true value can be assessed. Half of what you learn at Business School is how to deal with the big picture, not a particularly relevant skill for management-trainee-level positions most MBAs find themselves in initially. However, because most firms are interested in grooming managers, it tends to all work out in the end.

Holding an MBA from Michigan signals to management that you've invested considerable time, energy, and money in your career. It opens the opportunity for a fast track and identifies you as having long-term potential. Management will also be aware that you are highly marketable and liable to change jobs if more tempting offers come along. Michigan doesn't keep exact records on the number of graduates who switch jobs during the first years, but on judgment, the number is high. This marketability is a nice piece of leverage. Large increases in salary usually occur only when graduates move to a new firm.

But there are other advantages, depending on the specific industry or career chosen. In terms of service industries, for example, your MBA not only opens a career path to internal management, but also affords a better understanding of your clients and their problems, most of whom also hold MBA degrees. Consequently, one is able to provide more effective service and develop a strong personal relationship that is so vital in most businesses.

« *In advertising, for example, the product management teams in the large packaged goods firms are almost invariably all MBAs. While the advertising agencies themselves will swear up and down that having an MBA is not at all necessary for its own staff to succeed (perhaps partially due to the MBAs expensive price tag), according to trade sources some large packaged goods firms consider the number of MBAs in an agency as one criterion in awarding new accounts. Surprisingly, some agency staff who do not hold MBAs feel threatened by those with the degree. But you can't argue with the client. And in the case of the more sophisticated packaged goods accounts, the client is right. MBAs speak a language and have a common background all their own, for better or for worse. If you can relate to it, you're way ahead of the game.* »

SUMMARY OVERVIEW

THE Michigan MBA has many strengths and some weaknesses.

On the positive side, the program provides a solid, balanced general management program that is flexible enough to accommodate individual needs. The perspective of the general manager is developed via the core curriculum, which covers all the essential functional business areas within the context of a problem-solving approach. Balance and flexibility are achieved by permitting students to select fully half of the courses in the program. And the opportunity to tap into the greater resources of The University of Michigan at Ann Arbor provides an academic environment that further enhances your education. The program also strikes a good balance in terms of teaching method, employing the case method as well as the lecture method, depending on the nature and objectives of each course.

A second area of strength is the school's practical, nononsense approach. It is as quantitative as necessary, yet always in a pragmatic sense; it covers the theory, but always with an eye on the bottom line. And the overwhelming workload instills discipline and endurance that will stand you in good stead in the real business world.

The school's high standards, solid overall reputation, and excellent contacts with major firms translate to consistently impressive placement statistics. Once in the business world,

Michigan MBAs consider their degree as a continuing source of pride. It serves them well as they progress through the ranks of major firms, and many hold top positions in the upper echelons of management.

Finally, the school has modern new facilities, excellent renovations, and a major expansion program under way.

Every top business school has some weaknesses, and Michigan is no exception. As its student body has become older and more experienced, it has also become more aggressive and more competitive. While previously almost half of Michigan's graduate students came directly from college now only 12% do. As a result, there seems to be more overt competition for grades and jobs among these more experienced, older students.

Another possible weakness is that Michigan has no clear identity. It is a highly eclectic institution. Unlike a Harvard, for example, there is no dominant teaching style or single thread of research. This makes it difficult for prospective students looking at the school to get a full understanding of what Michigan offers. In short, unlike other top ten schools, Michigan graduates can't be easily categorized.

This eclectic identity, though, is also a strength, since Michigan follows the old Dallas Cowboy philosophy of choosing the best and then developing a well-integrated program around diverse elements. Michigan purposely seeks out diversity. This philosophy has evidently worked to Michigan's benefit, since its reputation has grown steadily stronger.

Overall, the Michigan MBA is an excellent degree, well worth the effort, and a continuing aid in climbing the corporate ladder. If you're looking for a solid, balanced program with no pretensions, Michigan is the one to go for. You certainly won't regret it.

Chapter 8

JOHN E. ANDERSON GRADUATE SCHOOL OF MANAGEMENT* (UCLA)

THE PROGRAM

« *There's probably some truth to the old joke that likens California to a bowl of granola — full of fruits, flakes, and nuts. So can there really be a top business school in Los Angeles? Don't people really go to UCLA so they can live in a wonderful, laid-back environment, stay close to the beach and work on their tans? Can anyone get serious about "Techniques of Financial Analysis" when it's seventy-five degrees every day and surf's up? Well, there really is a good B School in the midst of the Santa Monica palms, Malibu Canyon, and the Rodeo Drive boutiques of Beverly Hills.* »

Amidst the "tinseltown" reputation of Los Angeles, UCLA has quietly built one of the best professional management programs in the country. In fact, quietly is really the operative word here since the school's reputation is best known on the West Coast, where it has an especially active involvement with the business community. Although changing rapidly, its East

* BY CONSTANCE WILLIAMS, MBA

171

Coast image is less well defined and suffers somewhat from a lack of the "old boy" school network.

« *When I was first looking for a job and then working in the East Coast professional community, I found one of UCLA's major shortcomings to be its lack of a clear-cut image among the Eastern business community. In the beginning I sometimes had to sell the school as well as my own skills — although in practice UCLA had prepared me well for my professional choice. I have seen this changing rapidly. As more and more GSM students are making a big impact on this side of the continent, UCLA's image is catching up with reality — namely, that it is a serious, major-league business school.* »

Tough, innovative, and known for strengths in finance and information sciences, UCLA leads the pack in developing creative and sometimes unusual emphasis and special programs. This kind of innovative orientation has accordingly attracted a bright, forward-looking student body possessing widely divergent backgrounds and interests, but who are united in their desire for the broad management experience and program flexibility that is offered by UCLA. In fact, this flexibility is a genuine characteristic of both the program and the students. Anyone seeking a rigid, controlled program would probably not find their ideal at UCLA's Anderson Graduate School of Management (GSM).

UCLA's overall orientation is highly practical. Maybe that comes from its history as part of the public University of California system. At any rate, graduating students are well prepared to tackle hands-on analytical or line positions — rather than focusing only on conceptual, theoretical approaches to management skills. In addition to the analytical skills, there's also a heavy emphasis on other practical needs —

such as group management/interaction and experience with real-life fieldwork outside the classroom.

Because of the emphasis that UCLA places on versatility and uniqueness in its students, there is tremendous variety to the people in the program. Although UCLA is a California state school, and largely publicly supported, students come from every state, with more than half from outside California. Over 15 percent are foreign students, and more than 35 percent of the class is female. The average student is about twenty-six years old, has about four years of work experience, and probably has an academic background in the social sciences, humanities, or economics. Only about 15 percent of the students enter with a strict business administration major as undergraduates. No quotas are stated, but it is well known that the school makes an effort to seek qualified minority students.

« The composition of one of my first-year classes is an example of this diversity. About half of that class were women, including a banker from the Midwest, a black thirty-five-year-old former stewardess with a twelve-year-old daughter, and a designer/artist who was joining the Arts Management program; another 20 percent were foreign, with several Japanese, Korean, and Taiwanese, mostly on corporate sponsorships, a Swede who had experience in financial management, a Ph.D. in physics from Pakistan, and a French banker. The rest of the class was made up of people such as an Air Force officer, a sports coach, an MA in anthropology, a participant in the joint JD/MBA program, a couple of ex-teachers, etc. »

The school's reputation is largely financial and computer sciences based, and moving steadily toward even greater financial emphasis. The quality and reputation of these programs have consistently gained national recognition. According to a poll of the Chronicle of Higher Education, the finance faculty was rated as among the top five in the country by their peers. The professors are young, aggressive, and very accessible to students. There are an increasing number of endowed chairs, providing the resources to pursue important explorations into new financial areas, both empirical and theoretical.

UCLA has also benefited from its long-term and highly aggressive commitment to information sciences and from its location in the economic center of this new technology. The faculty members in this area are at the forefront of the technological revolution and have a strong relationship with the industry. UCLA has more classes in this discipline than any other top ten program — in such areas as telecommunications and data base design. Additionally, the student computer center is one of the most advanced of all the nation's business schools, and offers important hands-on experience with the latest technology for all business students.

The school also has several other extremely strong programs: probably the best Arts Management program in the country, an extremely well-respected Institute of Industrial Relations, and a new emphasis on entrepreneurial skills — including a new endowment specifically devoted to this area. A very solid marketing department provides for a well-rounded program.

The school's atmosphere is friendly, but academically intense. Part of the stress results from dealing with new kinds of academic experiences — beyond the usual lectures, papers, and midterms that most of us dealt with as undergraduates. Those are still there, but there are also case studies, group problem-solving exercises, and real-life field projects. While the experience of analyzing a business and helping a company solve some management problems is invaluable, it also contributes to stress, much as it does in the real world.

UCLA's program is designed around basic core course requirements. Beyond this, the class choices are highly individualistic. You take responsibility for designing a curriculum that will help you meet your own professional career goals. In fact, the program is flexible enough that you can take a somewhat evolutionary approach to its design. You can adjust the program and make choices among the more advanced classes as your knowledge and interests develop over time.

« *I came to the program looking for an advanced degree in industrial relations, which would offer a base in management and organizational behavior. But I had never had the opportunity to take a marketing class. I took my first marketing class as part of the core requirement the spring quarter of my first year. I was so stimulated by the experience that I completely changed my course of study in order to allow a second area of professional emphasis. I found tremendous receptivity on the part of my adviser and school directors to my need to change the direction of my program in midstream. This is typical of the school's attitude toward its students and their individual objectives.* »

UCLA's MBA program is made up of four basic types of classes.

1. *Management "Core"*: These are the basic business courses that make up the foundation of the program — and that everyone is required to take. This gives these classes somewhat of a "we're all in this together" feeling, which adds fun and camaraderie to situations with the potential for drudgery.

With a few exceptions for individuals emphasizing a particular course of study, the core is comprised of thirteen classes. Students are required to take at least eleven of the thirteen core courses in order to give them a broad management perspective. The thirteen courses are as follows:

Fall Quarter:
    Data Analysis and Decision Making
    Managerial Accounting

Microeconomics
One of: Human Resource Management
        Managing People in Organizations

Winter Quarter:
    Managerial Finance
    Elements of Marketing
    Two of: Managerial Model Building
            Macroeconomics
            Information Systems

Spring Quarter:
    Production and Operations Management
    Competitive Strategy

Second Year:
    Management of Organizations

Most of these classes are reasonably large lecture-style classes with traditional examinations and/or papers required. If you have completed graduate-level course work elsewhere in those relevant classes, you can sometimes waive the course in order to take the more advanced classes within that subject matter.

It is clear that UCLA is interested in developing managers with a broad range of skills. One of the first courses I took, Managerial Problem Solving — Individual, dealt with the more qualitative side of management. It showed how the areas of personality, motivation, communication, and group dynamics relate to your own individual management style.

« I remember the first paper I had to write for this class. The assigned paper's topic was an in-depth analysis of why I was in the program, detailing my professional and personal objectives and my own assessment of how my individual style and personality meshed with those goals. The paper was meant to go

far beyond the hyperbole laid out in application forms. It was a critical self-analysis. And we were instructed really to look into our souls to know our motivations and what we really wanted out of the program . . . now that we had gotten in. My first reaction was "Hey, wait a minute — this is more appropriate for my shrink than a business class." But, in spite of its touchy-feely, Californiaesque overtones, I really found it tremendously helpful. It focused my attention at the beginning of the whole program and helped to set the stage for accomplishing my objectives. And, in spite of initial apprehensions over the subject matter, most of my classmates agreed that it was a positive and motivating experience. »

2. *Area Electives:* These are the more advanced course opportunities, and probably the most intensive and interesting classes in the curriculum. These classes (at least eight classes in the program) allow you to develop much more specialized knowledge by choosing among different functional areas. The area electives are highly individualized and can be adjusted to focus in on one or two "majors" or can be pursued from a more general management perspective. Most of the classes here are small (ten to twenty-five), and the teaching styles vary according to faculty preference for either case study or lecture.

3. *Free Electives:* In keeping with the spirit of individualism in total program design, the final classes in the program (typically three slots in the two-year program) are not limited to the B School. They may be selected from management courses outside your area of specialty, or from virtually any upper division or graduate-level classes within the numerous other departments at UCLA. Thus, these credits can be utilized within or outside the management school to add depth to any area of interest.

4. *Management Field Study:* It's a hands-on management consulting experience where teams of four or five students

work with an outside business that is seeking independent management analysis and advice. A large number of highly prestigious corporations ask for Field Study groups to do studies for them, in fact far more than the school can oblige. This gives students a degree of flexibility in choosing the organization and type of study matter most appealing to them. And, since it is judged by the same standards used to judge professional-level management consulting, it serves as a very real final examination for the end of the program: proof of the management skills you are taking to the business world.

As a result, the graduate business student at UCLA is exposed to a broad range of basic business topics. The student then goes on to design a program around his or her own career objectives and special areas of interest. Finally, the student's "torture test" of his or her confidence and readiness to take his or her skills into the business world is the demanding management field study consulting experience, which gives students an opportunity to demonstrate analytical, communication, interpersonal, decision-making, and problem-solving skills. This provides a perspective on the student's abilities for a future employer. All in all, the UCLA program provides a well-balanced yet flexible, highly professional business education.

GETTING IN

IT'S not easy getting admitted to the program. The school typically receives over 3,000 applications for only 375 places. So it's important that a prospective student carefully consider all aspects of the admissions process and try to develop a highly favorable admissions application. In making its choices, UCLA looks for academic ability, previous experience, flexibility, and uniqueness. In other words, they're looking not only for the highest of academic and work standards, but also a sense of personality and individuality that will lead to both academic *and* managerial success: far beyond the man (or woman) in the gray flannel suit.

There are four major requirements for admission: demonstrated academic skills, work experience, references, and the actual written application. Interviews are not required or encouraged, but in certain cases they may be appropriate (e.g., unusual background circumstances).

Both academic record and test scores play an important role in the selection process. First, demonstrated academic ability is assessed in terms of undergraduate school reputation, the rigor of the undergraduate program, grade point average, and degrees attained. The school looks for demonstrated ability in whatever background the applicant possesses, not simply for previous training in business administration. In fact, undergrad business majors are not particularly sought-after, since the school is looking for more varied and well-rounded students. Good test scores on the GMATs are also very important (although there is a range in the scores and it is only one of the elements of evaluation). The median GMAT is in the mid-600s. Both verbal and quantitative skills are evaluated, although like most schools, the quantitative elements are weighed more heavily since they have been proven to be one of the best predictors of success in the program. Students are required to demonstrate proficiency in algebra and differential calculus through examination before entering the program.

« *There's a special summer program for students who need a refresher in math before the full-fledged MBA school gets started. It's basically a hard-core quantitative methods class — and although it's not part of the regular MBA program, it is a most difficult class. I'm not sure if it is designed to scare those of us who had been out of the world of calculations for a while, but it sure made us work harder preparing for the pro-*

gram. I never faced anything nearly as rigorous in the rest of my two years. »

Work experience is the second major criterion for acceptance. The admissions office actively seeks students with considerable business experience, preferably in some management capacity. The rationale underlying this preferential treatment is that students who have experience in business management usually have more focused career objectives. They also have a good perception of their own stengths and weaknesses in business, and have a more realistic idea of the skills they will need to succeed. The school believes experienced students can get the most out of the program.

The third area for evaluation is references. Two references are required for admission. But choose carefully: references can help an applicant a great deal, and it's important that the referencer know the applicant well and give an accurate, specific argument for why the applicant should be admitted. The referencer's relationship with the applicant and ability to describe the applicant are more important than the referencer's credentials. In fact, the more specific the information that is presented, the more weight applied to the reference.

The fourth area is the application itself. The applicant is requested to provide information (in essay form) about personal qualities and experiences which the applicant believes distinguish him or her from other applicants. Discussions of one's strengths, weaknesses, objectives, accomplishments, and reasons for entering an MBA program are required. Additionally, through the applicant's description of previous social and management experience, the school tries to get an impression of how the applicant assesses his or her interactions with other people. There are optional group interviews, which are information sessions that give the school a chance to observe an applicant's group skills. At the same time, these interviews provide the prospective student with information about the school.

ACADEMIC ENVIRONMENT

UCLA is a serious management school, and the individualistic approach it takes to program design carries over to the academic environment. You are responsible for designing a manageable workload, no less than sixteen units (typically four classes). Classes are tough and are run very much like a business: you are expected to be prepared for class regardless of other workload commitments. No excuses. It takes lots of work to keep up and to balance all the various requirements.

Grading is done on a letter basis: A (4.0), B (3.0), C (2.0), F (0). Pluses and minuses are worth 0.3 points. At least a 3.0 (B average) is required to graduate. There are no school mandated curves; theoretically it would be possible for all students in a class to receive all A's or all F's. The school does not try to fail any percentage of the class.

Failure, in fact, is not something you hear a lot about; the students who actually flunk out are relatively few. This does not mean that the curriculum is soft; there are some dismissals. (Students can be dismissed for failure to maintain a 3.0 GPA, or if their coursework falls below the sixteen units per quarter necessary to complete the program within the requisite two years.) However, the school really makes an effort to help students who are having difficulty. The school takes the attitude that it has a responsibility to help students in the program — unqualified students should have been screened out in the admissions process. Occasionally there are students who are not really committed and are thus dropped from the program, but those who demonstrate their commitment should be able to get through — and the school will help with tutoring and special assistance when necessary.

« *I had a friend in school who came to the program from a strong social sciences background, but who had difficulty with quantitative skills. She was extraordinarily qualified for the program in a number of other respects: she was a published author and had done consulting work successfully. She was also extremely committed to making a success out of the program. Before the program started, she took preparatory classes in quantitative methods and integral calculus. But, she ran up against problems in a couple of tough classes — in Operations Research and Computer Sciences. To help her through, the school found her a tutor, the professor gave her a little extra help outside the class, and she organized study groups. Today she's an independent consultant, with an impressive list of clients in organizational management — and she often calls on her skills in information sciences and operations research in her work.* »

The student interaction is friendly, although competitive. Class involvement is one measure of evaluation for a lot of professors, so the discussions in class can get pretty lively. The school puts a lot of emphasis on group projects, on the theory that long-term management success usually requires the need to work with others effectively, particularly in interdisciplinary groups. The atmosphere within groups is usually cooperative, although it's sometimes necessary to be assertive. The groups are frequently in competition with one another, so there's a lot of good-natured banter and inter-group competitive rivalry. In these games, the groups protect their plans and "business secrets" as religiously as any real-world competitors.

Student interaction with professors also is excellent. Professors are very involved with students both socially and professionally. There is no formal separation between the two and as with the rest of the school there is generally an informality to this relationship.

SOCIAL LIFE

THE fast-paced quarter system leaves little time for serious socializing, but even the most diligent students need a break once in a while. And, the Graduate School of Management places a lot of emphasis on activities and socializing, which complements other parts of the professional program. The very nature of the way classes are scheduled is designed to leave some time for students to meet and socialize. Classes run from eight in the morning to ten at night, but there are relatively few academic activities scheduled between noon and one and six to seven P.M.; with no formal classes on Fridays, school organizations use these times for social events.

There is an active Association of Students and Business (ASB), which promotes interaction with private and public organizations and gives students a chance to meet and talk with professionals in the field. ASB sponsors such activities as "Day on the Job," whereby small groups of students spend a day at individual companies learning more about particular industries and businesses (some are scheduled as far away as New York); "Firm Nights," in which representatives of various industries or functional areas speak with students at a cocktail party; "Student Executive Dinners," where senior-level executives of major corporations dine with students; and "Brown Bag Lunches," when students gather in large classrooms to eat lunch and hear informal speeches from prominent business executives.

« *One of the first of these events I attended was "Market Night." This was a cocktail party attended by one hundred twenty-five people. Sixty were from the business community. I enjoyed the chance to speak with advertising professionals, consumer products managers, marketers in retail banking positions, and high-level technical sales managers. I was able to ask questions about their job functions and responsibilities, interests, career paths, long-term objectives, etc. — all in an informal social setting. This added a realistic perspective on my own career options.* »

There also is an umbrella student association (GSMSA), which acts as the overseer for a variety of student activities and organizations. This association sponsors an extensive welcome and orientation for new students every fall, a spring talent show, *The Exchange* (the weekly newspaper), and at least twenty special-interest groups. Many of these special-interest groups, in turn, offer opportunities to meet with the management community in more specialized areas and provide a forum for meeting with other students with similar interests and career aspirations.

The school itself sponsors several large parties throughout the year and regularly schedules Thursday-afternoon "Beer Busts" to celebrate the end of the academic week. The latter are attended by MBA students as well as Ph.D. candidates, faculty, and the administration. These "Beer Busts" provide a good chance to do some informal networking, to gain additional perspective on classroom learning, and to speak with the academics about interesting management topics outside of the normal classroom subject matter. There is quite a bit of camaraderie among students, who socialize extensively both in and outside the classroom. Friendships often develop from this socializing and last far beyond the date of graduation.

« *One of the best parties I've ever attended was to celebrate the end of the first quarter of classes. It was strictly the thirty or so folks in my Nucleus class. Nearly everyone showed up with food or drink in hand, to talk of future career and academic plans and to relate tales of second-year student experiences. The party lasted far into the night. Those people formed the core of my friendship base throughout the rest of my master's program, and many still remain very close friends. »*

The whole B School process can be all-encompassing. While some single students dated each other (in fact, a few married after graduation), I wouldn't envy anyone married who tried to keep up with the coursework and the necessary professional networking and socializing. The demands left little time to seriously devote to outside family life.

UCLA offers a terrific environment beyond the classroom borders of GSM, too. Many of the social and cultural activities of the larger campus are open to students at the Management School. And the area around Westwood offers some of the best social and entertainment opportunities in one of the best environments of any school in the country. There's certainly no isolation problem at a place like UCLA — or, if you prefer, there are plenty of opportunities to get off campus for a change of company or scenery: to the beach, the mountains, artistic communities, restaurants, jazz clubs, etc. And, within UCLA, there are lots of other services that the larger campus can provide.

The housing office can help find apartments, roommates, etc. There's also inexpensive married-student housing and dorms (although the latter are not used much by graduate students). Housing around UCLA is extremely desirable and expensive, and so most students find it necessary to use the housing office.

If you live off campus, you'll have the pleasure of dealing with UCLA parking — make sure you get your parking application in early. Locally famous line from old movie: "I would have gone to UCLA but I couldn't get a parking space." Things haven't changed much in this department.

RECRUITING AND JOB SEARCH

UCLA's Graduate School of Management trains students to be managers, i.e., to combine the analytical, conceptual, technical, and business skills with a practical, worldly perspective and an ability to work effectively with people. In short, you know a lot more than financial analysis and accounting. You have both the abilities of the hands-on entry-level manager and the more expansive perspective and broad business abilities necessary to run a company. In contrast to the reputation of some of the other top schools, I believe UCLA grads know more than the theoretical ability to be the CEO of a Fortune 500 company. Because of their background, and UCLA training, they can make an effective contribution in their chosen fields when they enter an organization, which I believe better prepares them for the day when they're going to run that blue chip corporation or organization.

To be specific, UCLA places students in a wide variety of career fields and types of companies, although several general areas tend to dominate. First and foremost is the general financial area. In terms of functional job areas, the greatest number of MBAs enter such fields as commercial and investment banking, public accounting, and corporate financial positions. This is followed by marketing positions in consumer products and advertising firms, and then by management consulting.

Certain types of industries are favored. Since major California corporations greatly respect UCLA's program, the banking and electronics industries are heavily represented among the firms that students join. The leading industries by function are investment banking (32 percent), finance (19 percent), consulting (14 percent), and marketing/sales (14 percent). The basically national profile of employment patterns continues with representation among leading industries across the country.

Approximately two hundred and fifty international firms recruit and hire at the school. The Placement and Career Planning Office offers prospective firms a variety of services, from publishing a résumé book (a compilation of nearly all students' résumés) to coordinating workshops and receptions and scheduling open-bid interview sign-ups by students. It also serves as an information resource for employers who are not able to recruit on campus. The Placement and Career Planning Office is the principal liaison between employers and students at the school.

The Career Planning Office also offers the student information about the recruiter (employer profiles, annual reports, and other data such as a videotape library) and coordinates the scheduling of interviews, etc. It provides similar services in helping students with summer employment and internship opportunities during school. Nevertheless, a fairly large number of students with unique interests and/or abilities do their own career search beyond those employers who recruit on campus.

Recruiting starts early in the year. By November it gets rolling, and by January or February it's under full steam. On-campus recruiting is conducted by sign-ups or open bids for the more popular companies.

« There's a lot of competition for good interview slots and there is a lot of speculation about the best time of day to get on the schedule. Theories seem divided between the first slot in the morning (hoping the interviewer was a morning person who was starting out fresh and who hadn't been dulled by hearing students talk to him or her all day) versus later in the afternoon

(get them on a full stomach). Some even believed that the last slot of the day was best because if it was a good interview, you could keep going beyond the time limit. »

There is also extensive discussion about how many companies you should interview with. Some advocate very targeted searches, while others believed the shotgun approach is more effective. At UCLA both seem to work.

« *Personally, my strategy was to interview widely at first (for practice and to help narrow potential industries). Then, I targeted specific industries to really learn as much as I could about individual companies and job functions. It seemed to work out: I had eight offers by the end of March and had the luxury of cherry picking at the end of the process.* »

Students also do well salary-wise. In 1987, the range of salary offers was from $24,000 to $80,000, with an average over $45,000. And, this figure is somewhat depressed because a larger number than common for most schools enter the public accounting field and typically earn lower starting salaries than in other industries.

ON THE JOB — FIRST YEARS OUT

NATURALLY, the proof of the quality of any business degree has got to be career success. I think UCLA prepares students well for the corporate experience. In particular, it takes them beyond business basics and gives them the confidence in their analytical abilities to conceptualize and to be creative problem-solvers beyond "crunching the numbs." And those zillions of hours that were spent in groups really paid off, because a whole lot of corporate life is spent in group discussions, interaction, policy-making, recommending, persuading, rationalizing, pleading, etc. Thus, UCLA's emphasis on decision-making and group dynamics gives its students an edge when they enter the business world.

UCLA's program is also strong in teaching the basics. The basics enable students to analyze business problems within a larger economic, business, and political perspective. The fundamentals complement the individual areas of study so that students have both specific functional competence within a broader analytic framework. These skills are helpful on the job because they enable the UCLA MBA to be both a specialist with specific skills and a generalist who understands the big picture.

« *Beyond these skills, though, there have been other parts of the learning process not as evident or measurable as training in management accounting or operations research. For example, the negotiation and conflict management training in my Organization Behavior class has helped me better understand the inevitable give and take within the corporation and has given me knowledge about personal strategies for managing conflict. UCLA also emphasizes the importance of creativity in the management of a business. This provided me with a perspective that goes beyond what the numbers tell you is the most efficient or profitable solution, to understanding what makes sense for the business within its internal and external environment.* »

The broad business orientation offered by UCLA is valuable in some other areas as well. While most students form pretty clear-cut career objectives during their school experiences, it is remarkable how those goals evolve and change as more time is spent in the marketplace. Interests broaden or become more focused. New technology or socioeconomic shifts can create opportunities not even recognized previously. Additionally, geographic, personal, and life-style considerations probably become all the more important as time passes. The net result of all this is the need for flexibility and ability to deal with change. UCLA gives students the necessary training and preparation to deal with the change process.

The program at GSM has a strong grounding in the fundamentals, but it also encourages students to develop a facility in two or more areas of study. This enables students to make an immediate contribution to their first employer which goes far beyond what mere technicians and analysts can do. The discipline in the analytical thought process, the motivation to look beneath the surface, to question, to isolate and understand the real problem(s), give students the skills and the self-confidence to know that they have a plethora of options beyond their first career choice. Thus, UCLA business grads can show a prospective employer or even potential investor/financier that they have that flexibility and creativity needed to take themselves beyond the ordinary, the obvious, or the expected.

« As I talk with other alumni and think about the years since we graduated, I am struck by the truth of that promise of flexibility and creativity. Many of the people I went to school with have stayed with the initial employer. They are doing well and are very satisfied with their salaries and advancement potential. They seem to have very specific career objectives and are well on their way to achieving them. On the other hand, there's also a significant proportion who have made major changes in their career paths — from advertising to financial analysis or organizational behavior to arts management. Others have moved to new locales or chosen positions with more personal time flexibility. Their ability to make these changes successfully is evidence of the strength of UCLA's MBA program in preparing its students for top-level management positions in whatever field they choose. »

SUMMARY OVERVIEW

UCLA provides its students with an excellent graduate level management education. It offers them a wide variety of programs and opportunities. The strengths of UCLA's fine program are many.

Its academic environment is top notch. The faculty includes some of the foremost management and business professors in the country. There are many areas in which they lead the country in theory and application. Moreover, students have the opportunity to learn from and closely interact with these professors.

The coursework's individual flexibility allows students the opportunity really to tailor a program to their individual career objectives. While the program's foundation is strongly grounded in the fundamentals, there is ample time and chance to supplement the basics with advanced classes in numerous areas. The finance and information sciences departments are especially well known.

The school has a real-world orientation. Thus, there is emphasis on practical field experience, group analysis, and the kind of decision-making that most managers will encounter in their future careers. This provides a very real point of difference for a UCLA student compared to the highly theoretical, conceptual, all-case-study approaches of other schools.

The social network at UCLA revolves around a highly professional, career-oriented program. This approach helps orient students to business and potential careers by giving them plenty of opportunities to encounter working professionals. Additionally, it prepares students for the social and political networks that form the basis for all organizations.

The recruiting opportunities are myriad and are dispersed among a wide variety of industries and functional job areas. UCLA's reputation has rapidly caught up with the reality of the quality of the school's program. Additionally, alumni are expanding into all geographic areas, both domestically and internationally, giving new graduates an extensive and expanding alumni network to call upon when recruiting and seeking career information.

Its geographical location, while out of the mainstream, old boy business foundation of the East, nevertheless is importantly situated in the business center for the technological revolution. Los Angeles also serves as the international economic center for the entire Pacific basin. Finally, its physical beauty and weather make Los Angeles a terrifically desirable place to spend a couple of years.

However, the geographic location is a bit of a double-edged sword. Because it is on the West Coast, there is probably less access to the established East Coast business community — and conversely, they have less accessibility to you. However, virtually every major East Coast investment bank, commercial bank, and consumer marketing firm recruits on campus. Thus, each year, an increasing number of students choose to accept a job on the East Coast.

Another related weakness is the fact that because many students choose to stay in California, they tend to choose the industries that dominate the state's economy. Thus, banking, energy, accounting, and the rapidly expanding informations and EDP (Electronic Data Processing) organizations are well represented by graduates. While this reinforces the areas of specialty which the school is known for, a shift of emphasis might provide for a more well-rounded program. The program might be further improved by placing even more emphasis on marketing, public management, and similar programs.

UCLA is a publicly supported institution, and this can be negative. It tends to attract students who are more price-sensitive re tuition payments, particularly in-state residents who can get a top ten student education for a bargain-basement price. Students without the financial flexibility to attend other schools are probably less well-connected (via business and social/family contacts) when recruitment time comes along. While it's certainly not always "who you know" that opens doors of acceptance into organizations, it sometimes means that UCLA students have to rely more heavily on their business skills and hard work (as opposed to contacts) to land those job plums upon graduation.

Finally, public schools generally seem to have less alumni loyalty and ties (less use of the "old boy" networks). This means the school has to work a little harder to get the top professors, since it has fewer endowed chairs that can keep faculty salaries on a par with private institutions. However, both of these last two situations are changing. The school has worked hard the past few years to reinforce school ties among alumni, and actively to seek corporate sponsorships of faculty positions.

In summary, though, the strengths of UCLA's graduate management program far outweigh the negatives. If I had to speak for the majority of the class, I think most would agree that the MBA was one of the single most positive and powerful influences in their lives and that UCLA was, overall, a terrific place to pursue it.

Chapter 9

COLUMBIA BUSINESS SCHOOL*

THE PROGRAM

« During my first week at Columbia Business School, I met an economist from Brandeis, a business major from Notre Dame, an engineer from the Bombay Institute of Statistics, and an actress from Vassar.

Despite the diverse backgrounds, each person's objective in going to business school was remarkably similar: to get the additional training and credentials necessary to compete in the upper echelons of American business. Most importantly, they all sought that education in one of the fastest paced, most exciting cities in the world because they needed to be in the center of things, where the proverbial "action" is.

New York City offers many attractions: from avant-garde theater, dance in every form, and a plethora of museums, to professional baseball, basketball, football, and hockey. On the business front, New York runs the gamut from street-corner vendors to the loftiest bastions of America corporate power.

It is not surprising that my first group of acquaintances at

---

* BY VICKI TENCATI, MBA, COLUMBIA

Business School came to Columbia. The economist and the business major chose Columbia for the top-quality program and the chance to live in a city full of high-powered business opportunities. The engineer sought a good school in an international environment. The actress felt her future career choices would be greatly expanded by acquiring an MBA. At the same time, she wanted to continue working toward a professional life in the theater. Columbia Business School in New York offered her the unique opportunity to pursue both objectives simultaneously. »

Columbia Graduate Business School takes its cue from the city in which it is located. When 514 entering fall term students chosen from approximately 3,000 applicants arrive in Morningside Heights, they are faced with a comprehensive program that can be completed in as little as sixteen months. Many of them, however, take a term off to work or play and complete the program in two years. There are no provisions for part-time or evening students.

Twenty courses are required, eight of which are core courses that provide a general background in business skills and principles. Students are expected to complete seven out of eight required courses in the first two terms. These include Conceptual Foundations of Business, Business in a Changing Economy, Economics of the Firm, Managerial Behavior in Organizations, Accounting, Statistical Analysis and Inference, Operations Research, and Policy Determination and Operations.

Typical of the required survey core courses is the Conceptual Foundations of Business, which covers well-known business philosophers from Adam Smith to Eli Ginzberg. It combines lecture and case method, so there is opportunity for students to interact with each other and the professor without feeling pressured to do so. During my "Con Found" course on managerial rights and responsibilities, clear personality types emerged when we heatedly debated issues such as the relative responsibility of the corporation, government, and community in complicated pollution cases.

Statistics, another core requirement, is the basic quantitative course. My class was in a rather small amphitheater classroom that had a *Paper Chase* quality about it. Statistics is practically all lecture with some problem review. Weekly homework assignments were always a bane to me. The mathematical problems reminded me of dreary high school algebra and geometry. But I must admit the discipline required in the course has helped me to approach all kinds of nonmathematical problems more logically. As with most of the quantitative courses, a problem review session was held on Fridays. These sessions were particularly helpful since not that many students usually attended. In effect, it was tutoring without the financial outlay.

Students are also required to declare a concentration in one of eleven areas. Students must take five courses in their area of concentration. There are concentrations in Accounting, Business Economics and Public Policy, Corporate Relations and Public Affairs, Finance, International Business, Management of Organizations, Management Science, Marketing, Money and Financial Markets, Operations Management, Public and Non-Profit Management.

The concentration requirement provides the advantage of focusing on a particular area of business. Since most concentrations require just five courses, students still have plenty of opportunity to explore other areas of interest.

« *My concentration in marketing required a couple of basic courses, and then I had a choice of additional offerings to satisfy the concentration requirement. I took Buyer Behavior, which used computer models to analyze and predict consumer purchase patterns. I also took International Marketing and Sales*

Management. I had the interesting experience of having the product management/planning course taught to me by an advertising executive, while the advertising course was taught by a marketing executive! »

Many students concentrate in two areas. Popular dual concentrations are Marketing/Finance and Finance/Accounting. These double concentrations give students excellent background for banking, public accounting or Wall Street–type careers. I knew one woman who worked in a brokerage firm, then went to package goods brand management, using each part of her Finance and Marketing training. Another friend started out in public accounting and moved to retail credit where his dual Accounting/Finance background has served him well.

Students also must take seven elective courses during the four terms. Electives, outside the core and the student's area of concentration, give the student an opportunity to sample other disciplines or offerings of special interest. For example, many Business School students take courses such as tax law in the Law School. I also knew students who attended classes in the journalism, engineering, and architecture schools, as well as Fine Arts. However, most people had no problem selecting their electives within the diversity of the Business School curriculum. To promote well-rounded managers (and in keeping with the liberal arts orientation the university at large is known for), students must take electives in a number of areas. No more than four elective courses in a given field are permitted.

On the other hand, it is possible to utilize university resources and design your own concentration in a particular field or specialty (e.g., urban planning, world economics or educational administration). In fact, the Public and Non-Profit Management concentration has grown out of rising student and faculty interest supported by a cooperative attitude from other graduate divisions at Columbia.

« *During my first term at Columbia I took four required courses and the basic marketing class. Class size in the core courses is generally around fifty-five students. My first class of the Business School experience was a statistics course, which did nothing to alleviate the anxiety I felt, since I had not taken any math classes since my senior year of high school, six years before. My nervous state was compounded by the knowledge that the rest of my classmates had already attended two classes I had missed and most likely had completed homework assignments. As often happens in these cases, my worst fears were exacerbated by circumstances. Class started and several students immediately raised their hands, eager to strut their statistics expertise. But the professor called on a person who was hiding in the corner. The next hour and fifteen minutes was stark terror for me. I dreaded that my name would be called and I would be forced to reveal my total ignorance of the subject at hand. Fortunately, I slipped through that time and learned a valuable lesson for my tenure at the B School: Never go to class unprepared unless you're willling to risk playing the fool in front of the professor and colleagues. I also learned professors at Columbia can be tough and the work hard, and so my business education began in earnest.* »

Since a student generally completes core courses in the first two terms, classes the first year tend to be large. Quantitative courses generally use the standard textbook, lecture, and homework problem method. Most concentration courses, on the other hand, are small, use the case method, and allow for tremendous interaction between students and faculty. In my own experience, some of the best moments at Columbia were in these rather intimate seminars with gentlemen like Eli Ginzberg and John Howard. There are no designated standardized sections, so the student body mixes and mingles depending on intellectual inclination and propensity to awaken early enough for 8:30 A.M. classes.

« *Sometimes I felt that every Columbia Business School student was a future banker or broker of America. In fact, about one third or more of each class seeks employment in the investment community. During the recruiting season, I got the strong impression there were people who were considering homicide as a means to get on the interview schedule for those all-important Wall Street investment banking houses. You could always tell when someone got an offer from one of these highly desirable places; if he or she wasn't broadcasting the fact to everyone within a twenty-block radius, the beaming face and smug air of self-satisfaction gave the lucky student away.* »

Columbia is known for finance, accounting, and marketing. Faculty and alumni include a former chief accountant for the SEC, a consultant to the Federal Reserve Board, and Gordon Shillinglaw, noted author of accounting textbooks. There are thirty courses offered in Accounting, Finance and Money, and Financial Markets departments. Within the Finance concentration, students may emphasize Corporate Finance, Investment Management, Futures Markets, or Real Estate Finance. Over one third of most graduating classes obtain employment in banking, brokerage and investment. In 1987, 41 percent of the graduating class accepted employment at almost seventy-five different financial institutions. This connection to banking and finance is not surprising since Columbia is located in one of the financial capitals of the world. The Stock Exchanges, Wall Street, and headquarters for many major American banks are all in New York.

Columbia also has a strong marketing department, which draws on resources throughout the greater New York area. The large number of consumer packaged goods and communications companies in and around New York provides unique opportunities for Columbia students. Enterprising Marketing majors frequently obtain intern positions with packaged goods marketers, advertising agencies, and marketing departments of brokerage houses during their semester off. This allows students to get practical experience and make a good salary during the four-month break between school terms.

« One of the most interesting and useful courses I took at Columbia was a Buyer Behavior class taught by John Howard, a professor of marketing. At the beginning of the term, the small size class of about twenty students were told to organize into groups of three people. The next fifteen or so weeks were spent together analyzing a new product, Lean Strips, a soy-based bacon substitute from General Foods. We applied our various areas of expertise to the problem, analyzing the overall consumer decision-making process through a model developed by Professor Howard. At the end of the term, each group presented its recommended course of action to GF executives involved in the Lean Strips marketing question. My group consisted of two marketing majors and a finance man. We were lucky, because the other marketing major was a computer jock and the project required lots of time in the Computer Center.

We learned a lot in that class. We had the opportunity to spend considerable time focusing on a real-world problem and then to present our recommended solution to people actually making the decisions about the product. Additionally, the small size of the class allowed us to take full advantage of Professor Howard's extensive marketing knowledge and experience. Finally, it certainly highlighted the importance of choosing the right people for the team, a critical skill for top managers in the business sector. »

Columbia mixes classical Ivy League with contemporary urban reality. The university combines old ivy-covered red brick buildings and high-rise modern architecture on a campus spread over about fifteen city blocks. The Columbia neighborhood, sandwiched between Harlem and the increasingly popular West Side, maintains a middle-class gentility. However, there are the local characters who make the city life interesting and sometimes a little too exciting.

Columbia also has a well-deserved Ivy League reputation. The students are intelligent and talented. The faculty is committed and inquiring. Although the school turns out a large number of graduates each year, it maintains a quality approach and outlook.

One of the school's great assets is its diverse student body. The students come from all over the U.S. and the world, with a variety of backgrounds and skills. This mélange of people can make for very interesting and lively classroom discussions. Additionally, the range of professional and educational backgrounds helps students lend real-world insights to theoretical cases. While this diversity can make it difficult to develop friendships, the school sponsors social events to help promote camaraderie. Study groups, which are formed to cope with the workload, are probably the best way to get to know people.

All in all, Columbia has the advantage of being an excellent business school in the business capital of this country. The courses, the professors, and the students are all first rate. If a fast-paced, competitive environment sounds exciting to you, then Columbia Graduate School of Business in the City of New York is a stimulating and worthwhile place to spend a couple of years.

GETTING IN

« *I'll never forget when and where I found out I'd been accepted to Columbia Business School. I applied for fall term admission after closing deadlines and was placed on a priority waitlist to enter in September. In the meantime, I decided to quit my job and to go on vacation. On what turned out to be the second day of Columbia classes (two days after Labor Day), while I was traveling in Africa, I met my parents quite by accident in an island airport in the middle of the Indian Ocean. As my husband and I were dashing to make a plane, my mother said, "Columbia sent me a letter saying you got admitted and you should show up the first day of classes if you still want to go." We took off on a twenty-four-hour trek back to New York immediately. I still didn't get to school for almost a week but had no problem registering for classes.* »

Columbia uses a fairly continuous rolling admissions policy, since students may begin the program in any one of the three terms each year. Columbia admits a large variety of students to the program. For example, the entering class of 1987 was almost 20 percent foreign, 30 percent Ivy League/Seven Sisters, and about a third female. Although one suspects that quotas do exist, there is no official policy on the subject.

The school seeks bright and success-oriented people, since of course these types have the most potential to bring honor and contributions back in due time. Previous work experience and/or interviews can help a student get in, particularly if other credentials are a little weak. A father, mother, brother, or sister who attended the university or Business School can be helpful, as Columbia tends to support its own. Not surprisingly, it seems a tad easier to get in when you don't need help paying the tuition, which currently runs about $6,500 per term, not including books and other fees.

Columbia requires that prospective students complete a ten-page application, consisting primarily of four short essays. The questions are designed to reveal the individual's ability to sell him or herself. The students are requested to assess previous college and work experience and how it relates to their desire to attend the CU Business School. A long essay is required on the applicant's professional goals and how they relate to attending Columbia. Additionally, letters of recommendation from a college instructor and current employer are required.

A prospective student must also submit an undergraduate scholastic transcript and results from the Graduate Management Admissions Test.

This admissions system seems to work. The students tend to be intelligent, highly motivated, and very well qualified. The mix of men and women, foreign and American, some straight from undergraduate school and others with advanced degrees or several years of professional experience provides excellent stimulus for each other. While some may suffer from a certain "end results"-oriented myopia, overall the students are a well-balanced blend of grade-conscious achievers and sophisticated adults.

ACADEMIC ENVIRONMENT

« *Grades can be the Holy Grail for many Columbia students, and for others, grades aren't as important as Columbia's standard long weekends. These three glorious days can be used for skiing, going to the beach, or something more plebeian like a part-time job. Some students work extremely hard and will go to great lengths to get what they consider to be the all-important good grade. To others, grades are a means to an end. One friend cared little about grades since Business School was simply a vehicle to provide appropriate credentials to assume*

major responsibility, and later overall control, in his father's
successful electronics manufacturing operation. »

The current system consists of five possible grades: honors,
high pass, pass, low pass, and fail. In general, not many people
flunk out since a willing student can obtain tutorial help either
through study groups (virtually a prerequisite for success at
Columbia) or from the many MBA and Ph.D. candidates who
supplement scholarship aid and other income by tutoring.
Pressure is built into the system in many ways, which helps
students, particularly those with no previous executive work
experience, gain some understanding of the team player mentality so essential for success in most large corporations. Specifically, the academic workload is heavy, and study groups are
encouraged and even set up by professsors in some courses to
minimize duplication of extraneous effort and to promote
camaraderie and cooperation among students. On the practical side, if a person plans to work or play very much while at
Columbia Business School, study groups can be a valuable
and effective means to conquer the formidable reading lists
and casework assignments.

« *Most instructors do not assign people to study groups,*
preferring to let students align themselves according to their
own inclinations. This approach can help improve a person's
critical skills but doesn't reflect the normal working environ-
ment. Most entry-level positions provide the graduate with
little or no control over the choice of business colleagues.
   The process of putting together groups of students with com-
plementary skills can be frustrating and very similar to choos-
ing kickball teams in grammar school. There are the few expert
players everybody wants and then there are the unknown-
quantity types that people are reluctant to take a chance on. This
usually results in a couple of superstar study groups, a number

of teams with a realistic balance of good and not-so-good stu-
dents, and one or two "misfit" teams that have practically no
chance of competing adequately with the rest of the class.

While this "survival of the fittest" philosophy may reflect
real-world conditions, it can be very damaging to the unfortu-
nate few. In a competitive environment like Columbia, the
academic career can be severely hampered by negative percep-
tions of a person's ability to contribute to the overall good of the
study group. A new Business School student should be very
aware of the importance of the study group system and get to
know many people early on to insure informed choices are made
when picking the study group partners. »

Students tend to be very competitive as a general rule. Although there are a number of people with positions waiting for
them upon graduation, most students are at Columbia because
they want to make their mark on the business world. This
outlook is readily apparent in the beginning of the term as
students scramble to align with strong partners in study groups.
It also comes through in the classroom, where some people
seem compelled to speak out at frequent intervals whether or not
they actually have a contribution to make. While the atmosphere can be somewhat stifling at times, it stimulates many
rousing debates between students and teachers and among
students. Oftentimes discovering a new perspective or an insight
never before considered makes the student realize that the
drearier aspects of classroom interaction are a modest price to
pay for the positive side of the academic experience.

The faculty is a major drawing card at the Business School.
They respect inquiring minds and challenge most students to
exert themselves an extra measure. They are very well respected and often well known in their fields. By and large,
professors exhibit genuine concern for the students and make
themselves available for consultation outside of class. They

also provide references and valuable introductions to students seeking contacts in various areas of the business world. Like the student body, the faculty seems to run the gamut from urbane, sophisticated men and women about town to corduroy clad, almost absentminded professors.

Not surprisingly, professors have no set rules about grading; there are some classes that are graded on a bell curve with a few honors, a few fails, and most between the two extremes. In many smaller courses it is virtually impossible to fail, particularly if one is in a good study group, since 50 percent of the term grade is often the result of a joint project executed by the group. Most courses are graded on a combination of class participation (10 percent), performance on exams and quizzes (40 to 60 percent), and some type of group project (30 to 50 percent).

SOCIAL LIFE

THE social life at Columbia revolves around New York City. That can be very good and very bad. On one hand, New York City is the greatest city in the world, with more to see and do than any MBA student will ever have time or money to take advantage of. At the same, Columbia does not have as many tight-knit social groups as can be found at some of the other top business schools.

Columbia's social life is dispersed and decentralized. I suspect this can be attributed to a few factors. First, many students are from the New York area and aren't looking for a social life at school. Second, a fair number of students are married and their primary extracurricular interest at school is making potential business contacts. In fact, the Distinguished Leaders Lecture Series, the perennial favorite extracurricular program at the Business School, is held during the afternoon and draws a good crowd of people. Many go to hear captains of industry discuss a particular subject relating to their areas of expertise. More go to make contacts. Third, since the Master Degree Program for Executives (a program that allows executives sponsored by their companies to acquire an MBA while continuing their career) meets all day Friday, it provides regular full-time students with a weekly three-day hiatus, which can work against weekend socializing.

All of this is not to say Columbia Business School students don't get together. Sometimes they've even been known to marry each other! However, it seems that socializing is done in small groups, during dinners out or while having a drink at the West End Bar, a popular jazz music spot a few blocks off campus. One of the major advantages in attending Columbia is the opportunity it provides to explore New York City. The Big Apple offers a huge selection of intellectual, cultural, and sporting diversions for the hard-working Business School student. Despite the not altogether invalid assumption that it takes lots of money to enjoy the city, the energetic student will find there are many museums that offer student discounts (and often free admission one day each week), along with lecture and concert series that are included in the price of a museum admission. During the warm weather months, there are free concerts and plays in Central Park. Many off-Broadway theaters offer student discounts and most longer-running Broadway shows offer "twofers," allowing people to purchase two tickets for the price of one.

New York offers numerous opportunities for students who enjoy music. The selections range from opera to classical symphony, jazz, and hard-core New Wave/Punk concerts. Nightclubs and cabarets abound, although this type of entertainment is more costly and can easily run thirty to sixty dollars per person for an evening.

There are many dance companies based in New York and most major international groups schedule a series of New York performances on their American tours. Classical ballet and modern and folk dancing are only some of the diverse dance forms available to the city resident. And of course, everyone should visit Radio City Music Hall to experience the legendary precision dancing of the immortal Rockettes.

For any sports-loving prospective student, there is at least one professional sports team playing in the area any week of any season. New York boasts two football, two baseball, two hockey, and two basketball teams. There also are major golf and tennis tournaments throughout the year.

As this brief overview of available activities indicates, there're plenty of events for the Business School student to take advantage of in New York. With a little effort, one can plan outings that cost little money and simply require a bit of advance work or standing in line to obtain tickets.

There are opportunity and time to socialize at Columbia with other students, but you have to work a little harder than in other schools to do it. Study groups and living arrangements provide opportunities to know one another more intimately.

« *One of my favorite study groups at Columbia met in an apartment on Riverside Drive, a beautiful avenue looking out over a large park and the Hudson River. There were five young men, all single, all straight out of college, sharing this large apartment. Even though the place was big, they had to convert the dining room to a bedroom to allow for the privacy each fellow wanted. Only two of them knew each other before graduate school. But they were very lucky because they found a nice furnished apartment they could afford (about $700 a month, six years ago), even if it meant doubling up in one bedroom or sleeping on the living room sofa.* »

Students have the option of trying to locate their own apartment or living in university housing. If they choose to find their own place, they can start at Columbia's Registry of Off-Campus Accommodations, which has listings of available apartments.

It pays to get very friendly with the people who work there; go by every day to check on new listings and get there as much time before school opens as possible. The Registry of Off-Campus Accommodations is a source of leads for any university student, so the competition is fierce, particularly before the summer and fall terms. The university supplies limited housing for single and married students, and offers traditional dormitory accommodations along with suites and apartments owned and operated by the university. Students should be prepared to pay a minimum of $300 per month to cover housing expenses, more if you plan to live alone. For example, a small apartment with one bedroom in the Morningside Heights area runs $450 to $600 per month, plus utilities. On rare occasions it is possible to sublet faculty apartments for a year, which can either reduce rent or provide a larger place for the $400 to $500 monthly outlay. Additionally, there is a privately owned and operated facility, International House, open to both foreign and American graduate students twenty-one years or older. Again, plan to budget about $250 per month to cover rent in this building. There are recreational facilities and a cafeteria on the premises and the house provides the unique opportunity to live and socialize with students from other countries and other graduate schools within the university.

« *I had a friend in school who was always looking for a girl. Unfortunately, as an old married lady with very few unattached women friends, I could never provide much assistance. A continuous and vocal complaint among single men and female acqaintances throughout my two years at the B School was "How do you meet interesting people when you're not from New York?"* »

It seems easier to be married while going to school for a number of reasons. From a practical standpoint, if your husband or wife is working while you attend school, the financial burden is greatly alleviated. Additionally, you have another source of social contacts. If you're coming to New York for the first time it can be very comforting to have someone you love close by when the aggravations and pressures of school and the city close in.

Based on my discussion with unmarried students at the Business School, I would say it's not bad to be single, but it helps very much to have a steady relationship to offset the pressures that every student is subject to.

RECRUITING AND JOB SEARCH

RECRUITING is an integral part of the MBA program at Columbia. The placement staff begins working with students in their first term. Such projects as self-assessment, career planning, résumé preparation, and interviewing techniques are presented in group meetings and seminars. Alumni panels present insights into various jobs, careers, and industries. In addition, student clubs sponsor a wide variety of career-related meetings, both on campus and in the form of field trips.

Columbia has a very strong Alumni Counseling Board. This is made up of alumni from across the country, who volunteer to talk to students on a one-to-one basis, sharing insights into their jobs, industries, and careers, as well as the issues and frustrations they encounter in their work. Since so many of them are working in the New York metropolitan area, alumni provide an extremely valuable and readily available source of "real world" information to the students.

Still another, and perhaps the most valuable, way to learn about prospective career paths is through term-off employment. Most students do internships during the summer terms, but some few may elect to work full-time during the fall or spring. Summer and in-semester jobs are taken in a variety of functional areas, in such fields as investment banking, commercial banking, consumer goods, advertising, management consulting, manufacturing, government and not-for-profit agencies, and publishing and communications, to name some of the leading employer groups. In fact, one segment of Columbia's placement staff is focused entirely on helping students obtain these valuable training positions. Most of the students I knew spent summers on "The Street" in a brokerage house or an accounting firm.

The Columbia recruitment process has two seasons, fall and spring. Initial recruiting is done on campus in new facilities that are spacious and comfortable. The championship season is spring, when over three hundred companies and six hundred students make initial face-to-face contact. The process is computer managed, and students are assigned to desired corporate interviews by a lottery-type process. Each student has a computer form that allows him or her to rank order interview requests. However, with some persistence, one can manage to meet with almost any interviewer.

« I remember my first interview at Columbia. It was with a large, New York City advertising agency known for its "suit" mentality and a client list including packaged goods giant Procter & Gamble. I felt uneasy from the start and although I wasn't performing at my best, I knew there was more to the malaise than just "opening night jitters." Sometime later I realized that in those "dress for success" days, it was highly improper for a woman to interview attired in a red dress, sporting loose and curly long hair. »

At Columbia, the strong suit is finance. Roughly one half of employed students find work in banking and brokerage and investment. About one sixth of the students take industrial positions. Nearly 10 percent of the class enters the consulting field. In the past, students had been trained to be managers, not entrepreneurs. In recent years, however, it seems more students are showing an increased interest in entrepreneurial activities and entering such fields as real estate, specialized financial services, communications, and entertainment, with 15 percent of employed students in the 1987 class choosing careers in these fields. The one thing that stands out is that Columbia MBA graduates enter a wide variety of fields.

ON THE JOB — FIRST YEARS OUT

« *One year into my first job I had survived the crisis of beginner's nerves and answered the "What am I doing here?" lament. I was hot on the trail of a promotion and feeling ready to tackle anything Madison Avenue had to throw at me. I hadn't used a great deal of my Columbia education at first, mostly because the needs of a beginner in advertising are just not covered in the marketing curriculum at Columbia. The Business School teaches one to be a good client, but really doesn't focus on the development and evaluation of copy, which is the lifeblood of an advertising agency. But as I climbed the corporate ladder, I found the degree more valuable and useful.* »

The MBA is valuable as an admission ticket to the business world. It tends to overprepare a graduate for the first entry-level position. But if one could immediately begin in a Mary Cunningham–type position as Special Assistant to the President or Chairman of the Board, a Columbia MBA education would be very useful and immediately applicable.

On the other hand, a Columbia education does prepare the prospective tycoon with the credentials and know-how to overcome the most formidable of business situations (with a little bit of luck). In fact, Columbia provides skills that help the beginner grasp the proverbial big picture faster and thereby get an edge on the competition. Rigorous quantitative training prepares the new junior executive for numbers crunching. Months of analyzing cases are great background when evaluating the pros and cons of a marketing program or investment opportunity. Most of all, the education provides a framework for thought and analysis that proves invaluable for a career in business.

Additionally, the Business School experience allows for establishing an entire network of future business contacts. Of course, there are those people you meet in school and stay in contact with over the years, but there are also faculty members and thousands of fellow alumni, who you don't necessarily know as friends, yet can still call on. Alumni can help get you job interviews and give you information on various types of careers. The common bond of the old school tie can help break the ice at a business party or create surprising rapport with professional colleagues.

In that first year or two on the job, I found that my MBA education also provided some not so tangible benefits. It really did help me think faster than some of my colleagues. All those theories and cases were the basis for analyzing a variety of professional and personal situations. It gives the MBA graduate an overall perspective that translates into a real-world advantage if utilized effectively.

A fair percentage of graduates seem to switch jobs within the first one to one and a half years. Of my own acquaintances, about half had switched jobs within the first one to two years. The job changes were for a variety of reasons, but generally attributable to misunderstandings about objectives and the employer's mentality. Additionally, some students who have dual ambitions take the safer route earlier in their career and then tackle their higher risk ambitions once a track record in executive positions has been established.

My personal experience was that salary fell somewhat short of expectation. However, I went into a business not known for tremendous starting salaries. (Advertising ranks right above government as the second lowest paying industry in which graduates are placed.) Friends who went into more traditional areas of marketing, banking/finance, accounting, and manufacturing were pleased with their salaries or, at a minimum, felt they were being paid fairly. Salary can benefit from previous experience. The starting salary for Columbia MBAs now averages over $47,000 with the range being between $18,000 and $80,000.

SUMMARY REVIEW

COLUMBIA'S major strengths are a strong faculty, a quality student body, and access to all the business, social, and cultural benefits a world-class city like New York has to offer. The scholastic program is enhanced by its use of all the teaching methods traditionally expounded by one school or another: case method, lecture, and seminar. Importantly, there's a spirit of competition that encourages most students to achieve more than they might even have thought possible.

The faculty generally has outstanding academic and professional credentials. Many professors work as consultants to industry and government. As a rule, they are extremely generous with their time, providing counseling and additional help to those students who seek it. It is important to keep in mind that most of the faculty teaches because they want to teach. Many could earn much more practicing business than teaching business practices. There's a saying in the theater,

"Those who can't do — teach." In Columbia's case, the teachers can, and often do, do it all.

The student body is bright, urbane, and success-oriented. Many come to the school with exceptional track records in academics or business. The type of person attracted to Columbia and New York City is generally aggressive and savvy. The large group of foreign students adds in international flavor to the Business School experience and provides valuable additional resources for learning about how business is conducted outside the United States. Overall, one would be hard pressed to find a better group of people with whom to share the graduate school experience.

New York City provides a stimulating environment for Columbia students. The wealth of opportunities for business and pleasure are probably unmatched by any other city in this country. Any student who is interested in theater, music, dance, or art can pursue those interests to the limit in New York. For the dedicated future tycoon, there is the chance to interact with corporate movers and shakers through the Distinguished Leaders Lecture Series and special guest lecture meetings for some courses.

On the surface, it might seem strange that some of the school's strengths are also the source of its weaknesses. New York offers many opportunities for extracurricular distractions that can sometimes limit a student's academic achievement. It's very easy to push aside important project work that isn't due until the end of the term, in favor of more immediate social or cultural gratification. In fact, it seems that many study groups don't really start working until halfway through the semester, and the last couple of weeks often become a marathon of team meetings and "all nighters" to complete assignments. Since it can cost a lot of money to have fun in the city, many people find themselves looking for part-time jobs to finance their social lives. This can take important time away from the primary goal of going to Columbia — getting a high-quality graduate education in business.

Additionally, the students tend to be somewhat self-absorbed and highly competitive, so the atmosphere is not terribly conducive to making lifelong friends. Because of the number of students who are either native New Yorkers or married and don't live near campus, there is not as much community spirit at the Business School as on some other campuses. Some students mind this, others find it irrelevant.

My personal judgment? Columbia is a truly valuable and worthwhile experience. While it's not for people with thin skins, the experience is solid preparation for the corporate maze most graduates eventually face. For those without previous executive experience, the education is even more valuable. An MBA from a top school will be worth quite a bit even in a twenty-first-century world where postgraduate education will probably be as common as college degrees are today.

Chapter 10

AMOS TUCK SCHOOL OF BUSINESS
ADMINISTRATION*
(DARTMOUTH COLLEGE)

THE PROGRAM

« My Tuck experience began in the optional preorientation session that is offered the week before classes officially begin. It's really an intensive review of mathematics and economics. When the first session started with defining the union and intersection of sets and drawing supply and demand curves, I momentarily was lulled into a sense of security and confidence. As the sessions rapidly progressed into advanced calculus and the Cobb function, I was like many other students — humbled and nervous. Although the blitzkrieg of the first week orientation session let up, the sense of being on the battlefront lasts throughout the first semester. Luckily, my comrades in the trenches, especially in study groups, were all feeling the same way and were rooting for our joint survival. After the intensity of the first term's academics, we returned from Christmas vacation and were greeted by our grades in the mailboxes. All of us breathed a sigh of relief as we realized we could survive Business School. While other terms would prove to be very rigorous at times, the

* BY PETER AND KATIE DOLAN, MBAS, TUCK

academic program had to share the focus of our attention and anxieties with the search for summer or full-time jobs. »

Similar experiences have doubtlessly been shared by every entering class to pass through Tuck since the school was founded in 1900 as the first graduate school of management in the United States. Tuck students through the years had additionally shared the unique experience of learning in an environment that encourages personal relationships between its students and faculty. The relatively small size of the school enables those interactions to occur frequently both in and out of the classroom.

The typical entering class of approximately 165 students come from all over the United States and from about sixteen foreign countries. Women make up about a quarter of the class and minorities make up about 7 percent. About 96 percent of the class have at least one year of work experience prior to business school, and some students have considerably more. (One of the younger students observed on the first day of class that the person sitting beside him in marketing graduated from Princeton the same year he had graduated from eighth grade.) The mean age of entering students is twenty-seven. Most undergraduate majors are represented at Tuck, but the school favors applicants who have completed their undergraduate curriculum in the liberal arts.

While many of the entering students come to Tuck with extensive backgrounds in some areas, the first year consists of required courses in each of the basic areas of business administration. As a result, psychology and art history majors grind out the accounting courses with several CPAs, theorize about the money supply with students with master's degrees in economics, and determine credit decisions with former bank lending officers. In the second year, several students with J.D. degrees have been seen in the back row of the elective introductory business law classes! This mixing of backgrounds is intentional, since students learn from one another as well as from professors. And, because the three first-year sections are shuffled after every term, each student interacts with every classmate. Indicative of the cooperative nature of students at Tuck is the story of the CPA who held review sessions for anyone who wanted help the night before accounting exams.

The first-year curriculum includes work in economics, marketing, organization structure and human behavior, operations analysis and management, accounting and finance, industrial relations, probability theory, statistics, computers, management communication, and business environments. Reflecting the school's educational philosophy, these courses often utilize cases and problems as the basis for class discussion, with assigned readings providing detailed explanations of the relevant theories and analytical techniques. The Tuck School believes that both case study and theory have unquestionable validity and consequently blend the two teaching methods to varying degrees in different courses. As a result, no two classes are exactly alike. Financial Accounting, requiring a basic understanding of numerous techniques and theories, initially relies heavily on teaching theory and then later emphasizes analyzing specific financial statements from a case study. Marketing, while supplementing the cases with assigned readings, basically uses cases and a classroom style more typical of schools that rely totally on the case method. An often used but fairly accurate generalization states that "If Harvard and Chicago are at opposite ends of the case study and theory 'teaching style spectrum,' Tuck falls somewhere in the middle."

While it is true that no two courses are exactly alike, one course did blend the most common elements of teaching at Tuck and warrants fairly close scrutiny. Managerial Economics, a course taught in the first term of the school's six trimester program, in many ways proved to be an accurate overview of what was to follow. The subject matter itself touched on a number of topics that would be covered more intensely in later classes (regression analysis in Statistics and the allocation of joint costs in Cost Accounting). In addition, the combination of lectures, discussions, cases, and group projects typified the flexible format and mix of teaching styles that would be utilized in upcoming classes. But more importantly, the class encouraged camaraderie, not competition. Interaction between the professor and students was generally friendly and cooperative, not combative and hostile.

« *One particularly difficult assignment in my Man Ec (Managerial Economics) course was to summarize an economist's testimony of the cost of capital, a topic we had not previously discussed. The professor had told us he would randomly choose a student in each section to summarize the relevant information and field questions in front of the class. After hours of discussion the night before, no one totally understood the testimony.*

At the end of the first section, one of my friends went down to the front of the room to ask a question and happened to see my name at the bottom of a list of five names the professor had readied for the next section. As a practical joke, my friend told the professor to call on me. Afterward, when he realized that I might not find this too humorous, he sought me out to let me know what he had done. After expressing my disbelief over this sense of humor and vowing to repay him dearly, I waited nervously for class to start. "Someone in the other section recommended I call on a certain individual to begin today's class," the professor began. "Is Mr. Smiley with us today?" I went down to the front of the room with the notes from our group discussion the night before and reviewed our summary in front of the class. The professor asked me a few follow-up questions, which I answered as best I could, and to my delight, other students quickly vol-

unteered information to fill in the gaps of what I had missed (and to help me get off the hook). While I clearly did not have all the answers, the group's preparation the night before had been satisfactory. When one student tried to "grill" me, the rest of the class again came to my aid. After class, the professor and many of my classmates congratulated me on a job well done. What could have been a very unpleasant situation turned out to be a friendly exchange between both the professor and students. I found that cooperative environment to be a common theme in every class at Tuck. »

The Managerial Economics and Management Communication courses are the first introduction students have to group projects, an important element of the Tuck program. All the groups are chosen randomly by professors. In both courses, teams of six students act as consultants to local businesses. Students meet with the "client" to discuss the specific problem. The effort culminates in an oral presentation to this client, an outside consultant, and a Tuck faculty member. Both projects include a written report, again a group effort, and represent an important part of the final grade. These early group projects are very typical of course-work to come.

« *Of the twenty-four courses I took at Tuck, close to half involved group projects. The projects most often involved actual business problems and necessitated interaction with a firm. I worked with other students on projects ranging from an airport cost allocation scheme for the Lebanon Regional Airport manager to recommending and conducting a marketing research plan for an entrepreneur who wanted to mass market an Indian food product. I developed an optimization model for the Dartmouth College Endowment, looked at interest rate futures for a bank in Chicago, and helped General Mills try to reposition Hamburger Helper.* »

This practical application of concepts to real-world problems is a cornerstone of the Tuck curriculum. Despite the school's location, there is a tremendous amount of interaction with the business community. Most classes have occasional guest lecturers and the group projects bring in representatives who range from corporate giants to local businessmen to participate in project presentations. In true Tuck fashion, the second-year Entrepreneurship class combined the case method and guest lecturer techniques — cases consisted of a series of entrepreneurs discussing various aspects of their own ventures. At the end of that particular course, students presented their own business plan to the professor and an actual venture capitalist. (Usually every year or two a group project is actually offered some financing at the end of the presentation, and more than a few businesses have emerged from those projects.) The administration does its part to encourage executives to come to campus by sponsoring an Executive in Residence Program, which invites a top executive to spend a week at Tuck, to participate in classes and mingle with students on the tennis court and in the dining room.

Tuck prepares its students for careers in general management, and as a result, there are no majors at the school. The only requirement in the second year is the fall semester's Business Policy course. With its intense case study analysis (ranging from Lord Mountbatten's strategy in India to IBM's goals) and the week-long Tycoon game (in which students work around the clock running companies in a computer simulated market), the course makes the semester almost as intense as the previous fall. Other classes in the second year also rely more heavily on case study and are often much smaller (Auditing, although an extreme example, had only three students). The smaller class sizes foster strong faculty-student relationships, and as a result, students often invite faculty members to dinner or to play tennis and even socialize informally at parties with them. This interaction is one of the school's major strengths. Professors are always available, accessible, and approachable.

Working with peers on group projects, continual interaction with professors and the business community, and a blend of quantitative and qualitative courses are consistent with the school's objectives of helping students understand the relationships of business to society, encouraging them to develop a personal philosophy in dealing with others, and teaching them the most current analytical techniques used to help make decisions.

Students work hard at Tuck, studying Monday through Thursday nights and one day on the weekend, but there is also a realization that there are other aspects of one's life. Skiing, running, golf, tennis, and socializing are important too, and students find time to accommodate most of the activities that are important to them.

The Tuck School's reputation is that of a top ten school that is fairly quantitative, with a small student body located in a very out-of-the-way place. While the Hanover, New Hampshire, "outdoor" environment appeals to some students more than others, any perceptions that the school is too far away to allow for interaction with the business community are clearly unwarranted.

Tuck may not be as familiar to the general public as a few of the other top ten schools. But for many students, corporate recruiters are the only relevant audience, and as such, represent a yardstick by which to measure a school's reputation. More than 150 companies make the annual trek to Hanover, despite the vagaries of New England weather, to interview 165 students and offer them an average of four job positions.

The Tuck experience is more than just academics and job offers. Most students enjoy the location, their classmates, and the perspective "Tuckies" seem to have toward life in general.

GETTING IN

IN a conversation with several first-year students, a dean of the school once claimed, "Tuck is so selective that we could put you in a freezer for two years and most companies would still be lining up to hire you." Although Hanover does have several months of sub-zero weather, Tuck's academic program, as the previous section describes it, is far from a sterile deep freeze. Instead, the dean's comment is an accurate reflection of the effective admissions process at Tuck.

Last year there were 2,000 applicants for a class of 165 first-year students. With a ratio of twelve applicants to each opening in the entering class, Tuck continues to be one of the most selective schools in the country. The applications are reviewed in a rolling admissions process, which begins in December and ends April 15. As at other top ten business schools, the GMAT and recommendations are required. In addition, college courses in economics, a course in money and banking, and two units of college mathematics are strongly recommended, but are not required.

The school has five official criteria on which admissions decisions are based:

(1) motivation and leadership potential in management;
(2) scholastic achievement (with emphasis on performance during junior and senior years);
(3) aptitude for graduate business education (using the GMAT as a measure);
(4) maturity and a sense of purpose (which includes how an MBA fits into career plans);
(5) a personal sense of values consistent with the standards and purposes of the school's program.

As at most top business schools, prior work experience is a critical variable. Over 95 percent of recent classes have worked before attending Tuck. The school views time spent in the work force as a significant factor in developing a sense of purpose. Students applying directly from college should emphasize the applicability of experience gained in summer jobs and extracurricular activities.

Indeed, because Tuck is such a small, isolated school, significant emphasis is placed upon an individual's ability to contribute to the nonacademic life of the school. Therefore, extracurricular activities and "well-roundedness" may be more important criteria in the admissions process at Tuck than at other business schools.

While there is no quota system, Tuck has an affirmative action program and actively attempts to recruit minority students through alumni networks and membership in the Council for Opportunity in Graduate Management. Tuck also participates in the Johnson and Johnson Leadership Awards Program for minorities. However, Tuck's rural location makes it less attractive for those minority students who prefer the diversity of more urban settings.

Tuck also attracts a smattering of international students; our class included students from France, Norway, Canada, the Netherlands, South Africa, and Portugal.

Although not required, on-campus interviews are strongly recommended and are an important part of the admissions process. These interviews are half-hour discussions with either current students or with the Admissions Office staff. They provide both a chance for the applicant to learn more about Tuck and a chance for the school to assess some of the more subjective evaluation criteria.

One applicant, who later turned out to be a good friend, got a chance to demonstrate graphically his ability to "be cool under pressure" during an interview with the director of Admissions.

« After a half-hour talk — which he thought went really well — the director and my friend walked over to the closet to get his overcoat. They simultaneously pushed the sliding doors and my friend's fingers got pinched in between. He yanked his hand away and smacked his fingers directly into the director's left eye. He turned red and said good-bye sheepishly — trying to give the admissions director a handshake as he held his other hand over his eye! I think he's given a new meaning to the expression "blind admissions."

Despite this transgression, my friend was accepted and successfully completed the Tuck MBA program. However, he was careful not to wear overcoats to any of his job interviews. »

Besides going to an on-campus interview, one way to enhance one's chance of acceptance is by contacting students currently or recently enrolled in the program. The school's small size allows Admissions Office staff to know all recent Tuckies fairly well. A strong recommendation from a recent Tuck graduate could, therefore, be an added boost to an application.

Coming from Dartmouth College also helps. Dartmouth grads made up 10-12 percent of recent Tuck classes. Additionally, each year one or two Dartmouth juniors are allowed to skip their senior year and enroll as first-year Tuck students. These students, known as "3/2's," participate in a program that historically accounted for a much larger percentage of the entering class at Tuck. Years ago, Tuck was basically a graduate school for Dartmouth; today, however, students come from approximately one hundred undergraduate institutions.

ACADEMIC ENVIRONMENT

« Although it took me a semester to realize it, there are no quotas of students who must flunk out. Of a class of 165 people, it would be very unusual for more than three or four students to be forced to leave. »

This realization dissipates some of the pressure at Tuck, as students recognize that academic pressure is largely self-induced. No grade point averages are computed by the school, nor are students ranked, other than for Tuck Scholar recognition. As a result, students may be surprised to find less grade consciousness than at the undergraduate level.

The Tuck grading alphabet is H (Honors), S + (Satisfactory Plus), S (Satisfactory), LP (Low Pass), and F (Fail). Grading is on a flexible bell curve — professors generally give out F's or LP's to 1–15 percent, S's to approximately 50 percent of the class, and so on. The methods for determining these grades vary widely — professors can opt for mid-terms, finals, surprise quizzes, class participation, papers, individual computer assignments, and/or group presentations. Graduate business education encompasses such a range of skills and subject matter that this eclectic grading system helps foster diverse classroom atmospheres and course emphases. For example, grades in the second-year Business Policy class are based upon class participation and the results of two surprise quizzes. As a result, students attend classes diligently and analyze cases carefully. Meanwhile, Accounting grades are based upon a mid-term, a final, and written homework assignments. Such a blend of grading styles reduces academic pressure for students who afe not vocal classroom presenters or who get nervous on major tests.

In general there is less emphasis on classroom participation and decidedly more emphasis on group projects. Learning to work effectively in study groups and on group projects is clearly encouraged by the school. Students often begin Tuck finding it difficult to write collectively a two-page assignment and end up able to divide work up with amazing ease and camaraderie. Group projects also tend to reduce academic pressure and competition, since students are "all in it together."

This is not to say, however, that there are no late nights or seemingly impossible academic deadlines at Tuck. While there is diversity and there is camaraderie, the workload is significant.

« *Although I knew that classes ran five days a week at Tuck (unlike some of the other business schools I looked into), I was very surprised to find some tests scheduled on Saturdays. The faculty believed exams given on days of regularly scheduled classes detracted from preparation for other classes held on that day. I can't think of a better way to ruin part of a weekend.* »

Students do work long hours and strive to do well, especially in courses deemed to be most important and relevant to the business world. For example, in the second-year Entrepreneurship class, the student groups that develop business propositions and present them to actual venture capitalists for funding must receive prior approval of their project before taking the course. They also spend long hours researching the financial, marketing, and operational issues involved in preparation for the final presentation. One woman, whose resistance was reduced by many late nights of preparation, was hospitalized with a serious respiratory infection, yet, with a very wan face and minus several pounds, checked herself out of the infirmary to attend the final presentation, with a hospital ID bracelet still attached to her wrist!

Finally, for students seeking to become Tuck Scholars, the academic pressure can also be fairly intense. The students with the highest cumulative grades are recognized at the end of the first year, and after every trimester in the second year. A total of twenty-five students receive this honor by the end of two years.

SOCIAL LIFE

TUCK folklore tells of the student who, with squash courts, computer terminals, dorm rooms, laundry facilities, library, classrooms, and dining halls all connected by underground passageways, spent twenty-eight consecutive midwinter days without setting foot outdoors. This legend belies the typical Tuck student's attitude toward the outdoors and athletic activity, but does illustrate how the school's physical layout accentuates its small, tight-knit community atmosphere. The town of Hanover is isolated from the rest of the world — Boston is two and a half hours away — and Tuck's self-contained ten-acre campus is even more isolated. The resulting intimacy is the most influential factor in the school's social life. There are two sides to this intimacy — students are, on one hand, fully integrated into a community and experience no "anomie" at Tuck, yet there is also a strong rumor mill.

The examples of Tuck sociability and gregariousness are manifold. Tuck "tails," the Friday afternoon cocktail hour, attracts three-quarters of the student body. The same is true of the coffee breaks each morning between classes. A student's schedule would typically start with early morning classes; a midafternoon break for athletic activity; group meetings and studying until 11 o'clock; followed by late-night partying.

This late-evening camaraderie, combined with "free" Friday and Saturday nights, amounts to enough time for active social lives.

« *I worked hard at Tuck, but I also found time to relax. One of the social activities I enjoyed most was attending Dartmouth hockey and football games. Tuck students bought a block of seats and many students attended games diligently. It proved to be a great way to unwind from the pressures at Business School.* »

To organize students' free time, the Tuck Social Club, composed of six students, collects annual dues and sponsors events almost every weekend. These activities range from a spring talent show to a Casino Night, to road rallies, to a Bahamas Party — at which two tickets for a weekend in the Bahamas are the prize at the end of an all-night raffle. These events are augmented by the spring "Job Kegs," sponsored by students who have accepted jobs, and by occasional parties with the medical school or undergraduate fraternities. In addition, undergraduate activities such as film series and speakers are available for Tuck students.

An important part of the Tuck social life, and one which makes it unique among the top business schools, is the opportunity for athletic activities ranging from mountain climbing to kayaking. The school is located right on the Connecticut River (a swimmable part of the river), and is only twenty minutes away from the Dartmouth skiway. During winters with good snow conditions, Tuck students post a chart of their ski records and compete for the "ski bum" of the season award. Tuck students participate in intramural competition — with men's and women's teams in soccer, swimming, volleyball, softball, and football pitted against undergraduate or faculty teams. Those who have not mastered these sports prior to Business School can learn in Hanover — golf lessons, horseback riding, and skiing lessons are inexpensive and accessible.

This closed environment can sometimes feel too constraining and intimate. Two classmates, carrying on a courtship under the watchful eyes of 163 other Tuck students, resorted to throwing their coats and toothbrushes out of a second-story window in the middle of January to disguise their joint departure from parties. Courtship, however, is not impossible, and every year three or four couples get married.

The married student housing is located two and a half miles away from the rest of the campus. Sachem Village's "army barracks" and townhouses are a step above married student housing at other universities, yet will certainly never be featured in *House Beautiful*. Since Sachem Village is farther away from campus, study groups are initially composed of either all married or all single people. This dichotomy nearly vanishes as married and single students mingle in class and at social events.

The job prospects for spouses are fairly limited, although Dartmouth College, the Hanover businesses, and the Hitchcock Medical Center provide some employment opportunities. Some proportion of the married couples decide to use the two years "in the boonies" to start families.

RECRUITING AND THE JOB SEARCH

« When I first saw the listing of all the companies which come to recruit at Tuck, I felt like a kid in a candy store and thought that I'd never be able to decide which job looked most appealing. When else would I be able to pick out a totally new industry or new functional area and be pretty sure that I would get a well-paying entry-level job? During the interviewing and recruiting process, I gradually came to learn about the real differences between companies that had the perfect blend of opportunity, challenge, location, and atmosphere. »

As at other business schools, the recruiting season really begins in January of the first year, when students start interviewing for summer jobs. Although fewer companies recruit for summer positions than for full-time opportunities, all students find summer jobs. In addition to internships at investment banks, consulting firms, and Fortune 500 companies, students accept summer jobs with small New Hampshire firms, or with Tuck professors. These jobs are a chance to try out a new industry or locale.

In the structured programs of larger companies, students get a sense of how MBAs fit into the corporate structure. Interns are often given a specific project or are given a "smorgasbord" introduction to the company's business and departments. Companies usually treat their interns royally in the hope of attracting good candidates back to accept full-time positions, and to send company "ambassadors" back to campus.

« *My summer was spent with a major packaged goods company as an intern attending seminars and cocktail parties, and working on a new packaging concept. I was flown out to the West Coast to some of our test markets and was introduced to many of the company's top executives. It was a pretty heady experience, and I must admit that it left me with a good feeling about the company.* »

As a result of such internships, some students come back to Tuck with job offers "in their back pockets" — providing a real sense of security during the roller coaster of successes and disappointments during second-year recruiting.

The main elements of the interviewing process — reading up on the company, shaving off beards and buying new suits, the thirty-minute on-campus interviews, and the full day of interviews at company headquarters — are similar to the process at other top ten business schools. There are, however, some important differences, especially in the process of signing up for interviews. With approximately 130 companies recruiting on campus vying for the 165 graduates, students are free to sign up for interviews with as many companies as they wish.

Tuck has no "closed schedules" for recruiters. Indeed, the only constraint is one the school suggests — that students focus their job search and try to limit themselves to twenty-five interviews. Even this rule is waived in certain cases. Letters to companies are not required ahead of time, although résumé books are sent out in advance of a recruiter's visit. Companies often encourage good prospects to sign up on the interview schedule, yet the recruiters will talk to any and all students.

Tuck alumni connections are often very important and useful in the job search. Many times, recent graduates will come back to campus to recruit for their companies. A strong Tuck graduate often paves the way for new Tuck students in a company. This is especially true in smaller companies where Tuck has not become a "household" word.

« *Two time-honored traditions of the Tuck recruiting process are the "Ding" and the "Job Keg." At the Tuck School, ding letters are rejection letters from companies, which are publicly acknowledged by ringing a large bell in the mailroom. One day in the middle of the recruiting process, there were fewer "dings" than normally heard in the mailroom. One company had inadvertently sent out rejection letters to the five students they wanted to invite to company headquarters and twenty invitations to every student they wanted to "ding"! Each student receives his or her share of intended callbacks, however, and eventually everyone accepts a job. It's appropriate to sponsor, either individually or with other students, a Job Keg when the job choice has been made. During the spring semester in April and May, these impromptu parties occur almost every night.* »

What are Tuck students celebrating at these Job Kegs? Well, the class of 1987 had an average salary of $49,100 and students received an average of three job offers. Marketing positions attracted 15 percent of the class; finance, 50 percent; investment management, 7 percent; commercial lending, 3 percent; consulting, 7 percent; general management, 6 percent. Although the Fortune 500 companies, six investment banks, and consulting firms continue to attract the vast majority of Tuck students, an increasing number of students are going into smaller companies or are starting their own businesses.

ON THE JOB — FIRST YEARS OUT

« My job decision came down to two of the fifty largest Fortune 500 companies. These companies only hired from the very top business schools and made no distinctions in starting salaries based on the business school attended. These companies did, however, offer small differentials to reflect previous experience. This situation also proved to be true with most of my classmates. »

In general, financial remuneration is the first reward of a degree from a top ten business school. High starting salaries can represent a hefty increase from pre–graduate school incomes.

« Before I went to Tuck, I earned less than $10,000 a year. After graduating and marrying a classmate, we collectively earned more than seven times that amount. Talk about leverage! »

Getting an MBA was considered the right decision by nearly every graduate I know. Even students who went back to industries and jobs that were similar to positions they left suggest that the additional skills and acquired self-confidence made the decision to take two years off to pursue the degree well worth the "opportunity cost."

The usefulness of the degree is largely a function of the industry selected. Some jobs tend to give MBAs a lot of responsibility immediately, with little further training, while others have formal training programs that must be completed. Even in job situations that required formal training, students felt the MBA degree from Tuck helped get them the job, gave them a broader perspective on all aspects of business, and would be very useful as their management responsibilities expanded.

« One year after graduation, I found the company I worked for gave salary raises based on performance evaluations and future potential as product managers rather than the business school from which you graduated. While an MBA from most of the highly prestigious schools gets you on a rung of the corporate ladder, it is up to you to produce after that. As the years pass, contributions to previous jobs become a much better predictor of future success, rather than the MBA credential. »

If you are interested in changing jobs (as many MBAs are fond of doing), Tuck's alumni network can prove to be very helpful. Just as Dartmouth's alumni ties are strong, Tuck graduates tend to have a healthy sense of allegiance to the school. Classmates can provide access and information to the multitude of jobs and opportunities.

While some job switching occurs as a result of unfulfilled expectations, other graduates change positions because they simply do not like the day-to-day details of their job and still others change for personal reasons. About 15 percent of the class could be expected to change jobs after two years.

SUMMARY OVERVIEW

THE Amos Tuck School MBA program is similar to other top ten business schools in two important ways: the incoming students are a highly qualified group who have diverse backgrounds and experiences, and the graduating students are presented with a number of excellent job opportunities. The school differs from other programs because of the teaching approach, its size and location, and the opportunity to indulge in a variety of sports and social activities.

The school's flexible teaching approach is a major strength. The subject matter and the professor's own personal style determine the mix of teaching techniques. This results in a balanced curriculum and a multitude of different classroom situations. With no rigid adherence to either the case or theory method, no two classes at Tuck are ever taught in exactly the same manner.

The size of the school helps create a friendly, cooperative environment both in and out of the classroom. Interaction with the faculty is common, as professors attend parties, compete athletically, and, of course, make themselves available for academic discussions. Many second-year classes have only a handful of students, which fosters even closer faculty/student relationships. On the negative side, the school's size does prevent it from offering the same variety of courses as other programs. While Real Estate and Health Care courses are offered, more unusual courses are not.

The school's location is another double-edged sword. If you like the outdoors and skiing, golf, tennis, horseback riding, kayaking, swimming, etc., you will love the Hanover location. If art museums, Broadway, and a thousand great restaurants are more your style, then think twice. The New Hampshire winters can be cold and isolating. Interestingly, the school's out-of-the-way location is not a detriment to interaction with the business community. Possibly, the administration tries harder than most schools to bring executives from corporations and small businesses to campus. With the guest lecturers in classes, the Executive in Residence Program, and many of the group projects, the school is swarming with business people all year.

The social life is probably better at Tuck than at almost any other top business school. Despite a heavy work schedule, students manage to find time to engage in their favorite sports, socialize at numerous parties, and often buy season tickets to hockey and football games.

Job opportunities for Tuck MBAs are excellent. With more companies per student coming to Tuck than any other school, students can interview with whomever they wish. And students average three job offers, each at very impressive salaries.

After graduation from Tuck, you start a job at an excellent salary. You learned a tremendous amount in two years and you made long-lasting friendships and connections for the future. Importantly, the typical Tuckie enjoyed the Business School experience.

Chapter 11

SUMMARY OVERVIEW

THE nation's top ten business schools share a similar mission: to prepare the best and the brightest for the world of corporate America. The programs are tough, and the hours overwhelming, but the rewards are enormous. Graduates of the top schools leave with the skills, contacts, and credentials needed to succeed at whatever they choose to do. They may decide to work for a corporation or start up a new venture. It is this excellence in training and placement that distinguishes the top ten MBA programs.

There are basic elements common to all the top ten schools: a strong set of required core courses ranging from Accounting to Interpersonal Relations, a very heavy and demanding workload, a bright and aggressive student body, an emphasis on both formal and informal student interaction, a distinguished faculty with renowned expertise in one or more areas, a university with a reputation and obsession for excellence, and an active recruiting and placement program.

Beyond these common elements, however, each school has its unique set of characteristics and special areas of competence which define its niche within the top ten. For example, one business school may be noted for its finance program and another for its training of top-level general managers. All the top ten schools provide an excellent basic business education, but each does it in its own way.

COMMON THREADS

Required Courses

Required courses are to a business school student what exercise is to an athlete: basic training. The courses are long and they generally require a lot of work. They tend to be less interesting than many other courses in the program. But all in all, they do provide the basics necessary to compete in business.

Almost all the schools require courses in eight core areas: accounting, finance, statistics, marketing, human relations in organization, production, economics, and business policy. In addition, all the top schools now require computer literacy either through courses completed or demonstrated proficiency. Sometimes, there is a choice among a number of courses in a core area; most of the time there are no options. Occasionally core courses can be waived, but usually the exemption exams are very difficult. The core courses are the heart of the business school program and provide students with the basic skills and knowledge crucial to their education and future careers.

Workload

The top business school programs are tough and demanding. Long hours are the rule rather than the exception. Generally, more work is assigned than anyone could possibly do, and that is the method to the madness. In order to complete the work, it is necessary to manage time exceedingly well and to work cooperatively in groups. These are precisely the abilities that business schools want to inculcate, because time management and cooperative effort are key to succeeding in the business world.

Students

It is often said that the top business schools accept such high-level achievers that these students would have succeeded regardless of whether they went to business school or didn't. To a large extent, it's true; the top business schools can't fail. Students at the top schools are all bright and aggressive. They all graduated at the top of their class, have great business boards, and have done something unique and outstanding that sets them apart from the other thousands of unsuccessful applicants. They also are willing to put in the long hours and hard work required during business school.

The schools provide the structure, environment, and training; students make or break the program. Given the students' abilities and willingness to work, the programs succeed very well.

Student Interaction

While Greek mythological heroes and Western cowboys may go it alone, students at the top business schools rarely do. Most of the schools either require or strongly recommend that students meet together in study groups outside of the classroom in order to handle the voluminous workload. In addition, informal socializing is well organized (would you expect otherwise?) at most of the schools. Thus group effort becomes a critical endeavor at most of the top business schools. And since cooperation is the basis for almost all business activity, it is a skill and experience not to be underestimated.

Faculty

The persons you thought never existed, whose names you may have seen in business books and journal articles, are actually alive and well and teaching at the top ten business schools. The overall quality of the faculty at the top business schools is excellent. Many of these professors are engaged in "frontier" research, and teach basic or advanced courses for MBAs. They appear to teach quite well. Most of the schools emphasize teaching (as opposed to research) very strongly and most professors take their teaching very seriously.

University

Behind every great business school is a great university. The university generally has the resources, the reputation, and the commitment to excellence that carries over to its business program. In one sense, the business schools operate their programs fairly independently. But in another sense they operate within the confines of the university which offers business program administrators, faculty, and students exposure to other ideas and educational programs.

Recruiting and Placement

The ultimate measure of success of any MBA program, the bottom line so to speak, is its placement record. By this measure, the top ten business schools all have achieved unparalleled success. Graduates of these schools are highly sought after by major and minor companies, earn starting yearly salaries of $50,000 or more, and move quickly up the ranks of the organization to positions of power and influence.

DISTINGUISHING CHARACTERISTICS

Harvard

Harvard is intense. From its eight hundred cases to its demanding workload, from mandatory classroom participation to its West Point mentality, Harvard's defining characteristic is its intensity. Harvard is committed to having the best training program for general managers. And they have succeeded; Harvard Business School has traditionally been regarded as the premier business school in the country. Through its rigid adherence to the case method, Harvard teaches students to think analytically and solve problems. In essence, Harvard trains managers and develops leaders.

Stanford

Stanford does everything well. Its program strives for balanced excellence in training general managers and achieves it. The curriculum, the teaching method, the classes, and the workload are demanding, but not obsessively so. The curriculum has flexibility in choice, the teaching method combines the best of case and lecture, the classes vary in size and requirements, and the workload is tough but not crazy. Stanford's defining character is this balanced approach to high-quality general management education.

Wharton

Any school that used to have finance in its name has to have finance as its forte. Wharton's distinguishing characteristic is its strength in finance and the more quantitative subjects. For those who want it, it can be a number cruncher heaven. While in the past few years Wharton has broadened its scope and has achieved a uniformly excellent program, Wharton's capability in finance gives its program its excellent reputation.

Chicago

Chicago's program is distinguished by its finance faculty. Many well-known scholars with national reputations teach Chicago's finance courses. They consult, do research, and contribute to making Chicago's finance program one of the best in the country. Subsequently, more students from Chicago enter finance or accounting than any other field. Although Chicago has placed a much greater emphasis on general management in recent years, its strength in finance makes the degree very valuable in the business world.

MIT

The first hint of MIT's distinguishing feature, besides its reputation, is that everything — from the program (XV) to the buildings (39) to the rest rooms (39-059) — is numbered. MIT has a heavy quantitative orientation. Students are required to have taken calculus and economics prior to entering the program. Most classes, although not all, require some capability and facility with figures. In this vein, the school is noted for its highly quantitative programs in finance, economics, and MIS. While MIT has an excellent, well-rounded program with more than enough organizational behavior courses, MIT finds its strength in numbers.

Northwestern

What distinguishes Northwestern from the other top ten is that it is the only program that emphasizes marketing, which in itself is a clever marketing strategy. The faculty, courses, and research are top flight. Northwestern has developed this marketing expertise within a general management framework. By doing so, Northwestern has built a well-balanced and well-rounded program whose graduates subsequently excel in marketing and general management positions.

Michigan

Consistent with its midwestern roots and locale, Michigan's program is highly professional and without pretension. It does whatever needs to be done to provide quality training for general managers. Thus, Michigan's defining characteristic is its pragmatic approach. The program carefully balances both the quantitative and the qualitative, so that students are exposed to and understand both disciplines. In addition, Michigan requires that exactly half the courses be taken as part of the core curriculum, so its graduates receive well-rounded training. Finally, Michigan even established an evening program so that students would have greater options for taking courses. The result is that Michigan graduates subsequently do very well in widely diverse areas from finance to marketing to information systems.

UCLA

The hallmark of UCLA's program is its flexibility. Students design their own curriculum within the framework of basic core requirements and free elective courses. Students also undertake a field study consulting project to broaden and complete their management training. The school is strong in a variety of areas, such as finance, information services, marketing, and industrial relations. Thus the choices available to students are enormous and in some cases unique.

Columbia

Columbia is part and parcel of New York City: it is big, bold, intense, and decentralized. Columbia has the largest number of students in its program. Its finance and marketing majors are among the best in the country. Predictably, its social life revolves around the city. Columbia itself also offers diversity and flexibility. Students have a lot of choice in designing their programs, in scheduling their classes, and in taking full advantage of the social, cultural, business, and other opportunities that the city provides.

Tuck

Tuck is a world unto itself. While Tuck trains general managers as do many other schools in the top ten, its size, location, and atmosphere are its distinguishing features. Tuck has far fewer students than any of the other programs (with the exception of MIT). Tuck is located in a remote rural area in New Hampshire, and its personality embodies the small town where it's located: students are friendly, cooperative, and generally know each other very well. Tuck takes advantage of this close-knit environment by encouraging group work, fostering student/faculty contact, and persuading executives to come to the school to meet and interact with students. As a result, students not only learn a lot and get good jobs, but also enjoy the two-year program.

Any major investment involving two years and tens of thousands of dollars merits long and careful consideration. Once the decision has been made to go to business school, the choice among the top schools is difficult. While you can't go wrong with any of the top schools, not every school is right for every person. It is necessary to weigh individual needs and interests carefully. It is important to look beyond the academics and the reputation of the program to the cultural and

245

social environment, and to the personality of the school. Each school has its own identifiable strengths and weaknesses. Choose wisely and well, and be prepared for a demanding two years. It is one investment that will certainly pay off throughout your career.

II

BUSINESS SCHOOL TIPS

Chapter 12

TEN TIPS
ON GETTING INTO
BUSINESS SCHOOL

---

(1) *Make sure that business school is right for you.*

(2) *Get as much information as possible on the schools to which you are applying.*

(3) *Build up your college grade point average.*

(4) *Study for the Graduate Management Admissions Test (GMAT).*

(5) *Get a solid grounding in math, economics, and English.*

(6) *Pursue leadership roles in college and community activities.*

(7) *Apply early.*

(8) *Use any connections you have.*

(9) *Work for two to four years before you apply.*

(10) *Make the most of whatever opportunity you have in college or on a summer or regular job.*

1. MAKE SURE THAT BUSINESS
SCHOOL IS RIGHT FOR YOU

Business school requires a major investment of time and money. For two years you will earn no money, work twelve to fourteen hours a day under enormous pressure, and, to top it all off, pay dearly for the privilege. Is it worth it?

This is a question you must ask yourself and be able to answer to your full and complete satisfaction. Is it worth it for me to forgo two years of income? Given my previous skills, training, and experience, will I learn enough to make it worthwhile? Will I be significantly better off in my first or current job if I get an MBA? How much will an MBA help me in my future career or chosen line of work?

The facts are clear. MBAs from the top ten schools generally earn starting salaries averaging $45,000 to $50,000 a year. They usually have more than one job offer. They succeed in advancing within corporations or in starting up their own ventures. The MBA degree, like the American Express Gold Card, is a readily accepted credential. Finally, an MBA gives you a personal sense of confidence and security in whatever you do. It is something you have rightly and proudly earned.

However, like anything else worth having, it requires long and arduous hours. The process is sometimes enjoyable, but more often than not, it is just hard work. But in the end, you taste the thrill of victory.

An MBA is not for everyone. In order to get in, you have to decide that you really want it. You must spend a lot of time, effort, and money in the application process alone. And that's only the beginning. Therefore, make sure that an MBA is right for you. Once you have made the personal commitment, then be prepared to go all out for it. It is worth the effort.

2. GET AS MUCH INFORMATION AS POSSIBLE ON THE SCHOOLS TO WHICH YOU ARE APPLYING

Choosing an MBA program is an important decision. Whatever program you choose will occupy the next two years of your life and could well determine your future career path. Therefore, it is critical to get as much information as possible on the different schools and their programs in order to make an informed decision.

First, send for the catalog and read it carefully and thoroughly. Next, contact the school or its alumni office and ask to speak to recent graduates. Most of the schools will accommodate you by providing some names. MBAs from the school know more than anyone else about the program and its pluses and minuses. Finally, go to see the school, sit in on some classes, talk to current students, and interview with its admissions staff. In most cases these interviews are for information only. But it is worth the time and effort to learn more about the place where you may spend the next two years of your life.

After you have gathered all this information, use it. First determine if the program meets your needs. If it does, then try to figure out what the school is looking for in its applicants. Depending on the orientation of the program, the school may be interested in applicants who want to be general managers, or if the school is strong in finance, it may favor candidates who want to go into investment banking. The more you can tailor your application to the specific strengths and interests of the school, the greater the likelihood you will be accepted.

3. BUILD UP YOUR COLLEGE
GRADE POINT AVERAGE

If you have graduated or are a senior and have just taken your final exam, forget about improving your undergraduate grades. However, if you are a sophomore or a junior, read on. Grades are important to graduate business schools. They are one tangible piece of data that admissions officers can use to predict how well you will do in business school. While grades are not everything, they do count.

The higher the grades, the better the chance of getting in. Try to do well in all courses, but excel in some. Don't figure you can let your grades slide in math or English, assuming that they wouldn't count that heavily. All the top business schools require students in their program to take both the highly quantitative statistics or economics course and the nonquantitative human behavior or interpersonal relations class. The top schools are looking for the applicant who does well in both, and stands out in some areas. Someone who has had little business experience can favorably impress the admissions board by submitting excellent grades.

4. STUDY FOR THE GRADUATE
MANAGEMENT ADMISSIONS TEST
(GMAT)

While it is often too late when applying to business school to affect college grades, it is usually possible to improve your business boards. They count heavily and can be a major factor in the decision process. They are the one standardized test all applicants take and, therefore, are useful in comparing the abilities and potential of an overabundance of all seemingly highly well qualified applicants.

There are a few very talented people who could score 800 on the GMAT without doing anything. But for most of us a good score requires some work and study. Most people can improve their scores either by using a do-it-yourself book or by taking a prep course for the GMATs. In either case, it pays to do something.

If by chance you don't do as well as you hoped you would, take the boards again. It can't hurt you (unless you do worse) and most likely will help you.

5. GET A SOLID GROUNDING IN MATH, ECONOMICS, AND ENGLISH

No one ever said it was going to be easy. The top business schools have very difficult programs. They require highly developed skills in math, economics, and English. Regardless of which school you go to, you need to be able to crunch the numbers (i.e., be able to analyze and use quantitative formulas and data) as well as an accountant, and still be able to express yourself as well as an English major. While very few of us are equally adept with numerical figures and figures of speech, the more facile you are in both, the easier business school will be for you.

Therefore, if you can demonstrate extensive training or experience with numbers, and can express yourself clearly, your chances of getting in are improved. The top schools recruit heavily among engineers and numbers types, especially those who can speak and write as well as they can express themselves quantitatively. While it is not necessary to get an engineering or accounting degree, it doesn't hurt to take courses that will help you get in and also prepare you for the rigors of a topflight business program.

6. PURSUE LEADERSHIP ROLES IN COLLEGE AND COMMUNITY ACTIVITIES

All businesses are continually searching for good leaders because the essence of good management is the ability to lead or to motivate people. Therefore, a major purpose or function of business school is to train and to develop good managers or leaders. As a result, business schools look for applicants who have the potential to be good leaders.

The best way for an applicant to demonstrate this potential is to show leadership experience in college or community activities. This can be done in a number of ways: by holding office in a student organization, being elected captain of an athletic team, sitting on the board of directors of a local nonprofit corporation, and so forth. Being elected head of an organization gives you the opportunity to try out various management skills and to prove your leadership potential. It also shows that you are well thought of and respected by your peers and/or associates.

You don't always have control over being elected to a leadership position, so pursue those activities where you can exercise some control. For example if you were captain of a football team in college, you might coach a midget football team after you graduate. It also shows that you have a variety of experiences and can lead in any type of situation. This is the type of individual business schools seek.

7. APPLY EARLY

Several thousand applicants apply to each of the top business schools. Each applicant sends in approximately ten or more pages of information for the admissions committee to evaluate. This means the committee must read, digest, and evaluate over a thousand pages for each hundred students who apply. That is the equivalent of reading Clavell's *Shogun*. By the four hundredth application, a committee member has read the equivalent of Clavell's oriental quartet. And to think that process has just begun. When do you want your application read?

While there are no hard and fast rules and schools will vehemently deny it (at least officially), logic dictates that it is easier to get in the earlier you apply. Since most schools use rolling admissions, more places are open in the beginning of the process. Admissions officers probably take this into account somewhat. But when there are fewer and fewer slots available, judgments tend to be more critical. In addition, there is not as much time pressure on admissions officers early on in the process and they may tend to be more open than they will be in later months, when they may tire of the arguments and essays. While the edge in applying early may be small, in many cases the difference between being accepted and rejected is equally as narrow. Therefore, apply early.

8. USE ANY CONNECTIONS YOU HAVE

Business schools often rely on connections and contacts for alumni contributions and job placements. The top schools encourage the old boy network and often boast of the widespread influence of its alumni in the business world. Given this orientation, it is reasonable to ask whether contacts can help you get into school.

The official answer is no. In the ideal world admission to the top schools should be based solely on merit — on what you know, not who you know. And in one sense, it is probably true that if you are clearly unqualified for admission, no contacts in the world (short of a father who will contribute a library in your name) can get you into a top school. On the other hand, if you are qualified and competitive, a good reference letter from a heavy contributor or an alumnus who knows you will probably help.

9. WORK FOR TWO TO FOUR YEARS BEFORE YOU APPLY

Business schools, unlike the armed forces, want experience. It may seem curious that an institution established to give experience also requires it. But business schools are looking for well-qualified applicants who not only can benefit from the MBA program, but can also contribute to it. Someone who has had a few years of work experience is more likely to be able to do this. In addition, business schools prefer students who are more mature and more likely to have developed a sense of who they are and where they are going. And, an applicant with work experience can make a better case on his or her application when asked to state his or her three greatest accomplishments and career goals.

The percent of students coming to business school directly out of college is extremely small (2 to 4 percent at most schools). Except for Chicago, which has a special program for a limited number of liberal arts students to enter directly out of college, getting work experience is essential.

Given this propensity to favor applicants who have had work experience, does it make a difference what that experience was? The answer is yes and no. On one hand, positions in accounting, banking, and product management provide excellent preparation for business school. Jobs in these fields may make it easier to justify your decision to apply to business school. On the other hand, the schools are looking for a well-rounded student body and, therefore, accept their share of college professors, musicians, army officers, small retailers, and so forth. It is more important what you accomplish on the job than what job you do. (See the next tip.)

Generally, business schools prefer students with two to four years of work experience. It is difficult to determine whether schools purposely desire this precise amount of experience or whether the majority of applicants happen to possess that amount. Regardless, it makes sense for both the schools and the students. The schools benefit by getting experienced yet not inflexible students. Students with two to four years experience also benefit because they can leverage their degree more than their classmates who have a lot of or no work experience.

Some schools also offer deferred admission, an option which lets applicants have their cake and eat it too. Under deferred admittance, some schools grant acceptance to highly promising college seniors on the condition that they work for a few years before entering business school. Thus, a deferred admittee can work after college yet still be secure in the knowledge that he or she will enter a top business school two years later. It's great, if you can do it.

10. MAKE THE MOST OF WHATEVER OPPORTUNITY YOU HAVE IN COLLEGE OR ON A SUMMER OR REGULAR JOB

What sets successful applicants apart from their rejected counterparts is not so much specific grades or references as it is a total record or picture of achievement. Almost everyone who applies to the top schools has goods grades, good recommendations, and some work experience. In short, most applicants to the top schools are qualified. The difference is that the applicants who are accepted have done something special, unique, or outstanding and have achieved distinction or honor in doing it.

For example, it is not enough to have simply worked for IBM or General Foods. During your employment, you must have demonstrated your management potential by doing something that helped the company and that was unusual for someone at your level. And, if you don't have business experience, your college record should contain a similar accomplishment. Perhaps during your time at school you were president of the school's community service society and were instrumental in doubling the size of the program.

To set yourself apart, you generally have to create your own opportunity. Most of the time during college or on the job it is very difficult to do something outstanding. Great ideas and record-breaking success are not common occurrences. But these achievements can enhance the likelihood of acceptance to a top business school.

Chapter 13

TEN TIPS
ON FILLING OUT THE
BUSINESS SCHOOL
APPLICATION

(1) *Market yourself as a valuable addition to any MBA program.*

(2) *Be aggressive, both in style and content.*

(3) *Identify what you have done that is unusual, unique, or outstanding.*

(4) *Be justifiably proud of your accomplishments.*

(5) *Communicate that you are right for the school and the school is right for you.*

(6) *Keep essays short, interesting, and to the point.*

(7) *Make the application look professional: typed, neat, and error free.*

(8) *Use professional references/recommendations.*

(9) *Take your time and take it seriously.*

(10) *Be honest and candid.*

1. MARKET YOURSELF AS A VALUABLE
ADDITION TO ANY MBA PROGRAM

Applying to business school is the classic marketing or strategic planning problem. What do you as the applicant have to offer that makes you more attractive or better than the thousands of other applicants? Why should they choose you? The path to acceptance is good marketing, i.e., show your competitive advantages.

First, you must offer a good package, i.e., good grades, boards, recommendations, essays, etc. Second, you must offer something special that sets you apart from the crowd (see tip 3). Third, you must show how you can contribute to the program or why you are a more desirable candidate than others. This is important because business schools are often viewed solely as places where students learn or receive training, i.e., a one-way relationship. This ignores the fact that good business schools also expect a lot from their students in terms of classroom participation, group projects, informal interaction, etc. Therefore, your ability to contribute to this learning environment is as highly valued as your ability to learn. As a result you must demonstrate in the application that because of your experience, analytical abilities, or leadership capabilities, you can contribute to the program.

2. BE AGGRESSIVE, BOTH IN
STYLE AND CONTENT

The one common and shared characteristic of MBA students at the top schools is that they are aggressive. They know what they want and they go out and get it. While they all have a significant record of achievement, it is the aggressive attitude that distinguishes them. How do you show aggressiveness in an application?

First, carefully focus the content of your essays. They should portray you as a go-getter, i.e., someone who not only did well academically, but also played sports, held office in a major campus organization, and earned all his/her spending money for four years. Your major limitation was that you had to sleep for four hours a night. While this may be a bit exaggerated, you must communicate to the admissions office that you work hard and can accomplish whatever you set your mind to. Business school is difficult and not for the weak of heart or those lacking endurance.

Second, your writing style should also be aggressive. Use active verbs. Use short sentences and paragraphs. Use exciting words like "manage" and "accomplish." The application is the only place where you can really show how aggressive you are. Don't blow it.

3. IDENTIFY WHAT YOU HAVE DONE
THAT IS UNUSUAL, UNIQUE, OR
OUTSTANDING

Imagine that you are an admissions officer for one of the top ten business schools. You have to read a couple of thousand applications. Then you have to accept a couple of hundred students. Seventy-five to 85 percent of the applicants are clearly qualified with good grades, boards, and recommendations. How do you choose?

It's obvious you cannot make a judgment based strictly on grade averages, board scores, or favorable recommendations. So you review the applicants and try to decide which one has something unusual, unique, or outstanding to offer the program.

As the applicant you must determine what that something is. It does not have to be previous employment at a Fortune 500 company or honors from Harvard. Perhaps it's a small business venture that may have even made little money. It still shows that the applicant has the initiative and drive to do something that probably few of the other applicants have done. If you didn't start a business, maybe you had an unusual job. People from such diverse areas as television reporting, non-profit performing arts, government research, architecture, and other fields can make very attractive candidates.

Even if you had a mundane job, you can still highlight significant achievements or responsibilities. If you worked as a supply clerk for a large company but were responsible for millions of dollars' worth of inventory, that's significant. If you were an accountant but saved the company some money, you should highlight it. And, if you didn't work and have just graduated from college, you can still pinpoint an unusual or outstanding accomplishment. You might be the foremost Latin scholar in the nation. You might have run student services for a campus of ten thousand students. The key is to position what you have done in such a way that sets you far apart from a madding crowd of MBA applications.

4. BE JUSTIFIABLY PROUD OF YOUR ACCOMPLISHMENTS

The application to business school is no place to be modest. You are trying to convince admissions officers at the top schools that you are the greatest thing since sliced bread. Therefore, you must blow your own horn.

Whatever you have done, build it up and make it sound important. If you won the college debating tournament or were the youngest marketing executive at ABC Company and you feel that those were important accomplishments, say so. Never lie, but don't be reluctant to give the most self-enhancing interpretation of any job or accomplishment.

On the other hand, avoid the flagrant and egregious statements that cast doubt on your credibility. Case in point: one top business school applicant described a *summer* job as the strategic planner for GM. While this might be believable for a tiny company, it sounds ridiculous for a major multinational corporation. Just avoid straining anyone's belief.

5. COMMUNICATE THAT YOU ARE RIGHT FOR THE SCHOOL AND THE SCHOOL IS RIGHT FOR YOU

The top schools differ greatly in terms of academic strengths, teaching methods, general orientation, etc. Therefore, it only makes sense when filling out the application to tailor your responses to each particular school.

For example, Harvard is noted for its general management orientation. Therefore, you should stress in the application that you want to be a general manager and highlight what you have done that demonstrates general management potential. Wharton, on the other hand, is noted for finance. Thus, you might want to say that you're interested in the more quantitative side of management and that Wharton is perfect for you.

While it is not necessary to be a general manager to apply to Harvard or a finance jock to apply to Wharton, it is necessary to say why that particular school is right for you. Generally, the more you can tailor your application to each individual school, the better are your chances of getting in.

6. KEEP ESSAYS SHORT, INTERESTING, AND TO THE POINT

Admissions officers have to read thousands and thousands of pages. Moreover, they read the same story over and over again. They know all the reasons why applicants want to go to business schools, what each hopes to do after graduation, and so forth. Keep essays short, interesting, and to the point if you want to break through this paper log jam.

If the essay is short and interesting in both content and style, admissions officers are more likely to read it carefully. If it is longwinded with a lot of extraneous material, they are more likely to skim over it. Try to differentiate your essays in some way from the "typical" responses they receive. You might want to study stories, advertisements, or other documents that strive for an economy of style.

7. MAKE THE APPLICATION LOOK PROFESSIONAL: TYPED, NEAT, AND ERROR FREE

It would seem obvious that the application should look professional. However, it is surprising how many fail to satisfy minimum criteria of acceptability.

First, the application should be typed. Do it on a good typewriter with a good ribbon. Rent one if you have to. Second, be neat. All margins should be the same. Typing mistakes should be neatly whited out. The overall presentation should look clean. Finally, make sure there are no mistakes in the application; check spelling, grammar, and typing for errors. Typos indicate you're careless and indifferent. Proofread the application a couple of times yourself and then have a friend or family member look it over. Remember, since you are presenting yourself in the application, it should reflect the way that you want to be evaluated.

8. USE PROFESSIONAL REFERENCES/RECOMMENDATIONS

Many applicants submit personal letters of reference from senators, congressmen, and heads of corporations which begin "As a friend of the family I have known John [or Sally] since he was a child and I can unequivocally state he is a fine, upstanding human being." While these letters are nice and show that you are well connected, they generally carry far less weight than professional references from former employers, teachers, and anyone else who knows you in a professional capacity.

When asking someone to write a recommendation, give them an updated résumé. Discuss it with them. Tell them why you want to go to business school. Explain to them why you feel that their recommendation will help you get into business school. Ask them to be as specific as possible. Request that they highlight an accomplishment, such as the competitive marketing analysis that you did which everyone felt was outstanding and benefited the company.

The key is to get your reference to write more than just a perfunctory "Johnny did a good job" letter. Try to get a letter that tells why what you did was good and why it was useful. Try to get your reference to write as if your admission de-- pended on his or her letter, because it does.

9. TAKE YOUR TIME AND
TAKE IT SERIOUSLY

Filling out the application may seem to take forever. But wait till you get to business school, when the real work begins. Remember you will be spending two years of your life and tens of thousands of dollars at this school. It's worth putting in the effort on the application. Take time to think through each question in the essay section. Carefully consider who you want to write your recommendations. Study for the GMATs and take them twice if necessary. If an additional couple of hours are required for acceptance at a better school, it's worth it.

Although filling out an application is a pain in the neck and very time consuming, take it seriously; after all, it's your career and future. If possible, speak to graduates of the program, visit the school, discuss the application with your college professor or boss. While some people can fill out the application over a couple of beers during Monday Night Football and get in anywhere, for the rest of us it takes a lot of time.

10. BE HONEST AND CANDID

After marketing yourself and your accomplishments in the application, remember Shakespeare's immortal words, "And this above all else, to thine own self be true." Look over what you have written. Does it make the strongest possible case, and still accurately represent you?

This is important, because generally admissions officers can tell whether your essay is consistent with the rest of your file, or whether you are only trying to get in. For example, if you say that your one and only ambition in life is to be in finance, and yet you are twenty-eight and have never held a finance position, it's obvious you're lying. You should have a good reason for wanting to go to business school. State what it is. As in the rest of life, truth is always more powerful than fiction.

Chapter 14

TEN TIPS
ON SUCCEEDING AT
BUSINESS SCHOOL

---

(1) *Be aggressive and take the initiative.*

(2) *Learn to manage your time. Don't fall behind in your work.*

(3) *Form study groups.*

(4) *Get to know your classmates both academically and socially.*

(5) *Take advantage of the opportunity to know and work with faculty.*

(6) *Know where to get help if you need it.*

(7) *Get involved in school clubs and activities.*

(8) *Learn to write and speak clearly, concisely, and logically.*

(9) *Think conceptually.*

(10) *Keep it all in perspective.*

1. BE AGGRESSIVE AND TAKE THE INITIATIVE

The meek may inherit the earth, but not the nation's top business schools. The top business schools are tough and demanding. They seek out students who are tough and demanding. In order to succeed at business school, you too have to be tough and demanding.

Being aggressive means doing the work and more. It also means participating in class and taking the initiative in group projects, clubs, and activities. While being aggressive is usually a virtue, some students practice it to a fault. In other words, you must be aggressive but still cooperative, i.e., taking the initiative without being domineering. Business school, like business, is in many senses a cooperative venture. Students are constantly working together to do a tremendous amount of work no one individual could do by him or herself. Therefore, most students learn to channel and control their aggressiveness into accepted cooperative ventures. Those who don't soon learn the downside of going it alone when everyone else is working together.

Business schools reward aggressive students who show initiative. In order to survive and succeed, use your aggressiveness both wisely and well.

2. LEARN TO MANAGE YOUR TIME. DON'T FALL BEHIND IN YOUR WORK

Work is to business school what winning is to Vince Lombardi: it's everything. Almost all the top business schools require ten to fifteen hours of work a day. It's not humanly possible to do all the work that is assigned. Therefore, the key to success at business school is learning to manage your time.

Time management means prioritizing the work and then doing it. There is no way around putting in the time. One friend spent all of his time studying or attending class except for Saturday night and one afternoon during the weekend. While this is an extreme example, you will be amazed at how much time most people put in, even the super-bright.

Time management also means working harder and working "smarter." This involves forming study groups, letting recommended readings slide, looking for shortcuts in the readings or assignments, and so forth. Study hard early in the semester and learn the basics. This will make the rest of the semester much easier.

The cardinal rule at business school is never fall behind in your work. The work is cumulative and it piles up fast. Once you fall behind, you will be playing catch up the rest of the semester. Do the work on a daily basis; it's the only way.

3. FORM STUDY GROUPS

If business schools have one redeeming feature, it's study groups. Study groups are great.

(1) They help the student understand difficult concepts and material.
(2) They make it easier to cope with an overwhelming amount of work.
(3) They provide emotional support for the pressure-filled, anxiety-ridden aspects of the program.
(4) They provide a social group with whom you can share and enjoy the business school experience.

Study group members quickly become compatriots and close friends whom you can call at midnight when you are having problems figuring out tomorrow's 9 A.M. assignment.

Most study groups meet frequently, if not nightly, for the first semester and then taper off. They can be extremely helpful to new students during the first semester when the workload and pressure are the greatest. After that, most groups continue to meet on a social basis throughout the two years.

It's best to form study groups early in the semester. Pick class members with whom you feel you will be personally compatible. Select individuals with a variety of skills and experience (e.g., accounting, computer, economics, and marketing), so that each can contribute something different. Don't hesitate to use the study group for help with nightly assignments. Most of the top schools expect and encourage it, because most business organizations, by definition, are cooperative efforts and the experience of working in informal groups is invaluable.

4. GET TO KNOW YOUR CLASSMATES BOTH ACADEMICALLY AND SOCIALLY

The skills and training notwithstanding, the business school experience is meeting, getting to know, and establishing lifelong friendships with your classmates. Social contact and interaction is at the heart of the business school program.

It is often said, and justifiably so, that you learn as much both in and outside class from your classmates as you do from the professors. Your classmates form the basis for study groups, group projects, and early afternoon, late night, and weekend discussions. These classmates also make the rigors of business school tolerable by sharing the ups and downs of the program. Finally, these fellow students become valuable lifelong friends and contacts. Many of them will become heads of major corporations. Others are useful for jobs, information, and advice.

Actively pursue friendships and contacts with your class-mates. Informal socializing is as important as more formalized interaction or study groups. Take the time and make the effort to get to know other students. Short of having dinner with Thomas Jefferson, you will probably never meet a brighter, more interesting group in any one place at any one time.

5. TAKE ADVANTAGE OF THE OPPORTUNITY TO KNOW AND WORK WITH FACULTY

While professors are not the fount of all knowledge, they do know something. They are generally well read and knowledge-able in their field. They are a good source for advice and job contacts. In many cases, they are even nice and interesting people. Many are highly approachable and enjoy student-faculty contact.

Use the faculty. You might as well, because you are paying dearly for the opportunity. If you have questions about the course, consult the professor. If you have questions or concerns about grading, again talk to the professor. If you are interested in a field either academically or career-wise, faculty can provide guidance and stimulate your own thinking. Many have contacts in the field and will recommend someone to talk to about the industry or specific jobs.

While most professors are available and quite willing to help, avoid "brown nosing" them. They know as well as you do when you are just trying to impress them. It doesn't work. On the other hand, the faculty is an integral part of the educational process at business school and should be used whenever needed.

6. KNOW WHERE TO GET HELP
IF YOU NEED IT

Business school can be very Dickensian, that is, it can be both the best of times and the worst of times. It is the best of times in that you probably will never learn as much in such a short period of time, meet as many bright people in one place, and make as many friends. On the other hand, it is the worst of times in that you will never work as hard again while paying for the privilege, and be under such great pressure to perform or achieve against admittedly somewhat arbitrary standards. Most people can cope with it most or all of the time. But, if you can't, don't hesitate to seek help.

Business school is tough. Everyone needs help, some people more than others. If you are having trouble academically, seek help from your professors, friends, or classmates. If necessary, hire a tutor. Don't wait until the last minute. The cost of employing a tutor in comparison with the cost of the entire program is minuscule.

If you are having trouble adjusting or coping with any part of the program or life in general, seek out help. All the schools provide counseling or referral services. And you would be surprised at how many students and faculty take advantage of them. Remember the bottom line is getting your MBA. Whatever can help you do that is worth the additional cost or effort.

7. GET INVOLVED IN SCHOOL
CLUBS AND ACTIVITIES

It's very easy to just work at business schools. There certainly is more than enough to do and those who put in incredibly long hours are often amply rewarded by professors and peers.

However, business school is more than work and classes; it is a total experience. A valuable part of this experience is school clubs and activities.

First, school clubs and activities can expose you to another side of the business world through seminars, get-togethers with business leaders, and so forth. Second, these clubs can be a valuable source for job contacts, information about specific industries, new developments, etc. Third, clubs and activities are a good way to meet fellow students with like interests. Finally, these clubs and activities often provide a welcome respite and diversion from the intense pressure of the classroom and the workload.

Select a few activities or clubs in which you are interested. Devote a certain amount of time to them. Expand your horizons and enjoy the activities.

8. *LEARN TO WRITE AND SPEAK CLEARLY, CONCISELY, AND LOGICALLY*

Business school programs are two years long. During that time, you take at least twenty-five to thirty courses. Each course has a final exam. Most have midterms. Classroom participation is also graded in most schools. In order to get through the fifty to sixty exams plus the daily verbal challenges, two skills are necessary. First, you must be able to crunch the numbers and analyze the data. Second, and equally as important, you must be able to express yourself both orally and on paper. It is this latter communication talent that is sometimes overlooked by the more quantitatively oriented business school students.

Most business schools have a writing or business communication course. Generally, these courses are not highly regarded. However, the communication skill that is being taught in these courses is critical. This is often learned painfully in class and on exams during the first semester.

If you are not a clear and logical writer or speaker, get help and practice. Take courses either prior to entering business school, or seek some kind of help from the professor, the university counseling service, or friends during business school. Then practice, practice, and practice. Take the time to think through what you are going to say or to write. The same logical thought processes that go into analyzing a business problem should be applied to your writing and speaking skills. While out of necessity, these communication skills will improve during the two years at business school, the earlier and more time you devote to improving them, the easier those two years will be.

9. THINK CONCEPTUALLY

Never lose sight of your goal. Business school problems, like real business problems, are confusing and full of numbers and contradictory data. In analyzing these problems, students, like business people, often find safety in numbers. Numbers beget numbers. As a result, the original problem and goals you were seeking become obscured.

If you were a major company and had a couple thousand dollars to spend each day, you would call in a consultant. If you are a student and can't afford high-priced help, stand back, think, and try to view the "big picture." Try to identify the real problem and the concept or theory being examined.

Conceptual thinking and big picture planning are done primarily by top management in corporations. However, a big advantage of an MBA over a non-MBA is the ability to think in larger terms, i.e., to transcend the numbers and to think about the overall problem. The more you can develop this skill in business school, the more successful your career will be both in business school and in business later on.

10. KEEP IT ALL IN PERSPECTIVE

After you have overworked yourself to the bone, relax and enjoy. Keep repeating to yourself, "It's only business school, it's only business school, it's only business school." Keep it all in perspective. It's true you're going to have to work hard and put in more hours than you ever imagined. However, it's also true that you will learn a lot, make new friends, and even enjoy yourself sometimes. Plus, you get an MBA, which should not be undervalued in a highly competitive marketplace.

If you are admitted to a top business school and you accept, you are in for two long hard years. Few students flunk out. The failure or flunk-out rate averages less than 2 percent at almost all the top schools. While this may provide small comfort to you when you have five exams the next week and your entire grade for the course rests on those exams, from the overall view, these exams are merely interim hurdles that must and can be overcome.

Getting through a top business school program is an accomplishment. Like most achievements you have to work for it. The school certifies that you passed the rigors of the program. That in essence is why employers are paying top MBAs more than $50,000 a year as a starting salary.

During the heat of the academic battles, keep the "big picture" in mind. Admissions and alumni opinions notwithstanding, business school is not the only place to begin one's career. However, it is a very good place to start. Make the most of your business school years: work, learn, and enjoy.

Chapter 15

TEN TIPS ON GETTING A GREAT JOB AFTER BUSINESS SCHOOL

(1) *Determine what you feel will be a great job for you.*

(2) *Interview with numerous companies to learn what is available and what is best for you.*

(3) *Experiment with a summer job in an industry that interests you.*

(4) *Take full advantage of the school's recruiting facilities and programs.*

(5) *Use whatever contacts you can.*

(6) *Write a résumé that highlights achievement.*

(7) *Be knowledgeable in the interview about the company, its markets, products, and industry trends.*

(8) *Don't go only for money. Keep in mind flexibility, future opportunity, and personal fit with the company.*

(9) *Be aggressive and confident.*

(10) *Be persistent.*

1. DETERMINE WHAT YOU FEEL WILL BE A GREAT JOB FOR YOU

The primary reason for getting an MBA is to get a great job. And most graduates of business schools certainly are not disappointed. Consulting firms, the current rage at most top business schools, now pay new MBAs a starting salary of over $60,000 a year. Investment banks, a more traditional source of employment for MBAs, also pay well above the $45,000 to $50,000 starting salaries that new business school graduates now command. While these fields are lucrative, fast paced, and prestigious, they may not be right for you.

You must determine what a great job is for you based on your career interests, financial needs, geographical preferences, and personal priorities. Carefully think through your career goals, rank order and weight your needs, and then evaluate each field and position in relation to your goals and needs. Investigate a number of fields early on in the recruiting process. Then select a few areas in which to concentrate.

Too many new MBAs go for the almighty dollar or are swayed by the opinions of their classmates. While some students are willing to give their eye teeth for offers from McKinsey and Booz Allen or Morgan Stanley and Goldman Sachs, you may be happier in another field or even out on your own. You will be faced with many options and offers upon graduation from business school: only you can and should decide which to take.

2. INTERVIEW WITH NUMEROUS COMPANIES TO LEARN WHAT IS AVAILABLE AND WHAT IS BEST FOR YOU

When you are not at business school, looking for a job is a hassle. It is expensive and time-consuming. You may send out two hundred letters and get five responses. Then you may have to pay for a trip to an initial interview for a job that may or may not exist. Additional months may transpire before the company contacts you again. The whole process is neither encouraging nor enjoyable.

Now consider the situation facing top B School graduates. First, the companies come to you — not five or ten, but hundreds. Moreover, all these companies have jobs to offer at high starting salaries. Your problem is to decide which offer to accept.

While this description is a bit overstated, there are tremendous recruiting opportunities at the top business schools. Students have to work hard for offers, but it definitely is a seller's market. Take advantage of this opportunity. Recruit with numerous companies to sharpen your interviewing skills and to explore different career fields. Broaden your search as much as possible at the outset and then focus in when you can eliminate careers and companies that are not right for you. The advantage of looking at numerous areas is that you might uncover a good position or company you may not have initially considered. It also makes you feel more comfortable in the job you accept knowing you have considered all the options and picked the best one for you.

3. EXPERIMENT WITH A SUMMER JOB IN AN INDUSTRY THAT INTERESTS YOU

Students often go to business school to switch fields. Sometimes they know what they want to do. Other times they just know what they don't want to do. Classes may provide some help in picking a field, but to really know a job or industry, it is necessary to work in it. While a full-time job after business school is probably the best way to learn, you may want to try out a field during a summer.

Summer jobs represent good opportunities to experiment with limited risk and commitment. You can work for three months and familiarize yourself with a basic knowledge of the industry, the company, and career opportunities. If you don't like the field, nothing is lost. If you like it, then you have a leg up on the other students with no experience in the industry.

Summer jobs are difficult, if not almost impossible to get, especially if you have no experience in the field. The best way to get a summer position is to start early, be aggressive, send out numerous job inquiry letters, seek out as many potential job openings as possible, enlist the aid of professors, use alumni contacts, use family contacts, and then hope. It may take time to get a good summer job, but it's worth it if it helps you select a future career.

4. TAKE FULL ADVANTAGE OF THE SCHOOL'S RECRUITING FACILITIES AND PROGRAMS

The recruiting facilities and programs of the top business schools would make many top executive recruiting firms jealous with envy. The business schools have extensive libraries, job and company files, company contacts (alumni), and the influence and prestige of the school itself. The business schools run extensive recruiting programs in the spring, and anywhere from two hundred to five hundred companies visit the campuses in search of MBAs.

The spring job search is almost a ritual at the top business schools. Going through company files in the library, meeting recruiters at company-sponsored cocktail parties, and getting haircuts are all part of this process. However, too many students stick to the traditional paths and therefore miss out on other job opportunities. Because so many companies eagerly recruit on campus, not enough students seek out the smaller companies that don't come to visit. The schools' recruiting offices generally keep files on all companies, both those that come to campus and those that don't. Placement offices are normally more than willing to help students in nontraditional job searches. Faculty, whose school and consulting contacts are invaluable, are also often ignored by many students seeking jobs. Faculty are generally more than willing to help if asked.

5. USE WHATEVER CONTACTS YOU CAN

While in many ways the growth of MBA programs embody the rise of meritocracy, contacts never hurt. Many businesses still utilize personal contacts and the old boy network, especially in filling jobs. The top schools recognize this and do everything to try to strengthen their alumni contacts.

Use these contacts whenever you can. Speak to alumni in those areas you are interested in pursuing. Alumni can be very helpful in providing information, the occasional job, or referring you to other people who are knowledgeable in the field.

Never neglect family or friends' contacts. Don't be embarrassed about asking for their help. After earning an MBA, you are more than a friend or relative, you are a trained professional.

Contacts are especially helpful if you have a nontraditional background. Contacts may provide you with an opportunity to talk with people you ordinarily would not have gotten to speak with. Contacts also may be better able than the placement office to put you in touch with people in slightly nontraditional areas who can appreciate your own nontraditional background and experience.

6. WRITE A RÉSUMÉ THAT HIGHLIGHTS ACHIEVEMENT

A good résumé is like a good doorbell. If it rings loud and clear and people pay attention to it, it should get you in the door. After that it's up to you. Since you are getting an MBA from a top school, you have one item on your résumé to differentiate yourself from the competition. However, since your classmates also will have an MBA from a top school on their résumé, you need to distinguish yourself from them.

One way of doing this is to highlight your achievements. Do not merely list jobs, dates, and responsibilities on your résumé; show what you have accomplished that helped the company. Instead of stating that you conducted a marketing analysis, show how that analysis increased sales or cut down expenses. Even small improvements or ideas that show accomplishments will enhance your value to prospective employers.

There are plenty of good résumé writing books available. Some of the schools even publish their own guides. Use them.

7. BE KNOWLEDGEABLE IN THE INTERVIEW ABOUT THE COMPANY, ITS MARKETS, ITS PRODUCTS, AND INDUSTRY TRENDS

The interview can make or break you. Before your first meeting, the company has very little data on you. It has had a chance to look over your résumé briefly. But that's about it. The initial screening takes place in the first half-hour interview. It's at this point that the company decides to grant a second interview and invite you to the company headquarters or else to send you the well known bullet (rejection letter).

While your résumé may be great (see the preceding tip), you are competing against other great résumés, namely those of your classmates. To differentiate yourself you must show an interest in the company and the field. You can do this by extensive preparation for each interview. This means reading the company's annual report, collecting information on the industry and future trends, talking with professors and classmates, and whatever else you think will help. This tells the interviewer whether you are really interested in the company or merely gaining experience with the interview process.

The interview is not only an opportunity for the company to evaluate you, it also gives you a chance to critically evaluate the company. The more knowledgeable you are about the company and the industry, the better able you will be to make an informed choice.

8. DON'T GO ONLY FOR MONEY. KEEP IN MIND FLEXIBILITY, FUTURE OPPORTUNITY, AND PERSONAL FIT WITH THE COMPANY

One of the primary reasons people go to business school is to earn more money after they graduate. Therefore, it is only natural that money plays a key role in the job decision. After all, who would not be swayed by the $60,000 + some top consulting companies are paying new MBAs. This is especially true when you have just invested tens of thousands of dollars to get the MBA. The investment should pay off.

However, despite the happiness that money buys, don't go only for the almighty dollar. Jobs which pay a lot, demand a lot. Burnouts are common in consulting and investment banking. Look at your own personal interests. Decide what kind of life you want to live and what kind of work you want to do. Think about where you want to be in five or ten years. Certain companies with lower-paying jobs may be far more suited to your interests and needs. Remember, most of your waking hours will be spent at work, so you might as well enjoy them and find them rewarding.

9. BE AGGRESSIVE AND CONFIDENT

Business school students are often thought of as being very aggressive. In most cases it's true and in most cases it helps. In order to get through the rigors of the top business school programs, you need to be aggressive. In the job search, aggressiveness is also seen as a positive trait. Companies look for the archetypical business school grad: i.e., one who is young, bright, willing to work, and a go-getter.

Being aggressive means being enthusiastic and taking the initiative in the interview. Ask questions that show you are interested in the company and the position. Answer questions fully, but don't pad your answers. Show them the interview is a two-way process and that you are evaluating them as much as they are you.

Be aggressive, but not obnoxious. There is a fine line between the two, but generally it is easy to tell by someone's reaction which category you are in. Be confident. You are getting a degree from a fine institution and most likely will have more than one job offer. Sell yourself, but don't over-promise or oversell. Companies want bright and aggressive people, but they also are interested in employees who will fit into the overall organization of the company.

10. BE PERSISTENT

The recruiting process is like a roller coaster ride with incredible ups and downs. There isn't a business school graduate out there who has not gotten his or her share of rejections or bullets. Some schools even keep track of the more notorious ones. If you are really interested in working for a company or in a particular field, don't let a few bullets stand in your way.

Write to companies that rejected you and tell them you are still interested in them. Give them a reason to reconsider your application. Seek out smaller companies that may not recruit on campus, but may offer plenty of opportunity for the right person. Call alumni to seek information and possible job openings. Read the trade press, looking for major industry and personnel changes. Write the companies and individuals involved and offer them your skilled services.

Never take no for an answer and never settle. Business school graduates from the top schools are highly valued and over the long run will do very well. Take charge and be persistent. After all, it's your future.

APPENDIX

COMPARISON CHARTS
OF THE
TOP TEN BUSINESS
SCHOOL PROGRAMS

SCHOOL	# OF APPLI-CANTS	# OF STU-DENTS	% FE-MALE	% MI-NORITY	MEDIAN AGE	% DIRECTLY OUT OF SCHOOL	ACADEMIC STRENGTH	TEACHING METHOD
1. HARVARD	6885	785	25	10	26	0	General Management	Case primarily
2. STANFORD	4217	318	30.8	13.2	26.7	1.6	General Management	Combination
3. WHARTON	6000	750	27	16	26.5	2	Finance, General Management	Combination
4. CHICAGO	3327	528	28	16	26	13	Finance, Marketing, Economics	Combination
5. SLOAN (MIT)	1500	180	20	7	26	4	Finance, Economics, MIS, Technological Innovation	Combination
6. KELLOGG (NORTHWESTERN)	3600	420	35	10	26	2	General Management, Finance, Marketing	Combination
7. MICHIGAN	3000	375	22	17	26	12	General Management	Combination
8. UCLA	3700	385	32	14	27	3	Finance, Information Sciences, Marketing	Combination
9. COLUMBIA	3300	650	35	10	26	NA	Finance, Accounting, International Business	Combination
10. TUCK (DARTMOUTH)	2000	165	25	7	27	4	General Management	Combination Consulting Projects

SCHOOL	AVERAGE CLASS SIZE		ADMISSIONS REQUIREMENTS				YEARLY TUITION
	1ST YEAR	2ND YEAR	GMAT	REF.	GRADES	OTHER	COST (APP.)
1. HARVARD	85	85	No	3	Yes	2 yrs. work experience or equivalent, essays	$13,300
2. STANFORD	60	20–50	Yes	3	Yes	—	$12,960
3. WHARTON	55	15–120	Yes	2	Yes	Interview encouraged, College quantitative course	$13,354
4. CHICAGO	49	38	Yes or GRE	2	Yes	—	$13,500
5. SLOAN (MIT)	50–60	25	Yes	3	Yes	Calculus, Economics (Micro & Macro)	$12,700
6. KELLOGG (NORTHWESTERN)	56	30–50	Yes	2–3	Yes	Interview	$13,200
7. MICHIGAN	65	45	Yes	2	Yes	College Calculus I	$ 6,038 (In-State) $11,312 (Out-of-State)
8. UCLA	50	35	Yes	2	Yes	—	$ 1,851 (In-State) $ 4,280 (Out-of-State)
9. COLUMBIA	55–125	40–60	Yes	Yes	Yes	—	$13,000
10. TUCK (DARTMOUTH)	55	20	Yes	2	Yes	—	$13,000

SCHOOL	COURSE REQUIREMENTS		% COURSES OR AREAS REQUIRED		WAIVE COURSES	% OF STUDENTS WHO DO NOT COMPLETE PROGRAM
	1ST YEAR	2ND YEAR	1ST YEAR	2ND YEAR		
1. HARVARD	Finance, marketing, control, production & operations mgt, organizational behavior, business, government & international economics, introduction to financial statements, managing information systems, competition and strategy, human resource mgt & mgt communications	Management policy and practice	100	15	No	2–3
2. STANFORD	Financial accounting, decision making under uncertainty, decision support models and optimization, economic analysis and policy I & II, organizational behavior, managerial accounting, analysis of productive systems, business finance, data analysis marketing management, strategic management	Business & the changing environment	80	8	Yes	3
3. WHARTON	Accounting, finance, marketing, management, micro & macroeconomics, quantitative methods and statistics	Business policy, four major courses, advanced study project	80	60	Yes	3–5

| SCHOOL | COURSE REQUIREMENTS | | % COURSES OR AREAS | | WAIVE COURSES | % OF STUDENTS WHO DO NOT COMPLETE PROGRAM |
	1ST YEAR	2ND YEAR	REQUIRED 1ST YEAR	REQUIRED 2ND YEAR		
4. CHICAGO	Micro & macroeconomics, cost or managerial accounting, statistics, mgt science, behavioral science; 3 of 4: financial mgt, industrial relations & human resource mgt, marketing mgt, productions and operations mgt	1 of 4: business policy, the firm in internat'l mgt, health care mgt policies, policy problems in the mgt of governmental & nonprofit organizations	Student discretion		Yes, & substitute electives	Less than 1
5. SLOAN (MIT)	Applied microeconomics, applied macro & international economics, statistics, decision models, managerial behavior in organizations, accounting, information systems, industrial relations and human resource management, marketing, finance, operations management, strategic management, and communications	Concentration in one area and a thesis.	100	20 (Thesis)	Yes	1
6. KELLOGG (NORTHWESTERN)	Accounting, management, organizational behavior, mathematical methods, economics statistics, operations management, finance, marketing	None	75	0	Yes, and substitute electives	1

290

School	Course Requirements		% Courses Or Areas Required		Waive Courses	Students Who Do Not Complete Program
	1st Year	2nd Year	1st Year	2nd Year		
7. MICHIGAN	Financial accounting, organizational behavior, computer, statistics, applied microeconomics, managerial accounting, financial mgt, marketing mgt, operations mgt	Corporate strategy	90	10	Yes	2
8. UCLA	Managing people, data analysis, accounting, information systems, economics (micro & macro), model building, finance, production & operations management, marketing, competitive strategy	Organizational design, mgt field study	75	12	Yes, but units must be replaced	2
9. COLUMBIA	Accounting, macro & micro-economics, conceptual foundations of business, managerial behavior, statistics, operations research	Business policy	70	10	Yes	2
10. TUCK (DARTMOUTH)	Managerial and financial acctg, finance, applied statistics, intro to computing, mgt communications (1&2), managerial economics, marketing, decision analysis, organizational behavior, political economy, business environment, mgt science, operations mgt	Business policy	100	8	Yes	2

School	Top 3 Job Areas	# of Companies that Recruit on Campus	Avg. Starting Salary	# of Days/Week Classes Held
1. HARVARD	Consulting (20%), investment banking (30%), high tech and electronics (5%)	400	NA	5
2. STANFORD	Consulting (18%), finance (30%), marketing (9%)	245	NA	4
3. WHARTON	Investments (37%), consulting (16.7%), finance (15.8%)	420	$48,000 +	4
4. CHICAGO	Investment banking (23.9%), commercial banking (18.2%), consulting (10.7%)	251	NA	6
5. SLOAN (MIT)	Consulting (21%), electrical and electronic equipment (12%), investment banking (22%)	160	$50,000	4 with a few exceptions
6. KELLOGG (NORTHWESTERN)	Investment banking (22%), brand mgt (21%), consulting (15%), financial analysis and services (11%)	300	NA	4
7. MICHIGAN	Finance (34%), marketing (24%), consulting (12%)	438	$42,750	4
8. UCLA	Finance (19%), consulting (14%), investment banking (32%), marketing sales (14%)	200	$45,000	4
9. COLUMBIA	Investment banking/brokerage (20%), commercial banking (20%), publishing/communications (11%)	325	$43,000	4
10. TUCK (DARTMOUTH)	Finance (50%), marketing (15%), consulting (17%)	130	$49,100	5 (4 for second year)

COMPARISON CHARTS

SCHOOL	ACADEMIC PRESSURE	SOCIAL ENVIRONMENT	REPUTATION/MENTALITY
1. HARVARD	Intense	Section (group) oriented	West Point of business schools
2. STANFORD	Intense	Friendly, supportive	Balanced excellence
3. WHARTON	Intense	Good, supportive	Balanced, with strong quantitative leanings
4. CHICAGO	Moderately competitive	Good variety, integrated, friendly	Nobel quality
5. SLOAN (MIT)	Moderately intense	Small town atmosphere (without attendant intolerance)	Applied studies in an analytical context
6. KELLOGG (NORTHWESTERN)	Competitive	Best of both worlds city & suburbs	Balance of practical and theoretical
7. MICHIGAN	Intense	Section oriented	Solid professionalism with no pretensions
8. UCLA	Serious	Professionally oriented	A question of balance (analytical with group process skills)
9. COLUMBIA	Intense	Diverse, mix of school/city	Ivy League
10. TUCK (DARTMOUTH)	Competitive	Close knit	Well-rounded, balanced perspective

NOTES ON THE CONTRIBUTORS

Tom Fischgrund

(Editor and Contributor)

Tom is a 1980 graduate of the Harvard Business School. He has a Ph.D. in Political Science from MIT (1977) and a BA from Tufts University. He has directed a graduate program in public administration and done government research. He then spent six years in advertising. He currently is working as a senior marketing manager for Coca-Cola. His second book, *Match Wits with the Harvard MBA's*, was published in 1985.

PATRICIA HUDSON

Pat is a 1977 graduate of the Stanford Graduate School of Business. She received her BA from Stanford University and had worked for three years in banking before attending graduate school. After receiving her MBA, she worked for four years in product management for General Foods and is currently working for Bank of America.

MICHAEL DUGAN

Michael graduated from Wharton's MBA program in May 1979. While at Wharton, he was treasurer of the Wharton Graduate Association and majored in marketing. After graduating, he worked for a top New York advertising agency in both account management and creative positions. He received his BS in journalism from the University of Maryland. He presently is working freelance, writing screenplays for television and movies in Hollywood.

MARK SLAVEN

Mark is a 1982 graduate of the University of Chicago Graduate School of Business. He received a BS degree in Civil Engineering from Tufts University in 1978 and worked for General Dynamics as an engineer for two years. He has done consulting for Booz Allen & Hamilton on operations assignments, and currently works for IBM.

MAUREEN ROGERS

Maureen is a 1981 graduate of the Sloan School of Management at MIT. Prior to starting business school, she worked as a waitress, an editor and researcher, and an economics consultant. She received her BA from Emmanuel College in Boston. Maureen is at present a consultant in the corporate planning division of Chase Econometrics Interactive Data Corporation.

CHARLESANNA DAILY ECKER AND BILL ECKER

Charlesanna received her MM from Northwestern School of Management in 1979 with majors in Marketing and Finance. She did her undergraduate study in business at the University of North Carolina at Chapel Hill. After graduation from business school, she worked in marketing for a large southeastern banking institution and is currently working in product management for Pepsico.

Bill also attended Northwestern School of Management and graduated in 1979 with majors in Marketing and Finance. He has a BA from Pennsylvania State University, where he majored in advertising. Since graduating from business school, Bill has worked in product management for General Foods and Lever Brothers.

LEN SAVOIE

Len is a 1980 graduate of The University of Michigan Business School. Before entering business school, he received a BA in music from Brown University. He then spent four years playing in rock bands, recording, and writing radio jingles. Len is currently with Compton advertising agency, working in account management on Procter and Gamble business.

CONSTANCE WILLIAMS

Constance is a 1977 graduate of UCLA's Graduate School of Management. She had received her BA in history from the University of California at Irvine. She formerly worked in account management for Benton and Bowles and currently is a marketing manager with Heublein, a large food and spirits manufacturer. Constance also is Co-Director of New York's UCLA Business School Alumni Association.

VICKI TENCATI

Vicki graduated from Columbia Business School in 1977, majoring in marketing. She attended Barnard College as an undergraduate. Prior to business school, she spent three years working for United Airlines. She currently is employed in advertising as an account supervisor for Compton.

PETER AND KATIE DOLAN

Peter and Katie are 1980 graduates of the Amos Tuck School of Business Administration. Katie worked for a nonprofit organization prior to attending Tuck. She received her BA from Middlebury. She is currently employed as an administrator in New York's Health & Hospitals Corporation.

Peter went directly to business school from undergraduate college (Tufts University). He presently works in product management for General Foods.